WHY NOT ME?

WHY NOT ME?

A Lifelong Journey of 1%'ers & Becoming a World Champion

JESSICA DOUGLAS

Jessica Douglas

Photographer credits
Front Cover: Adam MacLeod
Rear cover: Paddy Lynch
Thank you to Norm Douglas, Adam Mc Grath, Russell Baker, Sarah O'Callaghan, Erik Peterson and other 'unknown' photographers who have photos in my book.

Copyright © 2021 by Jessica Douglas

All rights reserved. No part of this book may be reproduced in any manner whatsoever without written permission except in the case of brief quotations embodied in critical articles and reviews.

First Printing, 2021

A catalogue record for this book is available from the National Library of Australia

ISBN: 978-0-6453586-0-5
Cover image: Adam MacLeod
Cover design: Norm Douglas
Rear Image: Paddy Lynch

"Better done than perfect"

Thank you Norm, for believing in me but also getting the best out of me where I might not have found the courage to do so alone.

Jess Douglas

CONTENTS

Preface — 2

Foreward — 4

Introduction — 6

Chapter 1 - Believing — 9

Chapter 2 - Childhood Dreams — 25

Chapter 3 - Adversity is my blessing — 33

Chapter 4 - Living and Learning, Failing and Flying. — 44

Chapter 5 - 1% at a time — 71

Chapter 6 - Welcome to the World Stage young Padawan. — 110

Chapter 7 - Cracking the Code to Life — 126

Chapter 8 - Hard Work — 176

Chapter 9 - The Dark Side of Success	203
Chapter 10 - Ego is a dirty word	237
Chapter 11 - Kintsugi; healing with Gold.	280
Epilogue	313
Acknowledgements	315

1% RULE TO SUCCESS.

> Focus on 1 task at a time.
> 1 day at a time.
> 1 week at a time.
> 1 month at a time.
> Improve just one thing at a time by 1%.
> In a year's time, you will have improved.
> You cannot fail.
> Every Single Day, focus on the 1%'ers.

1% Life Philosophy

3 x WC & 3 x National Champ in 24hr Mountain biking which is a tough sport - mentally and physically tough.

I love sharing how adversity in my life created an inner strength and a philosophy to live by.

As I became a national and world champion 3 times over, it became very clear to me that there was a 'code I had cracked' and it was so very simple.

I ticked boxes that others were not.

I did the hard work, daily with consistency.

I followed a process, creating many small steps towards the bigger goals.

Then developed a simple rule that grounded and allowed me to overcome any fears and these can be applied to any situation, to any person for absolutely anything that might be holding you back.

My life has been a series of many consistent persistent efforts with so many lessons along the way.

My grandson Finley
Norm

Preface

After I won my first World Championship, the concept was floated, to write a book about everything I had done and how I got to where I was. I wasn't aware that people were genuinely interested in my story, and back in 2010, well I had another eleven years to gather even more stories.

The book never happened, though I thought about it constantly. Instead, I kept a blog that would ebb and flow with my energies and I am forever grateful that Norm created my website and nudged me in the direction of sharing my experiences with those that wanted to listen. But like most people in the world in 2020, I was in lockdown due to COVID-19 and I finally felt it was time to start writing. Funny how I still had a lot more 'shit to hit the fan' before I would get to this stage, nearly 18 months later!

As I wrote, it became apparent that I worked bloody hard and experienced a very blessed life. And life has a way of being quite balanced, there are lessons, not so good times and loads of adversity to get through, and as a result you find the GOLD. This period of the worldwide pandemic and lockdowns, whilst not ideal for anyone, certainly forced a 'reset' for many people, including me.

And so this book came to life, of course, not without more adversity, healing and self-discovery. By the time I press go on publishing it will be just shy of Christmas 2021, I am 48, about to be a grandmother for the 2nd time and starting the fine art/visual arts course I wanted to do at 18. I have loved the experience of writing my story. I could have gone on for another 6 months perfecting it even more, but for what? There are no literary awards I am seeking. I had to allow myself to be a beginner, to learn and grow from the experience. It has been HARD! Far harder than any suffering I have endured in my racing career that's for sure! **But if it was easy everyone would do it - right?**

What do I hope you get from this, my book?
Simply put, it's knowing that another human exists that shared her story, all the hardships and triumphs. That she found a way to navigate her life and make it how she wanted, even amongst adversity, but also amongst success.

My story is nothing more than a life well lived and it just so happened that riding a bike helped me live it a little more full-on than the average person.

The 24hr world championship winners - 2010
Adam McGrath

Foreward

There are two groups of people who should read this book; people who don't know Jess Douglas but want to and people who think they know Jess Douglas. That pretty much covers a fair portion of the planet. I fall into the latter group and I was both amazed and surprised to find out more about her story through life so far; all the extras that contribute to this person.

24 Hour mountain biking is something I have been involved in since 2000, racing in teams in the early days, then organising, but always passionate about this quirky arm of our sport with its enthusiasts all around the world. I love mountain biking, the 'WEMBO Family' we comprise, but I love the people who do it more. I was at Canberra Off-Road Cyclists' Scott 24 Hour in Kowen Forest in 2006 along with Jess and Norm Douglas and 6,000 other people but didn't meet them there. Not really surprising at the biggest 24 Hour mountain bike race in the world at the time. Our meeting would have to wait until the following year at the same event out at Stromlo Forest Park in some less than pleasant circumstances when they found their car had been broken into.

Over the coming years the interaction continued; Australian Solo 24 Hour Championship races in Canberra; pizza nights in Canmore, Alberta before Jess' first attempt at the world solo title; and visits to Forrest, Victoria for Jess and Norm's Forrest 6 Hour and their innovative Forrest Festival. Then her first world championship title in 2010 and her memorable second world championship title in 2012 at Finale Ligure in Italy when the Aussie riders schooled the rest of the world in the overall package of Solo 24 Hour riding; racing, pit time management plus the vital role of the solo helper.

With her win in 2013, Jess joined the USA's Rebecca Rusch as the only women to have won three elite world solo 24-hour mountain bike titles. Jess and Italy's Gaia Ravaioli are the only women who appear twice on the WEMBO world solo 24 Hour trophy, with Jess at the top. However, this book is about much more than mountain biking.

Jess' story is one of a path through life to achievement. A life filled with many peaks and troughs and also with her famous one-percenters. Her style of telling the story skilfully changes to match the times when things were more organised and times when they were less so. It contains some simple life lessons in a life and a story far from simple. Embedded in it is a planned path that took her to the top of the world three times in her sport, and all the unplanned paths that add up to the first half of an extraordinary life; a path that worked for her and maybe, just maybe, can work for you.

Always Solo. Never alone.

Russ Baker AM
WEMBO Founder
MTBA President

Russ Baker

Introduction

I have no idea how many times people have said, "Jess, you should write a book about everything you have done."

When we have achieved things in life that other people have not, or only dream of doing, we are considered talented, extraordinary or superhuman.

I am none of these.

My talent is a desire to work hard and an inability to see barriers in front of me. I am vulnerable and sensitive to the bone about what people think of me, yet I learned a valuable lesson, one of many, though this one stands.

Norm and I were freshly married, living in Sydney and on a five-week home honeymoon. I was not yet 19, only days off my birthday, young and scared, but so excited at what I might be able to do with my life. We were at a waterslide park in Western Sydney, enjoying the fun and sun in January 1992. Norm suggested we ride the speed slides. They are high, steep and straight down, landing in the pool at the bottom with super fast velocity. I was shaking on the inside, fearing the unknown, yet I wanted to do it, yet equally desperate to be sucked up by the ground underneath my feet and disappear. Norm was patient. He asked me, "Jess, what are you worried about?" I replied, "It's big, fast, and um...I don't know?"

His calm response was simple, "Ok, why don't we go have a look at people coming down the slide, and you can make decisions then. We can see how other people do it, and if it looks like fun, what do you reckon?"

Well, I couldn't argue against that. So we went and watched. It was a fair and reasonable approach to see if this speed slide was my gig or not.

For the next 10 minutes, half of me was nervous with fear and the other half jittery with excitement. I couldn't decide what to do. I knew I could and should ride this bloody slide.

Norm interrupted my thoughts, "So Jess, any decision? Any thoughts? Are these people having fun? Do you think you could do it? Do you want to do it?"

DAMN YOU! How can I say no? I can't.

So I say, "Yes. Let's do this."

And of course, I had a ball, and that was one of the most significant turning points in my life, where I learnt the value in role models who had done things before me, to gain strength and knowledge from their experience, and worry less about what people think as well. Perhaps the simplicity of a story is not in the extraordinary but rather the 'relatability' of a person.

If she can do it, then maybe I can too?

And this, my friends, is the very reason I must write my book, to share with others what I have done so they too can gain strength and perhaps a sprinkle of inspiration.

It's a pay it forward kind of thing.

Our wedding day in 1991

1km to go and I will be the World Champ - YES!
Paddy

Chapter 1 - Believing

There is often a magical point in time that we model ourselves on from this day forward.
Our future, our past, all makes sense at this moment.
All the hard work, adversity, dreams, financial investment, the lessons, the failures, the skills everything; delivers at the exact time you have only dared to dream.
The vision of what this dream would look like, what it would feel like, is here; it's in you, it is you.
You are here NOW. You made it.

This is a story about how I discovered something special inside of me, not talent, rather the capacity to turn adversity into a gift. I came to find out that my talent was to enjoy and thrive on suffering and longer than most. Maybe even to understand that this is even more important than anything else, for we are more likely to face many challenges over a lifetime.

To be a World Champion in the sport of 24hr mountain biking, you must be ready to hurt.

Let me start with the event that changed it all. The year is 2010, it's the 24hr World 24hr Solo Championships, in Canberra, Australia. Some magic is about to happen, it was my confirmation of what was possible.

The event will start at midday and finish 24hrs later, riding through the night. There is no sleep if you want to win, and you must eat and often drink, staying awake to ride through the night whilst keeping the sleep monsters at bay. You must possess a strong FOCUS and know YOUR why because when it gets tough, and it will, you need to have a damn good reason to keep the pressure on, that is, if you want to win. To win, you must be a skilful mountain biker, riding technical trails with your eyes closed. You've got to ride fast for the first six hours, then settle, ride fast again, make it through the night, and then, after 18hrs of racing, finish as fast as you can so no one gets a sniff that you might be tiring.

There is no finish point in a 24-hour race. Instead, you continue to race until the clock is up. The focus is intense; the mantras and mind chatter are nonstop, telling the body to do what it's told. To become a world champion 24hr mountain biker, you'll do well to enjoy suffering more than everyone else. I am grateful for the adversity in my life, giving me a solid foundation to embrace the hurt. My favourite mountain bike trail to race was always at Mt Stromlo in Canberra; the network at Mt Stromlo was part of the recovery after the devastating bushfires of 2003. Norm and I loved driving up the Hume highway from our home in Forrest, Victoria. We listened to good music, had long conversations, and planned our attempt to win the race. Often we would camp. It was the done thing. Part of the fun and excitement was being with all your fellow riders, preparing bikes, food, tents, registering for the race the day before and then going for a practice ride on the course was just part of the preparation. This process was cathartic—a rite of passage with 24hr Mountain bike racing.

This year was different, and we weren't camping. It was the 24hr World Solo Mountain Bike Championships, and it was going to be huge. This style of racing was at a peak. In October 2010, the field consisted of 300 men and 64 women racing with 59 elite men and 28 elite women.

Arriving in Canberra, we shared a small two-bedroom apartment with Ben Culton-our good friend, who was also racing. Once settled, we made our way to Mt Stromlo to do a reconnaissance lap of the course. An opportunity to test the bike and body out without pressure to perform. I can remember clearly that excitement of feeling strong and fast, enjoying the trail and all the technical features. In mountain biking terms, the distance covered doesn't accurately indicate the effort, though, in a 24 hour World Championship event, you can guarantee fast laps and lots of them. This course was challenging and technical, and I loved it. It was a perfect stage for me to test myself against the best riders in the World.

We spent lots of time deciding on what lines to take, especially the 'risk versus reward' features. There was a big slab of near-vertical rock at a trail called Pork Belly. There were numerous ways to ride down it and take the easier route, with a time cost. I spent over an hour in this location testing them all out. Would I have the mind and bike control at 1:00 am to negotiate this rock successfully? Would the trail deteriorate throughout twenty-four hours, making it even harder? We came up with an A, B and C plan. The default line to take would always be the 'A-Line, the hardest one, with the smoothest entry and exit and the fastest. But with the most significant consequence for error as well.

Trail features like this in a racecourse required processes to execute it well; engaging good technique and a calm mindset, using mantras or cue words to assert commitment. Doing this all the time to do the exact method at the precise moment, performing this with 100% undeniable confidence, now and twenty hours later. The mental plan and focus are all pre-made choices. Creating processes, doing them, moving on, next, and so on. The key was to tackle each section of each lap as a puzzle. I have always enjoyed this side of racing my bike. No matter how challenging the course presents, this practice brings calm and control. I am controlling the controllable. Where will I drink on this course? What thoughts will I choose to think? Where will I change the gears on my bike to optimise the terrain? Where can I pass riders on the trails if and when I need to? Where should I put in more effort, and where should I back off and recover?

The 2010 World Championship course had it all, twisting single track to start, pointing uphill for a good twenty minutes, punctuated with tough pinches, flow, technical rocky sections, then reaching the top of Mt Stromlo. Lots of opportunities to see your competition in front as well as behind. Then the fun unfolded, a fast flowy trail with rocky edges that could throw you offline before entering Pork Barrel, the vertical rock slab section. Many dropdowns, tight corners, small launches, brake ruts, pinch climbs encompassed by super close foliage and small trees whipping at your shoulders, giving a sense of speed and risk. Next comes the significant gravel fire road sections, time to drink before some steep climbing sections. Back at the top, the trail boosted you down into banked bermed tracks, flowing down the front face of Mt Stromlo for kilometres. A good time to focus, not a good time for drinking and eating. Solid work on the body and the mind. The course finally met the base of the hill and provided small climbs and fast-flowing downs in a final jump before re-entering the start-finish PIT lane loop. The course was around one hour long—challenging, fun and requiring a lot of concentration.

Canberra is my happy place, I get such a good vibe, and after a day of practice, I feel euphoric, content, full of energy, yet calm. Warm with anticipation. We went out to dinner as a big group and chatted excitedly about the prospects of the pending race. Tomorrow is Friday, with one more chance to embed the processes. The next day, we set up our pit area where Norm and the extra crew would assist with bottle changes, lights, general feed, and support. We rode one more lap at a leisurely pace, putting it all together in one hit.

"Norm, I feel amazing, and I love the course. I think I can win tomorrow", I say as we finish up our practice. It is mine to love, and I have a strong feeling that no one else will love this as much as I am going to. Today, I ride like I don't have a chain on, my legs feel weightless, and I am calm yet so wired. Every action is purposeful, every thought calm and controlled. Everything felt perfect.

On race day, I slept in, attempting to squeeze out more time in bed with my eyes closed. This time tomorrow, I would be finishing off my final hours of the race, exhausted and eager for sleep again. Breakfast is a simple meal, oatmeal porridge with banana and a coffee. Norm and I start preparing and packing what we will need for the race; it's never-ending. We had two bikes, as close to the same as possible, with spare wheels, tyres, helmets, lights, batteries, shoes, cleats, pedals, and a saddle. There are at least two of everything. Then the food; you need a buffet as food fatigue is real. What you desire at 6:00 pm on Saturday is different from 6:00 am on Sunday. Food is fuel; racing hard for 24 hours ruins your appetite. Some of my go-to options were peanut butter sandwiches on plain white bread with the crusts off, fruit in jelly, lollies, homemade risotto, pasta with a basic tomato sauce. The preparation is exhausting. It is best to pack loads of clothing, spares, extra warm gear for the night, socks, leg warmers, and jackets—the clothes needed for presentation if everything went to plan and towels and toiletries for the shower. For me to get out and race, well, the racing felt like the easy part.

The Race.

It is Saturday, October 9th, 2010, just a day, and it is up to me now to choose how I want it to play out—warming up on my road bike on my stationary trainer, with music and headphones, time to rehearse the plan. You see, I had spent the past six months creating a mental rehearsal of how this race would feel, what I would think, what I was going to experience and how I would deal with the highs and lows. I knew the trails well, overlaying my experiences onto a visual of me riding them simultaneously. As I sat on my bike now listening to music, I embraced everything that was about to unfold. I knew what I had signed up for; I knew it was going to hurt, I knew that I would have to put my absolute BEST on display and that all I needed to do was follow my process, have faith in them and be ready for the moment to go for the win.

A 24-hour mountain bike competition is a race of attrition. Many athletes can go fast in the beginning, for 6-8hrs. After this time, the race takes on casualties, not just crashes or mechanicals, instead, riders who went out too hard. Forgetting to drink or to eat, or just riding above their means and following the race plan of another rider. I am preparing myself for the first hour, the fast start with everyone pushing for the best position; I need to be ready for anything. I loved the strategy in this form of racing, the fear to perform propelled me into action. Investing the time to create a plan, a series of controllable processes and training to be physically in the best form possible to have an excellent chance to win and take control of the race.

It is 10:00 am; I am sitting on my bike, warming up and confirming my race plan, zoned in and ready for a big race. The morning sun warms my back and gives me energy. It is a cue, a process that I welcome. It is hard to explain the apprehension and excitement in the final hour before the start, knowing you will hurt and be sleep-deprived, willingly so, all whilst being ready to fight for it. At the top end of the elite field, right through to the age grouper just hoping to finish, the battle is with your mind first, as it tries to keep you safe and remind you what you are doing is not normal. It is by far the most challenging part of the race to control. However, I have not started racing yet; I am still aligning myself with my goals with less than two hours to go.

> This time tomorrow, I will be on my way to finishing.
> What do I want this result to be?
> This time tomorrow, 24hrs will have passed, the next day will be here, and right now, it is up to me to set in concrete what I want and how I want it to play out. What will this look like?

A day comes and goes. It goes quickly. I warm up my body and brain, making a pact with myself. No regrets, when it gets tough, never give up, when I start to hurt, invite it, welcome it, say thank you and that I have been waiting for you to come. As soon as I say this to myself, I am so excited; it's incredible. That warm feeling on my back permeates all over, and I know I can win this race. I am not fearful, and I am not nervous; I am excited. I am ready. My bikes are primo; Norm has set them up with race plates and given them a once over to ensure they are running perfectly. Two bikes are essential to winning, it gives us a chance to swap around, and one gets serviced whilst I ride the other. It was 11:00 am, and I was off for my fifth or sixth nervous toilet stop. We all need to be ready for the race briefing in thirty minutes. This is the final step; entering the arena; knowing you have agreed to fight it out, you may as well just make it happen and do it to the best of your ability. I have food in my pockets, sunscreen on, and have hydrated as much as I can—a final bite to eat and a sit down in the fold-up chair before the call-up. The day is hot, 29 degrees celsius, and a midday start implies we will be warm for at least another six hours. The calmness is still there, yet I am beyond excited; this is the most challenging time. Those final minutes before you are racing.

Today is a Le Man's start. *Le Mans-style start was used for many years in various types of motor racing. When the start flag dropped, drivers had to run across the track to their cars which were parked on the other side, climb in, start the car, and drive away to begin the race. (Wikipedia)* There is a briefing, and we walk over with our bikes. A support person holds the bike in a designated area. The riders start about 200 meters away and run to get to their bikes first, then the race begins. I don't enjoy this start regime; in fact, not many do. It does the job of sorting out the fast runners who will get into the single track first and the rest who realise that there is a whole 24 hours left to smash themselves. I want to win tomorrow; however, I also know that if I have a bit of a slow start, I will be behind slower riders than me in the single track. If I can get a buffer on my female competitors, even a gap of 2 to 3 riders between us, I will be happy with that. The tactic is to get out of sight of your competitors. All it takes is one or two corners, and you know the saying, 'out of sight, out of mind'.

It's now five minutes until the start gun goes off. I'm on the front line, a contender with a high rank. I look around at the other elite females and instantly doubt my ability; who am I to even consider that I could win a world championship? These women are stronger, faster, more skilful and experienced than me. What chance do I have? It was a fight or flight response. Right then, I wanted to fly away and hope no one noticed. But then I caught myself quickly, with a few firm words.

"Jess, stop it. You have done so much work and have put 18 months into becoming a World Champion. You have every right to go for it. Have you considered that they may be looking at you and fearing your skills and ability?" I promptly reigned these thoughts in and reminded myself; there are people everywhere in the World who are THE BEST at something. My dream was not unrealistic; I had every chance of winning this race.

Someone would become the World Solo 24hr Mountain bike champion at noon tomorrow; why not ME? I felt calm again, smiled and realised that, Yes, I had everything I needed to win.

The result was up to me. I would need to believe.
I would need to have focus.
I would need to be the one that was willing to suffer the most and for the longest. And I was up for it!

The start gun went off. We were all running, and it was noisy as we clip-clopped on the hard surface. I noticed some of my competition passing me but did not lose much ground. Finally, I saw Norm, and I was on my bike. The relief. 24 hours to go. The race had begun. At the start, everyone is redlining, breathing hard, legs full of lactate, and the adrenaline is in overdrive. This part of the race is always crazy; everyone at the front rides like they are only racing for an hour, and it's hard to imagine holding this pace for much longer. You've got to do it though, getting passed or missing a passing opportunity can cost you a minute here and another minute somewhere else. Sitting behind a rider who seems to choose nice lines can become mesmerising. You need to be aware of how you are feeling at this point. If you're starting to feel good, you're going too slow; it's time to put in an effort. For the next hour, everyone in the race is trying to find that place where they fit, the sweet spot of speed, but not too fast and not too slow. In all the 24-hour races I have competed in, the hardest part is the first hour. The pressure is on. You forget to drink. You push harder than you should, but it's just part of the race. Thankfully on target, the pace does slow down, enough to drink and get your breath back. Now it's time to chat with the riders around you, maybe the person in front is riding a smooth descent, and you get chatting. They ask if you want to pass, and you say, "No thanks, you are doing fantastic, "and so on like that.

The first lap saw Trudy Nicholas, a local Canberra rider, and me battling it out – she was way faster on the downhills, but I was quicker on the up. With one lap down, I was in the lead already.
The temperature was up, and the pace was hot. The first 5 hours brought on cramps in both legs on every section when I pedalled hard. I loved to smash it out in the big chainring, but now I had to revert to spinning easy. Coming in on my 4th lap, I was cramping in front of all my competitor's pit crews, and I whispered secretly to Norm as he ran alongside, "I am cramping!" We were in management mode. By nightfall, the cramps ceased.

I was in first place for around the first 5 hours of the race. Then late in the afternoon, Eszter Horanyi, from the US passed me, and she was flying. For a few minutes, I followed her but then smartly backed off as I realised I would cook myself too early if I did. Amazingly I would find her again somewhere at the bottom of Pork Barrel. I sat behind her on Skyline, thinking I could go faster but instead just sat behind her. Then on the descent, I took a sneaky pass on the high side entry of the berm and safely dropped in on her. I was back to first place. As I came back through the pits for another lap again, Norm told me not to stress as Eszter was coming into transition and rushing too much. Sticking to my plan, I sat behind her and watched. It was not long before Andrea Kuster, the Suisse girl passed me, creating a battle with her and Eszter. Perfect. I was delighted to see them push each other, wasting energy early in the race. It was not yet dark. They gained a few minutes for their efforts whilst I maintained my pace with far less energy expended.

After the heat of the day, the relief of darkness was welcome. Lights on, now it was my happy place. It was 6 hours in, and I was amazed that there was still such a battle going on. Around 9 pm, Jodie Willett passed me, silently without a word on the fire roads. I did not respond – yet. I knew that my time was from midnight onwards, and I was waiting for this. I was now in 4th place. I told Norm I was disappointed. He quickly reminded me of the big picture and was only four minutes down on 1st place. Time to refocus, how quickly that pesky devil comes and sits on your shoulder, putting doubt in your mind. My mantra was simple. You deserve it, you have done the work, and your time is coming, be patient, control the controllables.

It may well have been on my midnight lap; they are all a bit of a blur; however, it was dark, and it was late. I enjoyed the flow on the night laps, content with my own company and loving the trails. The gap was a few minutes between first and me. I had no idea I would catch the girls ahead on this lap, yet somehow we all culminated on the fire road climbs. At one point up a steep, dusty double track, I climbed quicker, and there was no one on my wheel. With no lights over my shoulder, no heavy breathing, no noise, nothing, I risked a peek about 100mts down the track and still nothing. It was now that I risked changing to a harder gear.

GO NOW, Jess, get out of the saddle and silently surge, find that 1% and more, pull away Go NOW! No one responds. I cannot believe it; the time has come to make my move. How nerve-racking and how very, very exciting. I have been racing for 12hrs, and now I get my chance to make the winning move. My patience and absolute focus are required to ensure I don't go too hard or crash. Initially, I kept the gap conservative, creating a two-minute gap in just half a lap.

Do I allow myself to dream of this win yet? It was past 1:00 am now. I was whipping out a 1:10, 1:12, 1:13, 1:13, 1:14, 1:18 and a 1:16 lap during the wee hours of the morning. Norm and I were transitioning like clockwork. I was eating, drinking, focused and highly motivated to win. I could see Norm was getting excited; he was praying that I would be safe, injury and incident-free. Many riders were crashing or having mechanicals. In these early hours, it's dark and cold, and the focus is on processes.

Find the Flow. Get off the brakes. Choose that line. Drink here. Change gears here. Get out of the saddle there—unweight front wheel, land soft. Repeat.

> **The pure joy of hearing the first birds sing before the sun is up. Nature's circadian rhythm inspires me to be hungry again, and I crave something real to eat, a welcome sign.**

Food fatigue and feeling like you can't and don't want to eat can be a real issue with long-distance racing, so when you willingly want to eat food again, it's time to get excited. Norm was starting to worry, doing the sums. Katrin Van der Spiegal, another accomplished local rider, was beginning to bridge the gap. I knew that as long as I stayed upright and incident-free, she would have to be superhuman to beat me now. I kept imagining her gap to me and what twenty minutes were in distance – not time. Twenty minutes took me from transition, almost to the top of Stromlo. It was a considerable gap to bridge. I now allowed myself to believe I would win with my final lap to go, even if only by fifteen minutes; it was a win. I had fought for an entire 24hrs for this. What a lap. I was so proud of myself. I quickly transitioned for this final lap, only changing over my bottle, riding slower on technical sections to keep it safe, pushing a little harder on the fire roads, keeping it smooth and final fast descent.

At three kilometres to go, I knew I had won.

In less than 10 minutes, I was going to be able to call myself a world 'freaking' champion. As I rode those last few kilometres, the feelings and emotions were a mixture of relief and disbelief. The words are hard to find; it is exhaustion, yet exhilaration, absolute fatigue and pain all over the body and the mind. Of course, I was excited about finishing this race. Finally able to get off the bike and not have to fight anymore. I do not let go of the processes; even though I could now, it is all about flow and gear selection and maintaining effortless momentum as I push towards the final moments. There is a section in the last kilometre where the trail picks up speed; there are braking bumps and a few jumps, fast corners and the chance to lose it here. Concentration is still required; everything hurts as I do my best to 'float' the wheels over the rough terrain. My feet are burning, so sore, as are my arms and entire abdominal region; everything has been working non stop absorbing the landscape for 24 hours.

Then I see it, the sign, 1 km to go. A friend is there, taking a photo, and I dared to take my hand off the handlebar and give a conservative fist pump. Now I start to celebrate.

There is not much more I need to do now. I could run the final part of the race if I had to and still win. I know Norm will be there, waiting for me, and I know he will be even more excited than me, which makes me happy. As I come over the final hump, I see him, hear him. Tears flowed down his face. **We did it, we won.** Russ Mullens passes me an Aussie flag taped onto a bike pump, and this is how I rolled over the finish line, dusty, dirty, so damn tired, waving the Australian flag to win my first ever World 24hr Solo Mountain bike championship. As I crossed the line, it was straight to the media, but I couldn't speak properly. Words fell out of my mouth with no filter and said what was on my mind. Right now, I am unsure I ever want to do that again and that I might retire from 24hr racing. Those that have worked harder than anyone else and put themselves through so much pain and suffering can understand; you just aren't sure you ever want to go there again. After the media commitments, I returned to our pit area with Norm, and now everything throbbed with pain. This part of endurance racing hurts the most, which I always feared more than racing itself—time to shower. As I wash off the dirt and grime from my tender body, it feels like the final stage in a tribal initiation. My body is so sore that my mind is no longer thinking with clarity, smashed beyond where ordinary people would choose to go.

> To be broken is where the gold shows up and is part of the drawcard to endurance racing. It is not in the act of the race where you gain the most. It is not even winning the world championship. Exceeding your comfort zone is where pure clarity is gifted, no matter what your place.

During this race, I began the actual journey, which I called 'Cracking the Code of Life.'

The CODE is simple. There are no barriers to success. There are no shortcuts to success. It's consistent hard work, becoming comfortable with discomfort so you can bear more than most are willing to. To get to the top where others only dream of, you must do more and be willing to do so. It isn't that much more, once you put yourself in the arena, you may as well fight for it, and when you are trying to be the best in the World, where everyone else is doing their best as well, then you have to exploit their weaknesses and capitalise on your strengths. But even then, there is just one more thing; you must not be content with a 99.9% pass rate. Simply go that 1% more; that's when you will find yourself at the top. The cracking of the code is so simple. When the light bulbs went off in my head today, the euphoria of what I was experiencing was like a drug that left me feeling so driven to do it all, yet so calm knowing I could do it all. I just didn't know what ALL was yet.

Winning today, being on top of the World, this itself was lacklustre; instead, my brain was in overdrive with the secret I had just unlocked. Of course, I was beyond stoked; however, my pragmatic self celebrated the processes, blowing my mind. What would I or could I do with this new information? Now to get ready for the presentation of a lifetime. I was now a World Champion.

How it really looks, 24hrs later
Adam MacLeod

Support from Norm through the pits
Adam McGrath

Media! I had just crossed the line to win
Adam MacLeod

My dad teaching me how to ride a bike
Mum

Chapter 2 - Childhood Dreams

Somewhere along the way, I chose the path to be strong and resilient, and I understood that it was far more productive to use any hardship or adversity to keep living my best life. However, this outlook didn't always serve me well. Fiercely independent, yet so very shy, I hoped not to go unnoticed in a crowd. My gaze held low with my shoulders rounded as though to help protect what I had so strongly my dreams and aspirations to be someone more.

The outside world was equally cruel as it was boundless with opportunities. My shyness was debilitating in the big wide world; no one enjoyed being made fun of or bullied. I remember finding solace in my own company, dreaming big, imagining a life where I could be the real me, with no need for the cliquy friendship circles, the useless gossip that glues them together. The pain of not fitting in did hurt. I am equally sad for that little *girl and proud and grateful for what she went through. I would often cry under my sheets and pray for tomorrow to wake up a different person. No, for me, I realised if I was to live my best life, it was up to me. I didn't need to be popular, but I hoped for acceptance one day.*

Me around 2 &1/2-3 years old

It might have been my 4th or 5th birthday; I know that I got a bike, which changed my world. We lived in the outskirts of in-nercity Geelong, with wide streets, laneways and sparse parkland. I was the eldest child born in 1973, my brother Ben, born in 1976. My mum and dad had been married for a few years. We were not far off moving into a new home in the suburbs. There were many happy times, family gatherings, going to the beach, swimming at the local pool after school. I was adventurous and open to anything, even when I was a lot shy. At 4 or 5 years of age, most children have no concept of failure or success or what people might think if they get it wrong. The memories mixed like a montage, no timeline, a burst of images and emotions. Our next-door neighbours were

American and loved having tomato juice with their meals. I was invited around for lunch one day; I ate what I was given and didn't complain. I drank this juice, gagging the entire time. I had a friend across the main road named William, and we used to play the Jessica & William show, where we would run across parts of concrete that were 'hot lava' and climb up a fence to safety and make it all up as we went. One day at school during recess, I was playing chasey, and another boy accidentally crashed into me, and my head hit the red brick wall of the toilet block so hard. We went back into class, and I couldn't stay awake. I was leaning my head on other children's shoulders as we sat around in a circle on the floor. I got to go home early that day. There was a monster that lived underneath my bed, I was sure of it, and the fear that would come over me was so intense I could not move. We had a backyard with garden beds, and I have vague recollections of eating snails, and my brother would eat cigarette butts from the phone box out front of the house.

Me, my brother Ben, my dad and our cat in Geelong

The day I was given my bike is etched in my hard drive though I was too young to have words. It was a rusty orange-red colour with 16-inch wheels, a second-hand gem that was repainted and repurposed for me—no training wheels, just my dad and me out on the front pavement. I hopped on, my hands on the bars and feet on the pedals whilst my dad held the back of the saddle. He told me to pedal and to keep pedalling to keep the momentum going. We may have tried this once, or it might have been days of trying; all I remember was that I was pedalling along believing I was being supported, then realised that I was doing it independently. I didn't have a library of words for this moment but rather a collection of emotions.

I knew I would ride a bike forever and be free so long as I was riding my bike, fulfilling me with a sense of adventure, the perfect tool for a shy loner like me.

We moved, and I left St. Mary's Catholic Primary School; it may have been an inner-city concrete jungle of a school, but it was small, and I felt like I fit in. As with any move when you are a child, finding your feet in a new school can make or break what happens next in your life. Not long into my transition to East Geelong Primary School in Grade 1, my parent's relationship started to fall apart, and it must have impacted me; maybe it was just the move in schools; I may never know. My memories from here, at 6, are of a slow build in debilitating shyness, feeling like a failure, withdrawing from social interactions and avoiding sport or being the centre of attention. I used to hold on to go to the toilet, wet my pants, and run home from school without telling anyone; later on, I got called names, bullied and bashed up by a girl who tormented me, and I kept that to myself. I would get all the way home from school before being told I had forgotten to pick my brother Ben up from his prep classroom, as he was only a few years younger. We did a lot of our schooling together.

I did have friends, a few, and got along well with my teachers. I loved art and writing, but I felt deeply embarrassed and inadequate for who I was as a person most of my days. Even when my name was called out to check attendance, I would blush beetroot red. There is no other way to explain this other than feeling like I was lesser to those around me. I was very much loved, cared for, and I had a home and family. We went to school in good clothing, and I was washed and clean. But I did not have snacks and drinks like the other kids, mine were wholemeal cracker biscuits, and a frozen orange cut up in tin foil with water from the fountain for free, brought to school in a plastic bag. All I longed for was an orange juice in a tetra pack, but it was never to be. In the end, of course, it never mattered, and we were doing the best we could at the time. As I write this, I ache for the primary school-aged Jessica if only she knew who she would become. She needn't have felt sad or wished for a better life. I had my mum write notes to be exempt from swimming sports. A teacher taught me how to breathe whilst doing an annual cross country run. I listened to him, and I still remember this today. I would never represent the school, but he showed me how to enjoy it, and I never avoided running or athletics again.

In grade 5 or 6, I can't recall exactly; we did a Bike Ed program. I needed to borrow my cousin's bike as I was at that stage where my bike was too small. I loved riding. So, of course, I was happy to learn more about how to ride my bike. We went out on the road and learned how to negotiate traffic, do hand signals, and turn right in the middle of a road. I was learning life skills, things that built my confidence in a tool I loved and already knew how to use. The program culminated in a bike ed camp. Providing me with this opportunity to excel and enjoy perhaps was the most critical thing that occurred in my pre-teen life. It would be very safe to say that this 'bike ed' experience was pivotal in creating the foundations of me as a World Champion. I learned how to be independent, take my bike on longer journeys, ride on roads, and communicate with other vehicles and traffic on roads. The bike rides were always on by myself and got longer as I got older. It seemed my prime purpose for riding was to get away from my life, to escape and explore and keep alive that pure unadulterated essence of joy I had when I got my first bike.

> As I was nearing the end of primary school, I cared less and less about what the cool kids thought of me as I developed independence and intrinsic focus. I found my niche and did things my way, and it followed me throughout life.

The end of primary school brought about the intense desire to move away from who I was or who others thought I was and create an authentic version. I chose a girls-only high school, Matthew Flinders Girls Secondary College. Located in the CBD of Geelong, I needed to ride my bike or catch a bus. It's safe to say that I took it all on 1985, the beginning of high school, no boys around to make fun of me, new friends and an abundance of learning to be had. I cared less about being 'sporty' or 'academic'; it was just school, a place to learn and enjoy a few close friendships.

I LOVED high school. There were times when I made mistakes, lost friends, was a bully myself and got into trouble with lunchtime detention. The introduction of boys as something more than just painful antagonists was revolutionary, and I was a fan. I never knew I would be interested in boys and them in me. Blue light discos, High school socials and other underaged gigs spattered over the year. They opened up a social life, what RaRa Skirt you were going to wear and if you had the latest Maybelline two-tone violet-hued lipstick sealed with the most amount of cherry flavoured lip gloss you could handle without it dripping off. These years of 1985, '86 played out like a never-ending summer. We were a larger family at home now too, my father was living interstate with his new wife, and my mum had met her new partner, my stepdad, Tony. Amber, my younger sister, was born in '82, with Thomas coming along in '85.

Life was pretty good, but it has a habit of throwing in a curveball just as everything seems perfect, and the grit I had developed in my early years was about to be given a test. However, until you reflect on situations, you can genuinely understand what wonderful gifts are inside many of our trials. The many experiences we have, the way we respond, and the personalities we develop add layers, creating our foundations; these are continually added to as we move through life.

I was about to add another layer.

Mum and me

My first bike

Sitting on my grandma's front porch handknitted everything

Chapter 3 - Adversity is my blessing

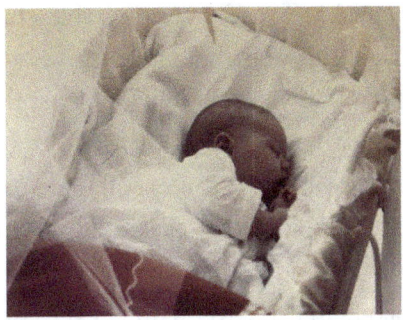

Baby Jess

If you were born knowing your life story and how it would play out, would you try and change it? What if you chose to embrace the good and the bad, knowing this was simply the undulations of a life well-lived? Appreciation of the good times is stronger when we have fallen upon hard times. Enduring hard work, sweat, and tears earn us a sense of achievement. We can't always win, and we will surely lose from time to time. Could it be the risk of failure and rejection to live your best life, which requires a good amount of vulnerability?

What if this was the only thing holding us back from being the best versions of ourselves to be vulnerable and to embrace failure?

I was 13. Toward the end of 1986, my best friend Angela recovered from Glandular Fever. I had missed hanging out with her dearly. Her family were very much Italian, old school Italian. Her mother, also Angela, used to spend weekends making homemade pasta and passata. Vegetables growing in every spare space in the block, plastic over every piece of furniture with lace on every seat or couch. Ever hopeful I would get asked to stay for dinner. Angela showed me the swollen glands on her neck, which resulted from her illness. I was amazed and wondered what mine felt like as a comparison. As I felt my neck, I found a considerable golf ball-sized lump and thought perhaps I now had glandular fever too. I went home, showed my mum, and we were off to the doctors the next day. Tests came back with negative results, and the GP suggested leaving it over the Christmas break and if it was still there in January to come back. It was still there. We went back, and now the tumour presented itself, located behind my sternum in an x-ray. My name went over the loudspeakers in class. My name never got called. My mum and Tony were there to pick me up. Bags packed, we were off to the hospital.

The news was that I had cancer; the tests would reveal if it were Hodgkins or NonHodgkin's Lymphoma.

There was no fear of what might be; at 14. It was February 1987, and I had started year nine at school. These tests were awful, with the worst being the lumbar puncture and the bone marrow sample taken from my hip. Then came the news.

I was diagnosed with Hodgkin's Lymphoma, and chemotherapy would start now. I could expect to feel nauseated, be sick and lose my hair. The cancer was stage 1, and the prognosis was favourable, with an 80% chance of a successful remission after five years. My thoughts were simple and practical, with a bit of rock star fame in my eyes.

I would be a survivor no drama.

I would deal with losing my hair it's only hair.

I had the C-word that would give me some kudos back at school.

And then the first chemo treatment happened. It was hard to predict if I would feel sick; everyone experienced different symptoms. The same day, my friends showed up, and I was ill; they promptly left; it was all very unexpected. Vomiting sucked. The chemicals gave an intense response. After these chemo sessions, I would be so sore like I had done a workout; it was hell. They gave me a drug used widely for chemotherapy then, nitrogen mustard, and along with this, I had another drug to assist with nausea and help sedate me. Always a horrible combination, sleeping and drugged-out as the chemo leached into my bloodstream, then without warning, I would be looking for the kidney dish to vomit into whilst half asleep. Then I would sleep, vomit, sleep, vomit until it was over. The following day was a write-off. By the third day, I was back to normal and attending school again. The treatment regime consisted of a 2-week cycle. Week one would have me in hospital overnight, knocked out solid and violently ill. A week later, I would have the follow-up dose, and I was nauseous but over it very quickly. However, it ended up being more complicated than this. Most hard-fought things require the ability to refocus, realign, and be ready for the unexpected. As each week went by, my body was taking longer to heal from the chemo, becoming anaemic at the same time. My veins, to begin with, were not exceptional. So they would put the IV drip in my hands' prominent veins each time, which hurt a lot. Poking and prodding, I was in pain and distress, gritting my teeth, crying in pain. Not too fond of this, I wished I could disappear. Though I knew eventually, I would need to face up to the invasion of this thin piece of medical grade plastic entering my veins to feed me the poison that would make me sick; yet cure me of cancer. My body fought hard, but it was my mind that got tired—tired of putting up with the pain, the vomiting, the tickboxes of all my treatments to be completed. I knew it sounded pathetic to be feeling overwhelmed by ten months of hardship, but at the same time, it put a chink in my resilience. It took much of my ammunition away, and my blood count became too low, often. There were always weekly blood tests to check on this, becoming harder and harder to extract blood. Sometimes taking blood from the veins in my feet or even resort to milking finger prick to get enough for the tests. I knew of young people dying of the same cancer diagnosis as me; pneumonia or an illness from their suppressed immune systems was often the cause. I was so grateful for my health.

> **At the beginning of my cancer diagnosis, the goals were to be in charge of my health. I became engrossed in nutritional literature and vegetarian eating and organic food, cooking most of our meals at home for the family. Nutrition was one area I could control, and I read a lot on mindset, choosing my thoughts and what I would do to improve myself today and each day.**

Not every day was terrific, and on those days, I would create. I immersed myself in art, design, cooking and making anything, drawing up patterns to sew clothes and spending days designing and making something to wear. Cooking dinner for the family, writing stories, painting on a canvas or drawing anything. I loved designing houses, captivated by images of walking through my dream house and plotting this down on paper in an architectural style plan. On these post-chemo days, I would also sleep a lot. As I was nearing the end, my oncologist said my prognosis was excellent, but there was no promise that this was it. There would be more tests and revisiting each month to ensure the treatment had done the job 100%. It was only nine months in, so close to the end, and finally, I cracked. I was 14. I thought I was invincible. I had backed myself unequivocally on this. Right at the eleventh hour, I was about to give up. I told my oncologist that I was no longer willing to accept this pain and suffering, and I needed out. I remember telling him, "I can do this on my own; I can do this with meditation and organic food and my mindset. I am going to the gym and working on my fitness. I don't want these chemicals in my body anymore. I am sick of being sick and feeling this way. I want to do it on my own"

He listened. My mum listened too. I lost it; the hardship I felt had pent up, and I was now a blubbering mess of tears and snotty tissues; well, they were probably hankies, my mum made sure we had hankies; I was the one that ironed them.

After listening to my 'get out' plea, the oncologist calmly said, "You have come this far and have only two treatments to go. Why don't you stick it out? What have you got to lose?"

Perhaps all I needed was a big cry to get out that emotion to clear my true thoughts on what to do next. I knew he was right. The final two doses took a bit longer than expected due to my blood count. As I clung to remaining strong, I knew that it was just time, and it would pass. In one month, I will be on the other side. That year, 1987, the year of vomiting and needles, will be a distant memory.

At fourteen, I was most proud of accepting what was happening to me, the adversity, and what would come from embracing it. It was difficult, but at the same time, I had learned to embrace the hardship and challenges and to learn to overcome them. I looked forward to the years to come and how this year would set me up for the future Jess; I was not through this yet, but my time to shine was nearly here. Eleven months later, I was done and dusted, had a big party in our backyard to celebrate with family and friends. I wasn't one for a celebration, let's have a party, and then what?

That was my year of cancer. I passed year 9, went a bit off the rails, met a much older boyfriend, and grew up.

The year was now 1988; now 15 years of age, I found myself in the next phase of the fiercely independent teenage years. Something had changed, that's for sure, mostly that I was a bit more assertive and a lot less tolerant. I got a casual job at Kmart to earn my own money and spend it on whatever I wanted. I was not a very nice person to my family; one minute, we would be getting along well, and the next, we tried to kill each other, and I wasn't afraid to push the limits. I still can't believe I turned out ok. The ties to my life with cancer were still active, and I attended Camp Quality events. One camp, in particular, was life-changing for me. We were at Hume Weir on the border of Victoria and NSW, with children from both states attending. People I had never met before. Friendships formed quickly, chatter about catching up over the school holidays. I started formulating a crazy idea to ride from Geelong to Sydney, carrying all my gear to stay with one of the families for a few days and catch a train home.

When I got home, I got a train timetable and bought a map and started to work out how much time and money I would need for this trip. I shared my plans with my mum, never thinking it was out of the question, though she felt that riding up the Hume Highway wasn't ok for a 15-year-old girl to do solo on a bike, instead she had a genius idea as an alternative. I needed to chat with a family friend, George, about the Great Victorian Bike Ride. He had done this ride last year and was heading back again in 1988. George said I should approach the school to form a group. I went to my favourite teacher, Mr Grant and told him my idea. He was keen and made it happen, with two teachers and six students. A few training rides and we were off on the Great Victorian Bike Ride. The GVBR was a nine-day 'touring' bike ride, your gear carried in trucks as you rode from town A to town B. On arrival, set up camp, shower and eat in an en masse style tour on wheels and repeat this the next day. The shortest day was 50km, and the longest was 120km.

> It was the biggest adventure I had ever done. Now all I wanted to do was ride my bike all day, camp somewhere and do it again the next day. I was in love with this concept and wanted more.

All the while, I loved school; my passion was Art, Design, Textiles and Home Economics. No one had to motivate me to get my work done, though I was still fiercely rebellious. My school was in the Geelong CBD, and often I would leave at lunchtime to get something in town or go home early because I felt like it, knowing full well I would happily get that assignment done in my own time at home that night. Consequently, lunchtime detention was a regular occurrence, but I used this time to get homework done. I hated toeing the line, a non-conformist. The following year in 1989, I went back to do the Great Vic Bike Ride again, with two casual jobs; adding to my Kmart employment, I started working nights as a waitress at a Mexican restaurant. I enjoyed the hard work of hospitality. Having two incomes allowed me the opportunity to buy a new bike. It wasn't anything special at $500, but it was mine with the pure purpose of riding long distances, and it even had toe clips. Interestingly, I had no cycling role models in my family and certainly not someone suggesting I get involved in the sport. To me, cycling was always a journey. I bought the magazines showcasing the Tour de France riders, but my interest was more about the gear and what I could buy for my bike. No one told me I could not or a specific athletic pathway to take, so I rode and found joy in cycling. I finished year 11 and sealed the year off with my final Great Vic Bike

Ride on my hard earnt bike and couldn't have been happier. I was 16 years old.

It was 1990, and I started my final year in high school. I formed a new friendship and a new boyfriend, Scott. The crew were friendly, but they too were a little off tilt, and I followed suit. The mix of hanging with 'the crew' and feeling out of love with school sent me in a downward spiral of disengagement. We were your usual gang of youths, not partaking in illegal stuff but undoubtedly insubordinate. It is most likely typical teenage behaviour, but it's perhaps how we value ourselves and the support we have that directs us positively or negatively. After the Easter break, I quit year 12. I had chosen some subjects that didn't align with me. The careers counsellor had an obligatory chat with me, and I said that I was out, done, and would find other career pathways to succeed; right now, I was not completing my schooling, end of the story. My mum said to me, "Jess, that's fine, leave school, but you must now get a job, and you will pay board." Fair call, so I got a job. Within the first week of post-school, I knew I would work for the rest of 1990 and then return the following year to finish Year 12 the way I wanted to, none of this 'career orientated' subject choice. I worked at The Reject Shop and had an excellent team and a great boss. He even suggested we do a fun run, 10km. That was a big eye-opener for me. I used 1990 to experience independence, spend some money, save some money and start planning for 1991. Part of my savings was my enrolment back into school and my books. The boyfriend, Scott, was probably never going to be a keeper, but I hung on, and it turns out that it was for a good reason.

In June of 1990, he joined the Royal Australian Navy, and I went to Melbourne to see him off one winters day. I sat waiting for Scott's processing at the recruiting centre for the final medical before leaving on the bus trip to Crib Point Naval Base.

> Sitting in a chair in the waiting room, minding my own business, someone else was checking me out. I had no idea. It was this exact moment that my future husband laid eyes on me and said to himself, "I am going to marry her."

Norm made it his only task to befriend Scott; then one weekend came home with him to meet me proper. I didn't like Norm. A week later, he had the idea to call me and got my number from Scott and made an excuse that he'd left something behind when he was down and needed to organise how to get it back. Instead, he had plotted how to contact me and whisk me off my feet, despite still being in a relationship with Scott. Within 2 hours, he was in Geelong; this was Christmas day of 1990.

It was March, only a few months later, when we decided to marry. I still remember it like it was yesterday. Norm and I were young and in love, you know how it goes, we would spend hours on the phone as often as possible—writing letters, pages long, every week. I couldn't imagine life without him. It was a weekend, and he was off duty. Norm was still at Crib Point Naval Base, not yet posted to a ship or naval base. Norm was driving, and as we often did, we talked about life and our future dreams together. I would look at him with so much admiration and love as he would me—squishy mushy love. But today, he looked a little anxious, like he was holding back something but also desperate to tell me.

"Jess, I have been posted to HMAS Hobart in Sydney and will be leaving next week".

In shock and unable to answer, except in a flood of emotion and tears, I didn't know what this would mean for us. We began exploring all options to make it work; the answer was simple. I would finish my studies; he would move to Sydney. It was a perfect opportunity to focus on school and him to focus on his career. We would catch up every month, sometimes me going to Sydney, and sometimes he to Geelong. But then Norm dropped the big bombshell, "Jess, what about if we got married at the end of the year? That way, we could be together forever."

> I looked at him and asked myself, "Can you see yourself at 80 years of age, growing old with him? Will he be your best friend and remain by your side for the rest of your life? Do you want to invest your heart and soul in this man?"

By Norm's side, I pictured myself cooking in the kitchen together, chatting and smiling, as an 80-year-old and felt the warmth of a friend. He was a keeper, he was my life partner, so I said Yes. After I finished year 12, I would move to Sydney and start university. And so 1991 was a year of finishing off my studies and waiting to go and start my new life with Norm. It was exciting that we had never lived together, having little knowledge of each other. Our life would unfold as we lived each day out, learning about our history but forming our future together. I completed year 12, got into the university I wanted, married on December 1st, moving to Sydney the next day with Norm.

December 2nd, 1991, was the start of the rest of my life.

On honeymoon, at our local beach, Bondi. So young!

Young Norm and even younger Jess, freshly married

Our wedding day, Dec 1991

Chapter 4 - Living and Learning, Failing and Flying.

When there is nothing to lose, you may as well aim as high as possible. Asking, "What is the worst that can happen?"
The worst-case scenario is often feared, avoided by inaction, procrastination, overthinking, losing momentum and the courage to try. I didn't understand this at the time, but I had nothing to lose and everything to gain. The life I had dreamed of when I was young wasn't living in a posh house with plenty of money, a nice car and expensive clothes. No, my dream was to live. To get amongst it and live each day like I was on holiday. It was not about travel or seeing the sights of the world; I dreamt about the excitement of life.

What was I capable of doing, and who could I be? When I married Norm at 18, I found a partner who wanted this too; the simplicity of being in Love with Living. The following 15 years had just the right amount of triumph as they did adversity; it was like a well-written TV soap opera. The act of living was so much fun; the only fear I ever had was losing my soul mate. There was nothing more I needed in my life, just Norm. One day I told him, "We could lose everything and live in a tent, but as long as I have you, we can always start again, from scratch I'm not afraid".

From failure, we grew, embracing adversity to pave new ways to enjoy life. Every blessing, every gift was within reach, and there was nothing to lose so long as we had each other. I wanted only this.

Before marrying and moving to Sydney, we had spent a total time together of 4 days, culminating in 4 weeks over the 12 months leading to our wedding day. I was 18, and Norm had just turned 21. Not knowing what you don't know is a liberating gift, and we were very young. United on December 1st and living together for the first time in Sydney on December 2nd. We were living in Rose Bay. Norm was working on HMAS Hobart at Woollamaloo. I was about to start a Bachelor of Design at the University of NSW in March 1992. We spent the next five weeks going to the beach every day and getting to know each other. We rode our bikes, doing laps of Centennial Park. We even rode to Woolongong, stayed the night, and caught a train home. But mostly we went to Bondi Beach every day, swimming in the surf and baking in the sun. We heard about a waterslide park in Western Sydney and decided to go. I loved the slides where you sat on a tube and landed with a splash at the end. I could have done these all day long. We progressed to the more daring slides from greater heights with faster speeds. I was doing well until Norm suggested that we go down the steep, super-fast speed slides.

Norm asked, "What are you afraid of? What do you think will happen to you? Do you want to have a go, even just a little bit?"

I didn't have a firm enough answer to back out, so I embraced the fear and had a go. All I had to do was stand at the end near the landing pool, watch for five minutes, and if I couldn't find a good reason not to have a go, then I would do one slide, and if I didn't like it, at least I tried once. Despite my best efforts to find a good excuse not to do it, I agreed, no one was dying; in fact, everyone was smiling and going straight back in line to go again.

> After a deep breath, I fronted up to the long flight of stairs, listening to the instructions intently, then closed my eyes and let go. Did I have fun? Did I do it again? You bet I did.

The day at the waterslide park showed me a straightforward way to determine what was possible. By looking for examples of people who had achieved anything, see how they did it, then go for it with my interpretation. Whenever I was fearful from this day forward, I knew what to do. Our 5-week post-marriage bliss eventually came to an end. I started University, and Norm went back to work. The Ba of Design was a wrong choice; I quickly knew this. I should have accepted the offer at the College of Fine Arts in Darlinghurst, but this wouldn't matter anyway. Norm went out to sea on HMAS Hobart and was gone for weeks, up and down the coast of Australia. I was missing him terribly, looking forward to his return home. We had planned to see The Violent Femmes at Coogee Bay Hotel; it wasn't what I hoped to hear when I found out that Norm was in trouble and had to do time on the ship. He wasn't coming home yet, as they docked back in at Woolloomooloo. Norm missed out on the Violent Femmes; one of his navy mates took me instead, who I shared my first experience of a death-defying mosh pit. A day later, Norm ended his naughty time on the ship. His brother Allan had died; the news ripped his heart out and would change his life forever. Allan had been Norm's closest sibling. We went to his funeral on the Gold Coast, and I watched Norm change. All that Norm loved and adored about Allan now became part of him.

We didn't know it yet, but we would face more adversity and decide on our actions quickly. Our lives were dynamic and changing fast, and we were often in a state of survival. We had enough money to pay the bills, we had time to do leisurely things, but we were in Sydney, entirely on our own, trying to find our way in the world. So young and quite naive. Norm returned to work after Allan's funeral, and I returned to University. We then found out that HMAS Hobart was on a 6-month deployment in two weeks. I decided at the same time to end my course and find work instead. After being married for six months, we realised that going away to sea and leaving me behind alone in Sydney was not a healthy option. Norm attempted to seek help and an appointment with a naval social worker. We both attended and emptied our hearts as newlyweds, totally unsure of our ability to survive being apart for this long. The social worker wrote a letter of recommendation for an Honourable Discharge. There were still hurdles to jump. There is a villain in every good story. Norm's XO (like a middle management role in the Navy) didn't see eye to eye. When Norm approached him with his request for Honourable Discharge, he avoided any action on it, hoping to have Norm come away on deployment. Norm had other ideas anyway, such as going AWOL (Absent without Leave) if he couldn't get out in time. The pressure was getting stronger each day. Norm went from being a model sailor to insubordinate, hoping to get kicked out. Then one day, the magic happened. He received his promotion from Seaman to Able Seaman with the ship's Captain and asked how is everything going Able Seaman Douglas? It was not the right place to do it nor the correct pathway. The XO was also in attendance, so he decided now or never and blurted out that he was not happy at all, and the Captain listened intently. It was the shit storm that needed to happen, and Norm got his honourable discharge that same day. As he rode his bike home that afternoon, I could see relief in his eyes that he was out of the Navy, just like that. And so our lives changed again, with many urgent things to address. We lived in Rose Bay with subsidised rent. Norm needed to find a job, and we needed a cheap place to rent. I hadn't yet left University, but this expedited my decision to leave and gain employment. We spent the weekend searching for an affordable rental and found a downstairs one-bedroom apartment at Bondi Junction. Our move happened the following weekend. It's funny how when you are so young, and everything is a barrier, you still go for it regardless. Norm went and visited many businesses with a resume in hand, then happened upon a job for a bicycle courier. He had no idea of the streets in Sydney, so he studied a map for a weekend, had the interview, got the job. Norm knew all the streets, but when he had a job to pick up from the MLC building, he needed to ask, "Where is that?"

He learnt damn quickly and loved this job. I picked up around 20hrs a week at the local Woolworths at Double Bay. Phew, we were okay and had averted danger, starvation and homelessness! It was as simple as that—survival mode. There was a problem; solve it. We lived underneath an Asian restaurant called the Mekong, on Oxford Street, Bondi Junction, eating many meals there. The price to buy a meal was stupidly cheap, maybe it was $5, and 20 cents to use a glass to fill it up with cold tap water. Our weekly grocery budget was $50. We no longer had a car either; it was just us, public transport and our bikes. Money was tight, but life was carefree, and we had each other.

If you ride a bike long enough, shit will hit the fan. You will have a crash, or hurt yourself, or someone will hurt you.

Norm's job as a bike courier carried this risk daily, and he would come home and tell me of buses and cars that he chased down to let them know what they had just done. Then one day, he was heading down Bent St, and a car turned in front of him. I am sure Norm wasn't going slow but certainly had the right of way. Norm tells me he went over the bonnet in a protective tuck and roll, but the bike was damaged, and he was beaten up, alive but hurt. Norm did get back to work with a new bike. It took ages to recoup losses from the person that caused the crash. Norm lost his nerve, eventually ending the job of a bicycle courier.

Hold tight; we are still in the same year, it is 1992, and within the week, Norm found a new job, managing a store in Westfield Eastgardens. The shop was a Saint Cinnamon franchise, making cinnamon buns and coffees. He found a job for me very quickly, and we worked together in the business, working hard every day. Riding our bikes from Bondi Junction to Maroubra on busy roads taught me to be decisive on the roads. It was fun, and we spent all day talking about the dreams of our future. But with no commitments holding us to Sydney anymore, Norm picked up the phone and chatted to an old boss on the Gold Coast to tee up work. And just like that, we had two weeks to finish up, pack up and leave. We had such faith in our decisions, coming from a place when there is nothing to lose; you may as well have a go. The next challenge was twofold. We sold much of our furniture and worldly possessions as we needed the money and didn't have the extra funds to take it all with us. Rent the cheapest but largest car that could fit our gear. Then fill this car with all our leftover possessions that didn't fit in the removal truck. With no credit card to our name, we had no choice but to pay a $1000 bond plus the rental fee for the car. Making this happen was tough, and we needed that bond returned in full as promptly as we paid it; there were no plan B or excess funds once we got to the Gold Coast.

We walked out of our rental, breaking the lease and leaving many things behind as we locked the door behind us. It was November, adios Sydney, hello Gold Coast. Our travel budget was tight; as fun as a road trip was, it was all about fuel and eating like a pauper to arrive on budget. There was so much anxiety; knowing we had $1000 on return meant we drove this car with so much care. Leaving Sydney on a Saturday, we arrived with one day of rest on Sunday. Things moved fast. Moving into our temporary accommodation that Norm's mum had organised for us on Mermaid Beach, Norm started work on Monday. Within a week, we moved to a longer-term rental a few kilometres up the road at Broadbeach. Our time on the Gold Coast was from November 1992 until June 1995. It was a challenge for me to find employment; I was now 19, nearly 20. To create a routine and stop feeling useless, I would go to the CES (Commonwealth Employment Service) and look on the job board first up and apply for at least one job a day. The outcome of the morning would then dictate what I needed to do next. Did I need to prepare for an interview? Or was my day free? I would explore the Gold Coast on my road bike on my free days. Within a few weeks, we found a long term rental, a new unit in Labrador out in the suburbs. I don't recall how we did it; however, Norm and I started riding super early in the morning with a bunch, leading to road racing. I was pretty raw, a hard worker, racing D grade with all the older guys who were smart and knew to sit on my wheel and sprint me at the end. On the other hand, Norm was always in the money in B grade meant we went out to breakfast and spent it all in one hit. Still, I loved it.

When you ride a bike long enough, you will experience coming off at one point, sometimes more than once, it seems.

I was happy fighting it out in D grade, and Norm had progressed to A grade with a good sprint on him. On the day of this crash, some of the Malaysian Cycling team were training on the Gold Coast; they were super aggressive. My D grade race had finished. I was on the finish line, excited to see Norm up in the front bunch as they turned the corner into the finish straight. He and one of the visiting Malaysian cyclists hooked arms and shoulders. He went over the handlebars and didn't get up. We were there with friends, and Leon raced up to see the damage. There was blood everywhere as the crash tore his left side skin with a lot of road rash and a broken helmet. I didn't enjoy seeing this. Soon after this crash, we talked about having children. We were married. We were young. We didn't have much money, so what did it matter? And I needed to see if I could even get pregnant after having chemotherapy. Norm's crash gave us both a fright, and we took a bit of time off-road racing whilst he recovered. Around this time, our friend, Pamela, wanted a road bike, and I wanted a mountain bike; we were the same height and even the same shoe size, so we did a complete swap. I got her mountain bike and she, my roadie. I had a spark of excitement and was keen to give it a go after riding mountain bikes with my brother in law at Nerang state forest on a loaned bike.

After many months of being unemployed, I finally got an interview at Movie World for a hospitality position working in one of the many cafes. I got the job, the relief of finally working and earning some money so we could breathe a little easier. We processed black and white film and produced prints. Norm was busy most weekends working with a modelling school and taking portfolio shots, a few weddings and corporate functions. I'm still impressed at how resourceful we were. It is how Norm afforded a new mountain bike, an Apollo Himalaya. Mine was a Shogun Trailbreaker. We were in the money now! We bought a bed. Previous to this, we were sleeping on the floor with sheepskins and blankets; our neighbours offered us an old foam fold out couch for our living room. Eventually, we purchased a car; it opened up our world, and we started going to mountain bike races. I will be the first to admit; there was nothing exceptional about my ability to ride a mountain bike. Mostly it was about watching others and seeing one skill I could master then building up confidence with this approach. Though if a feature was too big, like a log, there was no way I would try and ride over it; I just got off and got back on again on the other side. I was not fast at all. But what I possessed was the ability to endure the suffering for longer than many. I discovered this one day at a 3hr mountain bike race near Brisbane, showing up with no food and one water bottle. No one told me what to do, no nutrition articles in magazines and no Google search on eating for a race. Thank goodness for the random bucket of apples out on course, which I stopped to eat. That day, my water, my apple, and Shogun Trailbreaker won the Female Solo race and I discovered my most outstanding attribute was endurance and stamina. Still so young, still so unaware of what potential was lying inside me. I was also trying to get pregnant and not yet focused on investing in an athletic career of any sort.

The exact moment I was pregnant, I knew it. I bought a pregnancy test that day, and boom, I was pregnant. I was late in my cycle, and my whole body felt different. I made an appointment with my GP, and he confirmed another test and booked me in for an ultrasound in a few more weeks. The due date for our child was January 28th 1994. We worked hard, saving money and doing our best to set ourselves so I could leave work. Norm kept racing mountain bikes, and I would watch. I rode until I was eight months pregnant, only stopping because my legs would bump into my pregnant belly. Pregnancy was not my thing. Everything felt sluggish, and I was sure that Norm and I would only do this once. So we got on with it and knew this child would be the one go we would have at being parents. Saskia was born on January 28th 1994, her due date. Within the next day or two came postnatal depression. It hit me hard. No matter what I told myself, no matter how much I was in love with Saskia, I couldn't cope with the enormity of it. My daughter was now my responsibility for the rest of her life. Many people had opinions. I was too young, inexperienced, and should have waited until I was older, wiser, and ready for a child. Unsolicited advice was most unwelcome. Five days later, I turned 21. I got myself going, as best as I knew how. I thought joining a playgroup might help, but it was not my scene. I still remember slowly disappearing with Saskia out to the car whilst all the other women were making cups of tea, and I never returned. I was having trouble breastfeeding and sought help from the Nursing Mothers Association. They were like old fashioned matrons with the view of suck it up and, at all costs, succeed, leaving me to feel like a failure. I left that support network. So I chose a way to engage with the world, connect with people, have a breather each day and develop a daily routine that worked for Saskia and me. When she was four weeks old, I found a creche at a gym to take Saskia. For two dollars, I got 90 minutes of my time in the gym, and the carers in the creche loved looking after a newborn. At 9:00 am every morning, we would be there. On our way home, I would buy a few groceries, pay a bill just to be out and about, finally going home. Saskia would sleep, and I would run around like crazy doing the washing and cleaning, then quickly have a nap myself. Before I knew it, it was time to pick up Norm from work, and we would window shop for an hour or so. We then accessed financial assistance for childcare twice a week, and that's where my life changed. I realised there was an endpoint, light and hope, and parenting needn't be such a burden if you have support. Our families were in Victoria, and we were on the Gold Coast; childcare was crucial for maintaining good mental health. The freedom gained from childcare was indescribable. Using my time wisely, I would go for longer rides either by myself or with Pamela. When I would get home, it was a cleaning and cooking frenzy, along with a nap and Norm and I would pick Saskia up around 6:30 pm. It turns out that it was a fantastic outlet for her as well.

Now that we were a family, Norm gave up road racing altogether. Instead, on weekends we drove to the hinterland and took Saskia on bushwalks or went to the beach or found parks with swings and slides to play on. And twice a week, I got to ride my bike when and where I felt like it. As we started to find our feet with parenting and gained some fitness back, we returned to the mountain bike racing scene. Even though I was apprehensive in many situations, the amount of fun I had racing my mountain bike outweighed any level of fear I had. Norm and I survived the first year of parenting; by 1995, we had enough headspace, time and money for me to go back to study. I had started casual work as a waitress at Taco Bills in Broadbeach. It had sparked my interest in completing a six month TAFE Pre-apprenticeship course in cooking. I thrived on the hands-on learning of TAFE. We had found a secure and comfortable lifestyle. We were finally chiselling out a future until the winds of change came our way again, purely by chance. As my pre-apprenticeship course ended, I was offered employment in the kitchen at Sea World Nara Resort. A large kitchen with three restaurants and room service. I said yes to the opportunity. To be offered this from the Gold Coast TAFE class was a compliment, and I certainly felt optimistic about a future in cheffing. That would have been simple if the story had finished here. Whilst I was at this job interview, Norm had caught a Greyhound bus to Sydney to meet up for a job interview himself. He had just gotten back from 2 weeks in Germany representing Camera Town, where he worked, at the Leica Academy. Super expensive beautiful cameras and ten days of using them to travel the country, take photos, drink beer, and eat wurst. Norm had made friends with a staff member from Michaels Camera & Video in Melbourne, and it looked like he could get a job there if he wanted. If Norm could land a job there, we could return home to Victoria. Norm's bus trip to Sydney resulted from a quick phone call to the store owner the day after returning home. "Yes, I have heard all about you; I would like to offer you a job if you're able to meet me in Sydney for an interview this weekend; I will be there for a conference." We scraped together the money for a return ticket from the Gold Coast to Sydney and made it happen. Norm went to the YMCA, had a shower, prepared for the interview, got to where he needed to be, had the discussion, was offered the job and caught the bus back that night. All done on the weekend, and he went back to work on Monday.

> Just like that, we were planning our move to Geelong. He gave notice; we sold a few things and booked a delivery truck. Saskia and I flew back to Geelong, leaving Norm to pack up, driving down the highway with a car full of gear and a cat.

Arriving in a Victorian winter was cold, as we lived in my parent's garage for a few weeks. Norm started work; I found a full-time job too. We quickly found a quaint cottage to live in, close to the train station and work for me. It was beginning to feel like we had come home. I joined up in the gym up the road, and it wasn't long before we had found sport as an avenue to enjoy our new community. I still rode my bike around the river and road rides; it was just a bit harder to manage with full-time work and a toddler with Norm commuting to Melbourne daily on the train. Norm loved his job, and his financial incentives were a significant boost. But earning many bottles of wine every week for his hard work would prove to become a real problem in time. Norm worked hard at Michael's and further developed his reputation and career, leading him to apply for a job at Kodak as a sales rep. Usually, these roles belonged to people with marketing degrees, but he pushed on and succeeded. Quickly realising this was the wrong move, he got straight onto finding a more suitable job and 18 months later became the store manager at Camera House in Geelong. Finally, Norm could immerse in living instead of commuting hours a day. However, that sales target wine incentive would appear again, and complimentary alcohol in the house did not make for a healthy Norm.

With Norm working in Geelong, we had more spare time now. Saskia started ballet, gymnastics, swimming, netball and also basketball. Norm and I joined a mixed basketball team; I started learning how to row on the river and eventually rowing at Torquay Surf Life Saving Club in a surf boat. Immersed in sport, we were a busy but happy little family unit. Surf boat rowing was a huge turning point, facing more of my fears yet proving that the act of following processes could give surprising results. Surf boat rowing requires having faith in your team and knowing they rely on you to deliver your absolute best, as you do them.

My first crew at Torquay with Gary

When rowing out into breaking surf as the four of you work, the oars in unison feel like life and death, scary yet addictive. The sweep, the person who holds the big steerer at the front of the boat, can see the swell coming in and judge when we need to ROW

HARD, or hold water, or when we will get smashed and need to bail. Our sweep, Gary Pettigrove, had a saying, most likely passed down to him, and it was simple, "Eyes in the boat". Do not look out and worry about the swell or the other boats in the race; or things you cannot control. Stay focused in our cocoon, the boat, with our crew. These four words were calming—simple direction to maintain focus. Surf boat rowing gave me mental strength that I didn't know I had, improving my physical confidence in performing mammoth tasks. I was not the most gifted, the fittest or fastest, yet I understood the importance of technique and faith in the processes. It clicked with me, and from this experience, my self-confidence grew. If I could learn to do this and enjoy it, what else could I do?

Ah, Surf boat rowing. Steering me forward in my exploration of sport and what I could do. The girls I met and formed friendships with, Joh, Joan, Natasha and Jeannette, created a strong foundation. Our sweep Gary put us through crazy 'boatie' gym programs and stair running to improve our strength and fitness. We still had so much to learn and had come a long way from the first few times out on the boat. The first surf carnival we went to was both scary and empowering.

We were a bunch of mothers, giggling like schoolgirls, giggling with excitement and most likely nerves. We are at the beach early to get warmed up with the other surf clubs, with watercraft everywhere, skis, boards, IRB's, and surf boats. We are the 'boaties', clubbies that don't swim, the lucky ones that get to do their bronze requal on a calm day. Being a boatie and having this reputation suited me fine; I loved being on the outer and preferred doing all the yearly requal tasks when the swell was down. Our sweep, Gary, was calm, and we knew he could talk us through the processes with his easy-going nature. This gaggle of mums didn't respond well to anxiety or drill sergeant antics. We didn't have anything to prove; we did it purely for ourselves and had a good time. I set the timing for the crew. My position was stroke seat, the rower that sits almost at the feet of the sweep. I must listen intently to all instructions without falter or fear. It's also the easiest seat to jump into on the start line being in the shallows I was forever grateful for this.

> We held on to the inside of our seats, the end of our oars on the boat's gunnel. We are ready to jump when on the call IN! It was time to race.

"Half, half, three quarters, full", we heard Gary roar. We were off; the tide was running out and the waves were dumping. Did we have a good run out to the turnaround cans? We didn't know, don't look, eyes in the boat. You see, we are facing the shore. We don't know what swell is behind us; it's all up to Gary, his commands and the urgency in his voice. He calls out, "Hold water!!!" and we can sense a set coming through, and it's dumping. We need to get out in between the breaks, preferably without using the pump, emptying the boat of water; this will slow us down.

I like Gary; we all do; he has such a calming influence on us; when all around us feels like a war zone, he knows how to get the best out of us.

We are holding water, using the blade of our oars and body strength to keep the boat from moving, trying to stay in position, ready for the next call in the lull.

"Row! NOW, row, row, row, ROW!!!" Gary is serious, he calls out at the tempo he needs us to respond with, and we don't hesitate to give it everything.

We left the safety of the shore only forty seconds ago! Adrenaline pumping, with lactate screaming in my legs; we will be pushing this pace for at least another four minutes. But I now understand why the pressure is on; we are on a green wave, its peaking, about to dump, bow seat needs to stand up and get her bloody oar in, come on Joan, stick that oar in on the back of this wave, thump. The rear of the boat slaps down the other side of the wave; Joan can't get her feet back in the straps, but we are rowing, and we made it through the break. Time to find the rhythm, breathe, drive with the legs, steady up the slide, together. We are nearing the cans, the turnaround spot; now we get to see where we are; it's not too bad. Midfield is good; now to bring the boat back in. We can now see the waves; we know what is coming! There are now lots of runners to catch, steady. We need to catch every little bit of swell and get the boat moving ahead of the wave. Now it takes all our concentration, physical energy, strength and mental resilience, and always eyes in the boat.

We know the tide is heading out, and the waves are breaking on a sandbar. Are we going to luck out in between sets? Are we going to be asked to drop off the back of a wave and feel that dead water and go nowhere, watching another crew speed by us? The options are many; some are by choice, most are by chance; this is where the sweep uses his smarts, as often crews can win at this point from behind. All it takes is wrong timing, the wave brakes, crew trails oars and move up the boat, but still, it digs and broaches and gets hammered by the swell.

Today we seem to have landed a kind alley, a lane to race in that is predictable for the conditions. We miss a few runners, bumps of swell to use for momentum, but it turns out to be good, as the one wave we needed to catch, we nailed. We felt it; we were just ahead of the wave, our stroke rate had built to a bright and light tempo. We could hear the gurgling sound of rushing water passing underneath the boat. Right on cue, the wave started to break. We trailed oars as Gary called to "Come aft", heading up the centre of the boat, to sit at Gary's feet, smiling and giggling, that gaggle of girls doing epic shit. Back in our seats moments later, we rowed proudly to the finish line, alive and in one piece. That was so scary and addictive all at once. Today we had a few more races to do; we came third and progressed to the next final.

I fell in love with this feeling of focus; I had never experienced it before. Sure, I had ridden my bike, raced it and been regular with bunch rides. Still, this connection with a crew, the sweep with an intense focus on developing together as a unit, was exceptional. Rowing was fun, the gym workouts super competitive, and I got to invest time away from the role as a mum. I was in my mid 20's feeling like an athlete, and I would never have believed this possible for me. It was 1999. I enjoyed surf boat rowing for a few more years, living in Geelong and driving to Torquay a few days each week early in the morning, rain hail or shine to row in the crew, I didn't mind. But people come and go, and our sweep moved to Canberra; that 'team' vibe was never quite the same. Still good friends with everyone today, and we reminisce what a pivotal part of our lives that time was.

Rowing in the surf had opened up my mind to other possibilities. I saw an advertisement for women to join the East Geelong Football Club women's team, to play on weekends in the Victorian Women's Football League. I had become swamped running a small business and searched for something to do for me. I knew nothing and had zero skills, and was nervous as hell. The newspaper article did say no experience necessary, so I fronted up having faith I could learn. Mark Yeates was our coach; he used to play for Geelong in the 1980s. I loved the drills, the skills, the running, the camaraderie with the other women and younger girls. Our first year, we didn't get much of a look in and copped many thrashings, but we improved. I enjoyed footy so much that year both Norm and I took up umpiring football. We spent our weekends umpiring on a Saturday, playing on a Sunday. The following year Norm became the coach.

As soon as Saskia was old enough, she became a boundary umpire. We all eventually officiated a game together, along with my dad.

East Geelong FC Womens Team 2001

At the end of my second year of football, we played well and made it to the finals. We had one more game to play before the finals, against Hadfield. I was not the most skilful player yet had a lot of fitness and tagged a player and filled in space. I played out of the centre as an 'on baller' and had a few jobs to do, be a right royal pain to my opponent and fill space. The centre ball toss happened; I was going in for the ball that had spilled on the ground. A player from the opposition rushed for me, hip and shouldered me hard as I was picking up the ball, and that was it—twenty seconds of play. I knew I had broken something. The rucks contested the centre bounce, and the ball was tapped and coming my way. It was on the ground, with my name on it. Teammates were waiting, only meters away on either side, that I could quickly handball off to; I just needed to get it first. I had no idea I was a target, as the impact from the other player forced me to stop. Yes, I was in pain, but something had just happened, and I couldn't put my finger on it. Had I heard a crack? I simply felt weird, and when I ran, my shoulder hurt.

Yep, I was out. I hadn't even got possession of the ball. Hadfield was known for being rough, using every bit of body contact to weaken their opponents. I was their first casualty. The trainer came running out and took me off the field. Instinct told me to back out and get off the field, and I found myself holding my right shoulder. I didn't even make it 20 seconds into the game. I stayed on, watching the rest of the game with my arm in a sling, the pain slowly increasing as the adrenaline wore off. An x-ray showed I had fractured my clavicle, and it would be a good six-week recovery. Our team made the Grand final but lost. I never got to see it as I was so sick after the break, I came down with the flu and was bedridden. The following year, I played again but lost my mojo and didn't have the same attacking playing style. Our coach in the 3rd year was Janelle Cribb, "Cribby". I had developed a thick skin from years of umpiring and playing football, making decisions, being part of a team, and in both capacities being decisive and backing yourself at all times. I was far from perfect but proactive and always one step ahead of the game. Preparing for the next action was a learned skill that I took with me after these years. Failure, Bankruptcy, Alcoholism, a near marriage breakdown were all experienced in these next few years. Norm and I took on many opportunities. It became apparent that we were resilient and not particularly afraid of failure. If I was to reflect now, we were doing our apprenticeship in life and getting it done with a lot of enthusiasm. My boss sold his business to us, his two employees. Hindsight shows me now that getting into business with someone like that was never a good idea, but I learned so much again. We had very little capital to start, and our outgoings were more significant than our incomings. Start-up capital will only last a little while until you can no longer juggle the creditors whilst waiting for money to come in. We didn't have a Plan B. It got to a point where we were personally paying all the bills we could, taking it away from the business so it could keep running. After we paid expenses each week, Norm and I had $100 to buy food. We then started juggling our bills, ringing up to get extensions on phone bills and the like. I remember it got to the stage of making meals from tins of baked beans because that's what we had in the cupboard, and I couldn't spend any money just in case we needed it for something else. Thankfully Norm was working full time and earning a wage, or else we would have pulled the pin a lot earlier. It was inevitable, we both had a massive breakdown, and there was no end in sight. One day we were scraping loose change to buy milk, the next day, we could breathe. We weighed up our options and left the business, and declared bankruptcy. It may not have been the best way to go down at the time; however, when you are juggling everything to survive, it was the right decision.

I learned some valuable lessons during this time. I was a hard worker and enjoyed throwing myself all in. Starting a business with anyone because you can is not a sound model. Start-up capital gives you room to breathe. Grow slowly and have profit margins to grow and pay the bills. I was around 25, and declaring bankruptcy gave me a chance to reinvent myself. Norm got me an interview with Matchworks, an employment agency, as a Case Manager assisting long term unemployed people into employment. I got the job, and along with it was a company car and many perks, including a wage where we could live again. I was good at this job, and my main focus was always getting to know the person first. When I look back on our training to do this role, it was how to engage the person from Centrelink, link them to our online database, claim expenses and make file notes. Not much spent developing better relationships with people to get the most out of them.

Too much complacency and comfort in our lives brought back an old friend of Norm's. We now had expendable income, time and a bottle shop down the road. Many of our social interactions included celebrations and, of course, alcohol. I was often the driver to and from such events and would plan to get to the location on a route with no bottle shops and hope Norm didn't notice. I didn't want him to get stinking drunk and embarrass himself, and I didn't want to spend money on alcohol and feel crap the next day. I had no idea that Norm's obsession with drinking was a sign of an alcoholic. Norm's alcoholism was initially opportunistic and with an all or nothing binge approach. If it were there, he would drink it until he couldn't do so any longer, and many a time, we would have to leave early, and I would be embarrassed. He wasn't physically aggressive but had a tongue that said things he shouldn't have. Alcohol brought out all his insecurities and made him feel superior to those he might have otherwise not felt. One New Years eve party at our house, he got so wasted. It was around 11:30 pm; he walked to Eastern Beach with some others, as we lived close. I was exhausted and told everyone I was going to bed, and the party was over. I awoke the following day, and he still was not home. Now, I was worried; I was angry and all the emotions at once, with no idea where he was or where to start looking. When Norm finally got home, he had no recollection of where he was or had done; the whole experience was a total blackout. Yet somehow, he was holding down employment; somehow, we managed life. But more often, I was using sport as my escape from this life at home. Norm would happily drink in the house, and Saskia loved it. She was young enough to love the freedom that came with watching whatever she liked and eating whatever she wanted, whilst her dad drank cask red wine and sat on his computer and worked. Amazingly, many good things sunk into his brain whilst drinking into a stupor. It was a time when Norm immersed himself in learning, laying many foundations for his knowledge today. But when dealing with someone obsessed with alcohol, it's impossible to discuss why they are drinking and why they left the bread, butter and vegemite out again, for the 20th time, last night? To him, I was nagging. So I escaped and avoided him as much as I could. Weeknights were for taking Saskia to her sport or going to the gym until late, or footy training or whatever I was up to at the time. But whatever it was, I made sure I didn't come home until late, so I spent the least amount of time in his company. Every evening after work, he would walk to the bottle shop to get supplies, and every night he would be drunk, leaving not one drop.

Our relationship wasn't aligned anymore, having discussed that we were heading in separate directions. Norm wanted something different than I did, and I began to plan a way out. Budget sheets and all working out how much I could afford for rent and living expenses to go it alone. I still didn't know what was going on, even though it was staring me in the face. Norm threatened me that he would gain sole custody of Saskia, and I would have to budget for that too. I agreed to it, as he had led me to believe that my parenting was less superior to his. When I look back now, I can see his guilt and fear of being found out in his behaviour to gain control. That's what alcoholics do, deflect their inadequacies onto you; maybe I am the one with the issues after all?

But it all came to a head one hot evening in mid-October 2003. I was going to a Friday night drink and dinner with some work friends. Norm wasn't coming, but he invited himself, and the group said yes. Before going out, we walked down the street to the bottle shop and got a lovely bottle of sparkling shiraz, and I enjoyed having a glass. It was cold, bubbly and refreshing, the perfect drink to have on a warm balmy night. Norm quickly finished the rest of the bottle off. It sat there empty on the kitchen bench as we went out. We caught a taxi out to dinner. Norm was already drunk but ordered more red wine with our meal. To begin with, it was fun, and then it got nasty. I can't believe they didn't just tell him to go home. We went out to a pub, but within 5 minutes, I knew we had to go home; Norm had nothing nice to say, and I was exhausted being a part of this. Catching a taxi home, the abuse he was hurling at the driver; I was sure the driver would kick us out. Finally home, I was fuming. I had no words, I wanted to scream and say all the words at once, but my mouth wouldn't open. I only remember a feeling of total disgust, and I made a face that told him so—telling Norm that he was an embarrassment. Tonight's behaviour had potentially ruined me, my friendships and his employment. I had lost it and tonight was the straw that broke my little camel's back. What happened next was something I had only heard about, from stories of domestic violence. Norm's reaction was so unexpected.

I had forgotten about the empty bottle of wine on the bench. As he went to grab this bottle with anger, my eyes went wide with fear, and I ran out of the house, as I was, no phone, no money, no jacket, nothing. As I ran out the door, I heard the bottle smash on the bench and felt that gut-wrenching feeling of loss and despair, and I walked around the block trying to settle my thoughts and work out what to do next. I was cold, but I was numb with fear. I was devastated but had no emotions. The flood of adrenaline kept me from crying or being distressed. Instead, I focused on the solution of what I needed to do next. I couldn't control Norm, but I had to gain back my control. I decided to go back to the house. There was no way of knowing if Norm was angry and waiting for me with the broken bottle or if he held remorse and his actions. I decided to go to the front door and listen; I could still run away if threatened. The front door was open wide, and I could hear him cleaning up the glass. I stood there for a moment. Do I or don't I? I went back in, moving cautiously up the hallway and saw that his drunken bravado was gone, and he was now ready for my onslaught. I didn't give it to him. I did not want any more action tonight, so I asked for him to leave me alone in the spare room so I could have some sleep and that we would talk more tomorrow. Getting to sleep was not easy. The next day I got up early and assessed the damage. There was glass everywhere, and the coins Norm had thrown in anger from his pocket into the plastered wall that had left deep imprints; I could tell that a 50c coin had landed in one spot. I busied myself with cleaning, dreading the discussion we would have this morning. Would I have to come up with an argument to defend myself again? What blame would Norm be able to shift onto me for his actions? I cleaned, and I waited.

Norm was awake and walked into the kitchen; his first words were, "What are you doing here?"

It was my house too, and I had every right to be here. What he meant was, why are you still here and not packed up and left? I wanted to hear what he had to say and discuss our next steps in this relationship because this was not acceptable. Norm articulated clearly, "I am going to Alcoholics Anonymous tomorrow, and I will never drink again because I am an alcoholic."

BINGO! There you have it; I am married to a freaking alcoholic, okay, so now everything makes sense. My heart says to give him a chance, but my head says undoubtedly not? I am raw with hurt and can't fathom what recovery for Norm looks will be. I also want to give him a chance to be the man I first married. To live the life I believed we deserved to enjoy. If it meant he gave up alcohol forever, then there would be no more of this drama, and we could have another go. I was up for that. Norm attended AA as promised and has never touched another drink from that day forward. Life got better; in fact, it is always getting better. It's not what he was missing out on; it's what he gained back. It's what I have now too. Now that I could breathe, I was able to imagine a future. I began a Certificate 3 in Fitness and soon after finished a Certificate 4 in Personal Training. Before long, I worked as a Bootcamp Instructor with Physical Revolution and worked at Matchworks. It was here that the next level of learning occurred. Who was I, and what limitations had I put on myself. How could I use this knowledge to get the best out of other people? Waking up motivated to inspire other people at 5:30

am on a dark, cold winter morning was less than inspiring. I wanted nothing more than a warm bed and sleep. But I had a job to do, and people were relying on me to kick their butts.

I developed a motherly persona as a PT. One that was loving and nurturing, full of praise but reminding you to clean your room and get your homework done before you can watch TV. Kick butt now; reap the rewards later. Every morning I would thank my group for turning up. I admitted to them that I too wished I was in bed, but I looked forward to the group's energy, and their presence inspired me to be my best. It was true; I did rely on them, and them me. Consequently, we got the best out of each other, and they trusted me. What I share next becomes a pivotal part of my life and how I made things happen.

Often in Bootcamp, there would be many repetitions of exercises, like 100 burpees or push-ups, to be completed over the session, amongst other challenges. The typical response when under pressure is to say I can't do anymore, I am done. I would remind my group that all they had to do was one more push up or one more burpee; get one more done. Worry about the other 99 later. At the end of the 60-minute session, everyone had succeeded in getting 100 reps achieved. It did not matter if they had to modify them due to fatigue; they still got done. My catch cry to them was, "everyone has one more left in them." And it was true. It is only our mind that wishes us to stop. I loved being a Personal Trainer. Norm had left his job and become a Self Employed IT Consultant. Inspired by him, I knew I, too, could do it on my own and make it in the world of Fitness. I found work at Fernwood, stayed working as a Bootcamp Instructor, Box Fit & Spin Class instructor at Physical Revolution. My PT clients were spread over Fernwood, PR, outdoors, or in clients' homes and Neighborhood houses in Group training sessions. Back to working super hard, super long hours, and before long, both Norm and I put in 80 hour weeks. As crazy as our work was, we got out and enjoyed life. I look back and see the pattern of our actions; we were driven to succeed and relished in the opportunities. We were also parents, taking Saskia to her sporting commitments and bringing her up to be a good person.

One weekend in late 2005, we trained at the You Yangs, running up Flinders Peak and back, enjoying a trail run with friends. Norm and I had our old mountain bikes and the following week enjoyed the run and ride experience. A friend suggested that we go mountain biking the next week as well. We were instantly excited and made a return to cycling. Both of us had kept riding our bikes, but mainly as an exercise tool, and I also used it for commuting to work. Within the next week, Norm found a mountain bike race to enter, and we went and bought new mountain bikes. A large group of personal trainers and friends went with us to Whittlesea for an 8hr Mountain bike race in January 2006. We created Pairs to race, each person would do a lap whilst the other rested, then swap over and keep going until the 8 hours was up. I went first in my team; the course had loads of pinchy ups and technical log features. We came 5th in Female pairs. After looking at the results, I realised two things, I had the potential to improve, and the markers were not far away. I wanted to do this, and I loved it.

It was the beginning of a new year. I had just turned 33. The last time I had turned a pedal in anger was around 12 years ago. I regretted that I had given this up for this long.

> What if I had continued with mountain biking when I was living on the Gold Coast to now? What could I have done? Full of excitement for what my future held and all the possibilities that lay before me. Yet another shift in life. The catalyst for the next phase of growth and personal development.

In February 2006, had I known it was the first step in the path to becoming a world champion, I wouldn't have had the capacity to believe it. The hard work, the learning, and living are all just a steady investment in growth over time. If you stick at it long enough, you will find what makes your heart sing, and even that is not guaranteed to last forever.

But the magic is in the process.

It's so clear why my 1% Rule worked so well and changed my life forever onwards.

Me, Dad, Norm and Saskia umpiring a game of footy

Me Sas and Norm, she is about 6 weeks old here.

Chapter 5 - 1% at a time

"The best time to plant a tree was twenty years ago; the next best time is now."

An ancient Chinese proverb that needs no explanation.

It didn't matter that I was 32 now, wondering if I had continued racing bikes in my 20's. Yes, I did wonder, what if I had done things differently. Still, life had shown me many times over that every moment, every experience formed my roots. Each failure, simply a branch reaching out to see where it could go, strengthened my core values. Each success led me upwards, creating new opportunities to learn and grow. I had planted my tree twenty years ago, and it was still growing strong. Every adversity and success I had encountered in my life thus far shaped my future self.

After the mountain bike race at Whittlesea, I experienced a shift in passion and spent my spare time planning when and where I could ride my mountain bike next. I wanted to do it all and was highly motivated to make it happen. I told Norm and anyone who would listen, "I am going to do great things on the bike, just watch this space."

The game-changer that race at Whittlesea that started it all

But I didn't know how to take the next step, only knowing that I wanted to be an elite mountain biker. I was so keen to become a sponsored rider, improve my skills to match, creating cycling as a mainstay in my life where everything else revolved around it—turning my passion into my purpose, my job. I had a feeling that this was possible and had my name written all over it. But how? I was overwhelmed with this vision initially. Being a person who likes to be self-sufficient, I also didn't know or think about asking anyone for help to get there. I didn't know what the end game was going to even look like, just that this was the path I was born to take and perfectly positioned to see where it could take me. Being self-employed and working in the fitness industry, I'd experienced building things from the ground up and working with people to reach goals. Despite their fatigue or desire not to do so, I always asked my clients to dig deep and give me one more push up or burpee. The concept always worked; my argument to them was irrefutable. It was so simple; if it worked for others, then it would work for me.

I desired to improve my mountain biking so that I could race as an elite level cyclist. There were many elements: riding skills, confidence, nutrition, strength, fitness, and mindset, but I struggled to align with a plan, lacking the knowledge on HOW to get myself on this pathway. The road felt hard like it would take a very long time, and I could already foresee the roadblocks and challenges ahead. The problem was that I was looking too far ahead. I was trying to be perfect before I permitted myself to work on this project. All I had to do was allow myself the grace of being a beginner, to learn and embrace the process of upskilling in all its clumsiness. More importantly, I had an idea. A method that would allow me to learn without expectation yet, by default, achieve more than I had ever dreamt was possible.

I called it my 1% Rule to Success.
Focus on 1 task at a time.
1 day at a time.
1 week at a time.
1 month at a time.
Improve just one thing at a time by 1%.
In a year's time, you will have improved.
You cannot fail.
Every single day, focus on the 1%'ers.

Instantly this gave my mind so much freedom, releasing me from expectations. All I had to do was show up consistently. 1%'ers compounded quickly, with many small efforts often. I was also encouraged because I saw results. In this year of 2006, my goal structure was simple. Race two times a month, train on mountain bike trails two times a week and work on my fitness by running, gym, bike path rides or other opportunities. A simple example of how I used this was to brake a little later into corners and get off my brakes a little earlier out of the corner when riding my mountain bike. Simple concepts that anyone could do. I wasn't telling myself to use zero brakes or go fast, and I certainly did not focus on terms like don't brake early. I spent a lot of time eliminating words with negative connotations. These 1% efforts promoted more. The interest compounded, not just in what I gained, but how the attitude in the process opened up the mind to flow and continued the experience unimpeded because I was totally in the zone.

I swiftly progressed, investing small 1%'ers, finding my flow state, and the learning became fun. I was curious to know more and excited to keep investing my time and effort. When I felt fear or stagnation, I allowed myself to go back to where I was most comfortable on my last ride. Using that to cement the knowledge I had gained, I didn't always have to be on a growth mission. Whenever I felt overwhelmed or that the vision was too much to comprehend, I would ask myself, "What can I do now? What can I act upon today? What is one thing that I know can start the plan moving forward?" I was now using my 1% Rule in every aspect of my life. Was something too big and overwhelming? No problem, find one thing to act upon now and get the ball rolling. Need to put away all the clothes I have washed from being out on a muddy weekend of riding? Start with folding them in a pile. Worry about putting them away later. Afterwards, I would always find I had inspired myself to finish the job off anyway. I turned large tasks into small achievable ones that I could take action now and get done today, setting me up for my tomorrow.

I happened upon this brilliant quote by American footballer Jerry Rice.

"Do Today What Others Won't, So You Can Do Tomorrow What Others Can't."

WOW! It resonated with me instantly and solidified my passion for keeping up the 1%'ers. I felt like I had stumbled upon a secret CODE to living a high-performance life and was amazed that no one else I knew was doing life this way. By the end of 2006, I had completed 26 races, podiumed in 13 and won 6. I bought a road bike and started doing ergo sessions 1 or 2 times a week at Cycle Edge with Donna Rae-Szalinski, learning more about improving my fitness. But what I found by the end of this year was that the longer the race went on, the stronger I seemed to get and the more fun I had. I could endure the suffering for longer than most and embraced this. The penny dropped in October of 2006, Norm and I joined a six-person mixed team in the Scott Australian 24hr Mountain Bike Championships at Kowen Forest in Canberra. The event was a huge affair, with 3000 people in attendance. It was exciting to imagine sharing the course with many riders and setting up camp with everyone—a party with bikes in a forest for two days.

The 24hr race would be my first experience of riding with lights at night. I had never done anything so significant as this and had never done any riding in the dark, ever. My naivety was proving to quell any nerves; I didn't know what to expect. We arrived the night before; I tested my lights for 10 minutes and accepted that I would just learn on the job. Night riding turned out to be the most fun part of the whole experience. A team of six in a 24-hour mountain bike race has the first rider complete a lap, then relays onto the next person and so on for the entire 24 hours. We were in a mixed team, so there were five males and one female, me. I was last in line to go. With the race starting at midday, my first lap was not until 6:00 pm, with the light beginning to fade but not requiring my lights yet. The course was dusty, with challenging fire road climbs and twisting single tracks with tight corners. With my first lap done, I quickly went and had a shower, got some food into me and tried to get a bit of sleep. My next lap was sometime after midnight. Darkness fell, it was freezing, but I was laying flat, resting as best I could. Around midnight, it was time for my 2nd lap. The quiet of the night, fewer people riding, and the pure focus of the light shining the path in front of me gave me such a sense of happiness. I could have ridden all night long; I loved it so much. When I came back in from that lap, the temperature had dropped even more. Back to the showers to warm up and another attempt to sleep. As I lay down in my sleeping bag, all I could feel was the flow of the trails, and as I closed my eyes, my brain was constantly riding twisty tree-lined single track and would not stop working. Sleep didn't happen.

The sun rose, and it was time to see what the new day looked like. I still had one lap to finish off for the team, but I went and had a look at how the rest of the riders were fairing as they were coming into the transition area. I walked to a part of the trail to watch everyone coming through a technical section. I was entranced by the solo riders, riding all by themselves lap after lap after lap for 24 hours straight. What was more exciting was that they didn't sleep at all, and the biggest attraction to me was how beat up and exhausted they looked. These solo 24-hour riders looked trashed, and I wanted what they had.

> I knew then and there this was what I wanted. For no other reason than it looked fun. A lot more fun than getting up out of a warm sleeping back twice through the night to do a lap.

It was now time for me to do my third and final lap out on the course; all I could think about was how it would feel to keep riding and not stop? What would I feel like now at 6:00 am if I had been out there for 18 hours riding solo? I was not saying it out of fear or worry; instead, I was starting to hatch out of pure excitement for the plans. As I watched James Williamson and Kim McCormack cross the line as Solo 24hr winners, I had found my why. The reason I needed to get better, get fitter, more skilled and open up opportunities to experience long-distance rides and races. I had found my niche in the enjoyment of voluntary suffering, and I wanted in on this club.

"Norm, did you see James and Kim come through at the end? Did you see how wrecked they looked? It was amazing. I am in awe of them both. Racing in a team of 6 was a bit boring, but that solo 24hr stuff looks amazing. I think I have found my calling."

We had a nine-hour drive home to talk about the next steps to make this happen, Norm was in full support.

That was October; I now had eight weeks to prepare, as I signed up for the Kona 24hr at Redesdale in Victoria as a Solo entrant. In 2007, these races were often held on private properties with some hand-cut single track weaving through the exciting features of gullies, creek crossings, technical rock gardens and steep uphills.

The Kona, 24-hour course, had a serious mix of everything, including loads of sharp random rocks. Victoria was in the midst of a drought, and country Victoria was very dry. The course would get dusty and rutted out, which made it even more difficult. Norm also entered this race solo. Some strong female riders were on the start list, and I knew that my task in this race was to complete it and learn. Yes, I did allow my mind to wander and think, "what if" I got on the podium. Still, with zero experience in a solo 24, I could not yet conceptualise finishing, let alone winning. At this point, Norm was fitter and faster than me as a cyclist, but as we would find out, he lacked the desire to suffer when the race got tough.

The race started with us on foot, a Le Man's start, in a dry and dusty field where cattle had caused many holes and imperfections in the ground. We negotiated this carefully to get on our bikes. Here I was, only eight weeks later, after watching with awe, the solo riders at the Scott 24 in Canberra, doing it myself. I had not yet even contemplated what would happen at 1:00 am.

So I rode, Norm would be ahead of me at least 5 to 10 mins most laps, but I would find him at our campsite sitting down, looking exhausted and eating something. I would come in, grab something whilst standing up, hop back on my bike and go out again. He would inevitably catch me partway through the next lap, taking around 1 hour to do and repeat the process. Eventually, as the night wore on, he was asleep in the tent and unfortunately, I followed suit. After about an hour of not achieving any sleep and my legs aching, I decided to get going again and felt much better for it. I guess I did not know if I could ride through the night non-stop, so the concept of resting was a preventative measure just in case. As the laps wore on, I slowed down a lot. All the 'first-time 24-hour' learnings came to the forefront. Not feeling hungry, so not eating and forgetting to drink. Making errors on technical trails, cramping in the adductors and wanting it to be over, walking the hard parts of the track as a reward to self. I would soon learn I could be overcome all these things, but I had to experience them first. With around 2 hours to go, I was sitting down, contemplating the hard fact of going out again for another lap. My gut told me this is not how you would want your first 24-hour race to end.

"Jess, I just found out that Katie can't continue, but if you get back out and ride, you can finish third today! Come on, get up, you might regret this if you don't."

That was Norm, watching out for me today and for many races to come in the future. Damn him, I know I must get up and keep racing. I would have to go out and fight for it now, as Justine was closing in. My energy reserves kicked in, and whilst I was hurting, I found speed and enthusiasm again, finishing off my race with two great laps. My first 24-hour solo race resulting in a podium had me in disbelief, and I was so pleased that I had to fight for it. This experience had everything, all the highs and lows, all the lessons I needed to get back to the drawing board and do it better next time. One year into my racing career, I had ticked so many boxes and was able to finish it off with the hardest thing I had yet done. Now that I had a vision of what was possible, how would I take on 2008? I had learnt so much this year; it was a bit of a fairytale to look back and see what I had achieved purely by focusing on 1%'ers. I knew I would have to step up, enter the Elite category and go to the next level with my skills on the bike.

I have to admit that I was scared to embrace this next challenge. I started to conceive all the hard work I knew would be involved, the new skills to learn, the crashes I would have, the physical pain of suffering in a race that I would experience.

At that moment, I could have said, "Nope, too much, let me enjoy this space I am in now and I will progress later, maybe if it works out that way." Instead, I took a deep breath and reminded myself, do not overthink this; you will be learning all over again. Allow yourself to be a beginner in the Elite field. Once I gave myself that permission and removed the expectation, I felt the excitement return. I now focused on the opportunities these challenges would offer me rather than fear. All I needed to do was to show up, to turn up to the start line, and I would learn. My daughter's grade 5 & 6 teacher, Ian Rae, had taught her this valuable lesson, and here I was reminding myself that. "80% of success is turning up."

This small win provided a lot of comfort. Turn up, line up and ride until you are finished. I then devised a mantra I would offer to myself upon starting a race to relieve the weight of expectation I had on myself.

You won't always be THE BEST.
You won't always be at YOUR BEST.
However, you can always DO YOUR BEST.

This became my focus for the next year of learning, keep up my 1% investments, turn up to the start line, do my best and no regrets. The repertoire of mental skills was growing along with my bike skills and fitness. I was doing what I had set out to do and succeeding at it. Each setback taught me more about what I wanted and how to get it. Whenever I had fear or uncertainty, I was building a resume of experience to draw upon. My trusty 1% rule always simplified my anxieties and focus. Initially, the fear of what this year would look like filled itself with new opportunities to expand my race experience. So I said yes, and worked out how to do it later, or as it were on the day.

The mountain bike race scene was booming in Australia. Mountain bike marathons, 100 km long, were on offer in most states, including Forrest, Victoria. It was called the Otway Odyssey, and it sounded challenging. I was instantly attracted to this and signed up with a few friends. We did loads of training over the summer and raced in February. It was tough. I wasn't the fastest out there, but I started to pass people in the race's later stages. It would be a common theme over the coming years for my cycling career; the longer the race went, the happier and more positive I felt. The experience was like an extended meditation retreat, broken to the point where the pain was numb, and I could think and act clearly. The answers to all my problems would come at me, and I would finish big races or rides like this with so much enthusiasm to dream about what else was possible in my life. The act of these rides gave me a similar feeling to what someone might get taking drugs. Either way, it was a very healthy addiction for me, as it added more reason for me to train and ride. It would quieten my mind, clear the clutter and give me clarity on my purpose.

So I rode until it hurt, then waited for the calm.

Year two of my apprenticeship to becoming a World Champion started many new pathways and opportunities. I gained my cycle coaching qualifications; I also did a certificate in outdoor education with components for mountain biking: a personal trainer, group fitness instructor, and Bootcamp instructor. I started to train more and more on the bike and fill my weekends with racing. I had bought myself a road bike again to improve my fitness, so I was racing this as well. Norm and I started a business called MTB-Skills.com.au. The rollout was nice and slow, learning how to teach and break down the elements of technique, enabling riders to improve their skills. Norm had a real knack for being able to do this. Getting like-minded friends involved who were educators, we started to develop a curriculum with sequential, repeatable, and teachable methods at any level. We ran our first paid skills sessions quickly, with online bookings via our website and our first camps at Anglesea and Mount Buller. Then, with my training and Bootcamp instructor experience, I started up the MTBSkills Bootcamp. This led to the Race Development Squad, an inclusive group of riders who would turn up to training and racing to join teams or join teams or solo but ultimately support and learn from each other. We were working around 80 hours a week each. What became quite apparent to us was that if we wanted to make something happen, we could, and so we did.

The rest of the year had lots of racing. Norm and I chose to do the Scott 24 hour Australian MTB Championships again; this time, we entered as a Mixed Pair. The plan was to give me a perfect experience at riding a bit faster but with no sleep but sharing the load with Norm as we would each do a lap on lap off for the 24 hours. With a massive turnout of 3000 riders, we raced at Mt Stromlo. The course had a 'blue' lap and a 'red' lap, and after our practice lap, I decided I would do the blue and Norm the red. It was just us, our bikes, a tent with our gear and the concept of no sleep; keep riding when it's your turn, rest and prepare for your next lap whilst the other is out on course for the entire 24 hours. Norm devised a set of solid processes to follow to ensure neither of us missed a beat.

Everything was going great early on. We were fighting it out for 1st place with another mixed pair. I think it was taking away the enjoyment for Norm as he was fatiguing. His lap was 30 minutes, followed by a 10-minute descent. My blue lap was rugged, with many ups and downs; the concentration was intense, with many of the short climbs also rocky and technical. I kept fighting but could tell that as I would come in to swap over with Norm, his enthusiasm was waning quickly. Our position changed to 2nd place now, with 3rd place smelling our plight. Darkness was falling, and this would prove our undoing.

The concept was to wait five minutes before the other came in at the transition area. As the race progressed, fatigue grew, so the laps became slightly longer in duration. I was worried about Norm on one lap, as I had been waiting more than 10 minutes past his due time. I went out to ride as fast as possible, trying to hold onto our 2nd place, but Norm was nowhere in sight when I came back to swap over. I then heard a big whistle alerting me that he was back at the tent. Now I was worried. First of all, was Norm ok? Second thought was, all this effort for what?

Norm was in the tent, wrapped up in a sleeping bag, shivering cold; he had not followed any of our plans or processes. He was toast. I was cranky at him, got him dressed in warmer clothes, forced a Red Bull down his mouth, put some lube on his chain and sent him off with the promise that when he got back, I would do a double lap for him.

I would never ask Norm to do something like this again. I had the motivation to go deep, race hard and focus on the processes to get the job done, but he did not. When it got brutal, cold and dark, Norm was ready for bed, to call it a day and stop racing. I wasn't angry at him; this was an experience no matter our result. If it was to be, it was up to me. Norm returned from that lap very slowly, he went back to the tent, took off his shoes, dropped his bike on the ground, hopped in the sleeping bag, and slept hard. He wasn't there as I rolled in for the changeover around two hours later and there he was, needing a kick up the butt to get going. With only a few laps to go before we would finish at midday on Sunday, he perked up. Now he was on the blue lap, and me on the red lap up the long climb. We held onto 3rd place, despite Norm's best efforts to have us stop and sleep. When reflecting on this experience, it's laughable, but it wasn't at the time. Racing as a pair for 24 hours was far more demanding than doing it solo, further consolidating my vision to pursue this mountain bike racing discipline.

The following two months, I trained hard because now I wanted to know if I could win a 24hr solo, and I had just the race to test this out. The Kona 24 hour Mountain bike race was moving to Forrest in Victoria and a fun format. Three different laps to be raced for 8 hours each. I learned not to waste time in the pits and to have an array of food on offer because what you like at five hours is not what you want ten hours in. I learned that I enjoyed riding throughout the night; I would gain time on my competition and find my happy place. Norm made an excellent support crew and could easily stay up all night and look after me. He wanted to see me succeed. We had the perfect team and sponsored support from Torquay Cycling Factory.

Two years after deciding to pursue mountain biking seriously and see how far I could take it, I was about to put myself to the test and go in for the win. My rival would be Alex Kiendl, a very accomplished rider who won 24 solo races. I felt confident I could ride hard, ride through the night and enjoy the competition. If the result meant I came 2nd after giving it my best, losing to Alex would be an honour. It was a hot day in December, over 30 degrees celsius, with many exposed sections of trail on climbs that drew the energy from you. I was cramping in the first six hours of the race, so I focused a lot on slowing down a notch and getting back on top of my hydration. The course included many single tracks, which makes it difficult to drink or eat whilst riding. In the first six hours, I could see Alex in many parts of the single track, she started in front, but I passed her in the pits on an early lap. She was always there, close by, fighting to stay with me. I was interested in why she seemed to be struggling. I wondered if it was due to the 24-hour race she had won in October, the same race Norm and I raced Pairs in. Whatever the reason, I started to pull away from her and lost sight, now well ahead doing my own thing. With the night starting to creep in, my body cooled down and functioned better, with the cramping disappearing altogether. I would ride through the night, and Norm would feed me, replace my drink bottles each lap, change my light batteries over and give me time checks on how I was travelling.

The dawn lap is the best. You hear the birds chirping, your stomach reminds you to eat breakfast, and you finally start to believe there is an end to this madness. Until this point, whilst racing, you learn that thinking further ahead than a lap at a time can be dangerous. Laps are a series of achievable processes: eat, drink, breathe, relax shoulders, get off the brakes, stretch the lower back, repeat a mantra, ask yourself, "can I go faster? Can I push harder? Is this all I have?"

Is it tough riding around for 24 hours? The physicality is brutal. However, the most exhausting part is its impact on your mental toughness, inviting the hurt, staying focused, and not diverting from the plan. I learnt a few times over in the years to come that turning up to a 24-hour race without the proper mental health and wellbeing, no matter how fit and strong you are, is fraught with danger. The final few hours hurt a lot; your body battered from holding itself strong on the bike, absorbing all the imperfections on the trails. Even suspension in the bike and wide low-pressure tyres have little impact on supporting the body. Pedalling the bike is the easy bit. The end is near but not near enough. At this time, you will see people riding along at a snail's pace, hanging around transition for too long and trying to find a valid reason to stop. The mind is exhausted, tired of thinking and being on guard, tired of working out the math of how many hours to go and how many laps that might equate to.

When you are winning, the pain is there, but you are winning, which overrides everything.

I won my first 24 hour Solo mountain bike race on this day; now, we are onto phase 2. It was time to invest. Our next move would expedite my growth as a mountain bike rider and take us in another direction. Over the summer, we went to Lorne to watch and be involved in some friends doing the Anaconda Adventure Race, a swim, paddle, run, and ride. Norm myself and Saskia watched on. As we were walking down the main street to get ice cream, Norm and I were looking at the real estate prices of Lorne just for kicks. We then saw houses for sale in the Otways hinterland, like Barwon Downs. In late 2007, you could buy a place for $200,000, so we booked a time to inspect two properties. We were living in Geelong but felt a connection to the Otways. I knew that this would be the place for us to live and also for me to invest my time in mountain biking. The concept was born, and now I was on a mission to find us a place. I wanted to move from Geelong and live in the Otways.

With the seed planted, it was too late now; we sold our house in Geelong within two weeks and now had to work out where we were going to live. I looked into Colac real estate agents and found a beautiful rental in Forrest. What happened next was so quick, but it had to be; the school year had just started, and Saskia was in year 9. We needed to get her into school in Colac at the beginning of the year to make friends and settle into her new life. Of course, she wasn't too happy, but it was a done deal. We were moving to Forrest, a tiny hinterland village of 200 residents, beautiful Australian bushland and lots of mountain bike trails right at our doorstep. The move created a lot of work, vacating our house, having time off our businesses to move and settle in and get Saskia into her new routine. I saw around 40 personal training clients a week, working as a Bootcamp instructor and group exercise classes at Anakie Neighborhood house. We had also started running our MTBSkills courses a few weekends a month. Norm was doing tech consultancy work, building websites, hosting, and umpiring football and basketball.

Forrest was only 50-60 minutes away from Geelong, so we were able to maintain a lot of our business for the first year until we had to rip the band-aid off. Travel, early mornings, time wasted was all getting too much. We finally, as most people who move to the country eventually realise, had to immerse ourselves in our new home town. Once we let go of what we had, we grew our other businesses such as MTBSkills and my cycle coaching and Norm, focusing more on web design and hosting. More importantly, though, I rode my bike every day and headed out onto the trails with marked improvement in my skills and fitness. I also rode long road loops around the Otways, building up a solid endurance base. The evolution of me becoming a full-time cyclist was happening. Not your typical professional cyclist though I made my income through cycling and nothing else.

I gained further sponsorships with Giant, Jet Black products, Shimano and Bike Box. Opportunities, media spots, recognition and acknowledgement was happening fast; it was a bit of a shock. All I ever did and wanted was to ride my bike, get better at it, and have fun. My growth and investment were intrinsic; I wasn't looking for this amount of external involvement. Norm made me a website, jessicadouglas.com. I was almost embarrassed, as I was the cyclist who vowed never to put my name on a sticker for my bike or helmet (I never have to this day). Preferring the understated, 'nothing to see here approach'. I soon learnt that the gifts from sponsorship needed a platform, and I was one of those now; this was a job, albeit a very fun one. I rode bikes, raced bikes, taught people how to ride bikes, coached cyclists, and that was how it was from now on. I was now living the life I had set out to achieve in February 2006, just a mere two and a half years later. What had I done to get to this place in my life? I had to pinch myself. I was able to pinpoint a few key steps that got me to now.

Passion, the pure joy of riding my bike, drove me to find the space where I could find success and my platform to turn it into my life, not just a hobby.

Vision and Direction, I knew what I wanted and why I liked it. I also knew that all I had to do was decide. Then take action. Then work hard, invest energy and do it often enough; it will pay off.

Consistency became the most crucial element of changing my life direction to how I wanted it to be.

Daily practice, daily affirmations, daily "ok I will just do it, and I will become it, live it, and this will be me."

Blind Faith, relinquishing some control and allowing things to go wrong or right or just be what they will be. You can plan all you like, but eventually, you have to test out your theory or execute the plan. There was a lot of "let's just do this and work out how later!" Then drilling down into the nitty-gritty, it purely was about executing the 1%'ers, the little things I did not want to do some days. A few fun memories come to mind, I would go to bed early when the Tour de France was on and get up at 10:30 pm, and ride on the rollers in front of the TV for 2hrs to get extras in. I would do my core workout daily and make sure I did one extra push up each time. Or when I was out riding, if it were a 2hr ride, I would sneak in an additional 5 minutes ride time. They might not seem like huge things, but they helped my mindset. I was focused and wanted to do better. These small investments reinforced the behaviour of someone who wanted to achieve some big goals. I wanted to create a robust and unshakeable person that would become the athlete I was dreaming I could be. I had passion, purpose and direction. I started seeing results, which gave me the confidence to take more action and have a bit of blind faith. Moving to Forrest was one of these Blind Faith adventures.

> It would prove to pay off more than I could have ever imagined.

2008 was a big year of consolidation. My experiences were growing, and of course, I would encounter failure, disappointment and what comes with it. Realising how much further you have to go. The mind starts to tire with constant application, thinking too far ahead, with thoughts like, why bother, is it worth it? I should just get a job and be happy. Some days I would wake up so excited to be alive, whilst others would be overwhelmed and ready to pack it in. It was not just the act of cycling to pursue excellence; this was the fun bit. Norm and I were entering a phase of growth in our businesses, and everyone seemed to want a piece of what we had. How can you complain about that?

Saskia was in year 9, with her wants and needs. She was getting involved in the netball scene in Colac, building new friendships and all the responsibilities that come with parenting. Norm was making more and more websites, turning his business into a seven day a week affair. Then the two of us were running MTBSkills courses nearly every weekend, at Forrest or the You Yangs. We received invites to travel to other regions and interstate places like Townsville to run classes. There were invitationals to come and race all over

Australia. In our 'say yes now, work out how later' attitude, we travelled, taught and raced, and did a bit of parenting too. There was a lot of travel involved, too; it was at least one hour to get anywhere from Forrest and a two-hour drive to Melbourne. These little add ons would make a trip extra arduous and why we both gave up our Geelong connections to business this year. As much as I loved doing the personal training and group classes, eventually, you need to sleep.

The pattern of working hard, resting little and Norm and I trying not to drown was carving a solid groove. There was so much hope and excitement about what we were doing. As a result, we forgot to note that our relationship and energy was taking a hit. Initially, we were juggling this with no drama. However, we didn't have time for friends or family, and we became a matter of fact with interactions with those we cared about. I guess that's how we survived. We headed off for our regular Scott 24 hour mountain bike race in Canberra in October. I would be racing solo this year and wanted to win. We travelled with a group from our MTBSkills Race Development Squad, enjoying time away from working for a weekend. October in Canberra can be freezing or super hot; race day was the latter which always messes with my stomach and pacing. Things don't settle down until the sun goes down where I can eat again. As the race started, it was over 30 degrees Celcius. Philipp Rostan, a local rider, went out hard, and we raced neck and neck for the first few hours. She was a very fast descender, so most of the time, I just let her set the pace and hoped she wouldn't be able to sustain this for too long. Finally, on one lap, we went into the pits to get assistance from our crews, I came out back on the race course, and she wasn't following me. I found out later that she spent a lot longer in transition.

That's part of the unknown in 24-hour racing; put on your best poker face and hit the laps hard, to begin with, the hope that one of you will concede, at least for a few hours so the pace can drop a little. Especially as the race starts at noon, the afternoon sun is taxing. Many riders will forget to drink or put off eating, ride too fast and end up being sick or unable to dig deep later in the race. It's not only how fast you can ride, but how well you know your own body. Self-preservation is vital, as is the ability to push right to the edge without going too deep, occurring many times throughout the race. For me, on this day in October 2008, Philippa had conceded in the first six hours, and I was going to win. But winning a 24-hour race still requires you to ride and keep riding whilst looking after your bike and body and fueling yourself, staying alert and in the game for 24 hours. This aspect is what makes the racing so hard, mentally and physically. The fastest rider doesn't always necessarily win, and you have to possess outstanding mental toughness. Going into a race without a good reason or feeling under the pump and emotionally vulnerable has the potential for a bad outcome. It's not the kind of thing anyone wants to do when other more important issues are going on in your life. The win on this day came easy as far as 24 hour wins go; it was just about me riding around at a sustainable pace. Making sure I lapped around enough times to finish in the top 10 male placings, always a good measure of success, and today I would have come 8th overall.

I loved visiting Canberra on these trips, and it was always a rush to get home. I had to learn to enjoy the whole experience as though it was a holiday, so it worked for me. When we got home, not only did we have washing and unpacking to do, but there would be work to catch up on and life to get back to. It was a bit of a bad habit I was getting into, go to a race, win or podium, come home, work. I had forgotten part of the process, that of celebration or reflection, and as you can imagine, this led to a feeling of all work and no play. There was more racing to do, though, and that included another 24 hours, the Kona, held in Forrest, our hometown, on our wedding anniversary in the first weekend of December. By the time December came around, I was exhausted on every level. Expectations were high from everyone around me that I would win this Kona 24 hour race. Still, I wasn't even interested in racing, feeling like I was doing it out of obligation. Norm and I, whilst not harbouring any marital issues, were like ships in the night, working hard, barely discussing things, including what we both wanted from this race. He was my pit crew, my support person, the shining light at 2 am when I was tired; he gave me that spark of purpose and excitement to get the job done. He was my teammate, the non-riding one.

On the day of the race, I could sleep in and get prepared at home, knowing it was a five-minute drive in the car to get to the event centre at the football ground. We didn't discuss what the goals or plans were today. It was like going through a well-rehearsed program, just forgetting to have our pre-game pep talk. We knew so many people and wished us well, wishing me well. I found this a bit overwhelming. My racing goals and results were mine, and I still didn't understand why others were interested or cared. All the same, it was a great community of riders, and everyone looked after each other constantly. If you broke something and you needed a spare, someone would always loan you their spare part. We did it many times for other riders too. The Kona 24 hour hosted another three-lap course, 8hrs in each variation, to spice things up. This was going to be easy, fun, and how could anything go wrong today? It was my home trail; I was in good form. All I had to do was ride hard to start, make an impact, then settle in. Eat, Drink, Ride. How wrong I was. The race started; I went out hard as planned and was winning from the get-go. I knew every lump and bump in the course, and finding the rail trail return was boring and unengaging. As soon as it got dark, my brain gave me messages like, "why bother?" I processed this as I wanted to quit, go to bed, and I was bored. I was telling Norm this; he was not listening. We were both talking in a different language to each other. He wanted me to finish this and win badly because that was what we did, and he wanted the best for me. I was unmotivated, bored and had no desire to be out there still. I learned today that just because you should win, just because you are the best and have all the tools at your disposal, doesn't mean you will. You must want it even when it's coming at you super easy. I was six laps up, that is six hours up on the 2nd place female. I could have gone to sleep, got up the next day, rode around and won. But my heart wasn't in it, and I hated myself for it. Norm hated me for it. It was such a horrible experience. I pulled out even as I was winning and quit, with no passion, no purpose and certainly no desire to continue racing. I was embarrassed, yes, and emotionally burnt out. I needed a break, time to refocus, to rekindle that passion.

> Sometimes your most significant failures are your most valuable lessons. I failed hard on this day, and it hurt Norm. He never wanted to support me at another 24-hour race again. In his eyes, he couldn't trust me, his time and investment were valuable to him, and I had wasted this for nothing. It took a long time for me to explain to him what happened, why, and what lessons I had learnt.

The gift of failure comes with a lot of emotional unpacking to be done. The awkward race failure at the Kona 24 hour would prove to be just the catalyst we both needed, especially me, to have a most magnificent 2009. I never seemed to have an issue accepting when things didn't go as planned. Perhaps it was a life skill. The easiest way to deal with the fear of failure was to imagine the worst outcome occurring and devise an action plan, take steps to ensure that the option of failure was removed or minimised. I knew that if the worst-case scenario did happen, I had already prepared for it. It is all about creating control of the situation, even if it is unpleasant. Often situations like getting a DNF against my result at the Kona 24 hour race were silver linings. Catalysts to push me in a new direction. To take stock of what went wrong and why? I allowed myself a day to feel crap and emotional about it, then a good night's sleep. I would be motivated as hell by the following day, pumped with a new perspective on what happened and what to do next.

Norm and I reflected that the lead up to the Kona 24 hour mountain bike race in 2008 was hectic, both exhausted from every aspect of our lives. I am happy to admit; we were most definitely overdoing it. The solution didn't alter our work-life balance, but we made a promise to each other to talk things through, to get inside each other's psyche before a big race and to discuss each other's goals and align them, and openly discuss the bad stuff, the what-ifs. More importantly, I decided that I was not superhuman and needed to work less in the lead up to big races to prepare myself mentally.

The year started with the Otway Odyssey, not a race I was ever likely to win, just a bit on the short side of only 100km, but it was always a good hit out and something to train for early in the year. Saskia was now in year 10, and we had been in Forrest for a year. We were no longer working hard to gain new business to survive in the country without the travel to Geelong; new business was landing on our doorstep. Busy with travel for skills courses, camps and racing almost every weekend. This was our life, the new normal. We had created this life, and it became the only thing we knew over time. I think I was aware at the time, but it was so much fun. Norm and I were involved in the Forrest Mountain Bike club and took juniors away to racing our MTBSkills clients, which was on top of my racing goals.

National Championship waiting to be won
Adam McGrath

It was the first time we would travel to Canberra for the Easter Australian National 24hr Mountain Bike Championships. It had never occurred to me before to attend this event; it was now evident, could I become a National Champion? I had started working with a coach, Brendan Rowbotham, an accomplished road cyclist who spent a lot of time helping me get stronger faster and sustain a higher output for longer. My training was now 50% on the road and 50% on the mountain bike. Planning for the Easter champs was an excellent opportunity to see where I was and what I needed to work on. I also knew that some other high-ranked women would be there, namely Katrin Van der Spiegel. Katrin had raced the year before at the World Championships in Canmore, Canada. She came in 2nd to Rebecca Rusch, the current world champion; she was also the current Aussie champ. Racing her would give me a firm indication of my current form. Was I fearful of the competition? I would say I was respectful; she had the runs on the board at a World and National level. I was a relative newcomer in this arena, but I was learning quickly. I didn't know much about Katrin, only that she was fierce, strong and fast. Norm and I devised a game plan that stemmed from that. See if I could match her starting speed, stay with her and watch and learn. The only way for me to reach the top of my sport was to learn from my competitors' strengths and be there to take advantage of their weaknesses.

To do this, I invested a lot of time and effort into riding long, riding fast and building strength and stamina—simple hard work. We also had two race bikes to swap out, and if anything went wrong, I would be able to keep moving and racing. The other element of our race plan was to spend very little time in transition to eat and drink and swap out lights and bikes. Essentially to keep moving for as much of the 24 hours as I could. Every minute lost being still in transition was another 100 meters lost on the track—such a simple plan. Ride as fast as I could. Put pressure on the Australian Champion. Continually eat and drink. Ride through transition as quickly as I could. Waste no time and fight until the end. I was the underdog here; I had nothing to lose.

We travelled to Canberra this time as a family, with Saskia in tow. Arriving on Friday always gave us a chance to ride the course as a big group and reconnaissance, discuss any issues and sort bikes out. Plus all our mountain bike posse. The course was at Majura Pines, and there were many exposed roots, gullies, tight corners and pinch climbs. But it was fun, and I loved it. There is nothing more confidence-building than feeling the joy of a race course you are about to ride for 24 hours. I felt so good about it, and when we rode around for one more short lap, I whispered to Norm away from the group. I told him that I felt terrific, I felt strong and felt this course was made for me and that tomorrow would be a fantastic race. After the disappointment of the DNF in December of the last year, Norm and I had spent a lot of time working out our partnership and what it meant for us as a team. It was my job to ride the course as hard and as best as possible. I was only capable of doing what I could do, nothing more. But what I was keen for Norm to communicate to me was factual information that I could use as motivation and assist in adhering to our race plan. Information such as Katrin is 5 minutes up on you, but you put in 2 minutes to her on that lap. Keep riding as you are; it will only be a matter of time before you catch her if you sustain this pace. Ultimately, our team goal was to have no regrets, leave no stone unturned, and be in a position to get my best result on the day. Of course, if we followed our processes, we were a chance to win. So back to my surf boat rowing days, we were aware of our competition, but we "kept our eyes in the boat".

Easter Saturday and the morning was chilly and the tree roots slippery. I went out for a mini practice lap to give my legs one more test and enjoy what I came to know as the "warmth on my back" feeling. This was present when everything aligned as it should have. An inner sense of contentment and what I had to offer today was enough. So long as the warmth was there, I felt calm. The race started down in a gully which meant a gradual climb to get out onto the race course proper. This meant I needed to ride hard, fast and with a lot of effort in the first five minutes to ensure a good start. The first hour of every 24-hour event I had ever done was always like is. The fight for position felt futile, knowing we would have all day and all night and tomorrow to sort it out between us. The effort showed who was here to do business, who was in good form and who wanted to put the pressure on. Today I was that person; I was there to win. The corners, the twists and turns, the slight rises, short pinches, flowing trails and fast descents were perfect for my riding style. Today I wanted Katrin and everyone else to know I was here to give it my best shot; I wanted to win and was not afraid to show my cards early. I reasoned that we already knew Katrin's strong points, and this fast start would give her a chance to counterattack. In the best-case scenario, I would be able to pull away and win. There was nothing to lose; it's a fun and exciting place to be coming into a race as the underdog. The laps went by, around 30 minutes long. About 60% of the way through, the course passed close to the transition area where Norm would be there to give me any input or feedback that was necessary and I to him as well. Very early on, he told me that I had put time into Katrin. All was going great, better than expected, and I had nothing to lose. It started to get dark, and it began to rain a lot. Perhaps I had not eaten enough or was starting to feel the effects of going out too hard as I had a few crashes in the wet. I was not thinking as well as I should have.

Katrin was starting to reel me in, lap by lap, minute by minute; she was catching me. It was now dark, and she finally caught me and started to put in the time.

This is the story of how the race panned out via Norm's mobile entries onto my TWITTER page, an insider's rendition of a 24hr race, not so glamorous, eating, drinking, riding and needing to go to the toilet. A week later, I added my thoughts at the time.

This was how it unfolded.

NORM: Good weather in Canberra. Heading out shortly for some practice on the course at Majura pines.

Jess: Happy to be here, excited, nervous, a bit tired, hanging out to race.

NORM: Finished two laps of the course. Fast, flowy & hardly any climbing. The tight single-track will hopefully suit me. Bike prepared & ready.

Jess: The course is incredible, very fast, just up my alley. I mean, 95% can be done in the big chainring, only one hilly section.

NORM: Good sleep 8 hours, slightly overcast weather.. cool conditions. Looking forward to getting started.

Jess: Awesome sleep, no nerves, just want to race & put all the hard work and preparation into action. Whoop whoop!!! Bring it on!

NORM: Good start... 20secs up on Katrin, the Claire Graydon, then Phillipa.

Jess: Can't believe it, no one is going with me. I expected Katrin to be on my wheel, breathing down my neck. But as soon as we entered the single track, I felt her presence lessening, then I could see I had a break on her as the trail wound back on itself. I feel great!

NORM: 3 laps down... Jess & Katrin riding around together. Justine Leahy is not far behind with Claire & Phillipa.

Jess: Every lap, I have this marker point to see if I have gained or lost on Katrin. I keep seeing her at the same location, so the gap is still the same. No problem, I am willing to race her for 24 hrs; that's what I am here for.

NORM: Jess still holding a 1 min lead over Katrin, 1min back to Claire. In the men's Jason English from John Claxton.

Jess: In a rhythm now, feel in control and so happy to be racing. Life is good.

NORM: Jason English opening up a bit of a lead now... Jess is lapping at 33 mins. Katrin has reduced the gap to about 30 secs.

Jess: Still cruising, eating well, drinking well, stopping every now & again to get the chain lubed. The race MC is excited. Each time I ride through, he keeps time on how much lead I have on Katrin. As I am in the single track, I can hear him tell the crowd that Katrin has left for her next lap, so I know she is coming to get me. I stay steady, knowing that she will catch me soon. Stick to my plan, go out hard, set the pace, race my race.

NORM: Jess holding two min lead. Katrin has started on the Coke already... Jason English is now about 5 mins up on Claxton at 4:30 pm.

Jess: I am unaware of the need for Katrin to turn to Coke already! But Norm does tell me next lap. Same thoughts as before. I still have a count of what lap I am up to at this stage. I listen to my breathing, settle, think to myself constantly that no matter what, I deserve to win; it's a long race; just relax and enjoy, prepare for a race until the end.

NORM: Night laps started... Jess is still in the lead, but Katrin is putting on lots of pressure... Only 30secs at last split; it's now heading onto 6 pm.

Jess: It's heading into the night now, and the trail is losing light. Turned lights on, it's that "limbo" time of not quite needing lights, but a bit of extra vision is necessary. Far out, I love this course!

NORM: Jess and Katrin just left transition together... just as the rain starts to fall at 6:15 pm

Jess: Katrin passes in single-track. We talk. She says," Why did you make it so hard?" me, "what do you mean?" I have no idea what she is talking about. It's about going out hard. "Oh", I say, "What did you expect me to do, Katrin? You can lead for the next 6 hrs now." Yep, I am having fun now. The game begins. Woo hoo. This is why I came to Canberra – to race Katrin good and proper.

I am looking forward to showing her who has the mental game under wraps here.

NORM: Heavier rain now. Katrin and Jess lapping together, with Katrin leaving transition first. Jason English opened up a 10+ min lead; it's now 6:45 pm.

Jess: It is wet, and the trail is getting nasty. Roots are slippery, and ruts become waterfalls. I make the conscious decision to slow down a bit as I do not want to have unnecessary stress on the bike or myself. Vision is challenging as glasses reflect water & become fogged up on uphills. Getting a little despondent for 20 minutes or so. Realising that I have ridden over 100 km, I could have finished either a 100 km MTB Marathon or a 6-hour solo race by now & be having a hot shower. But it's all in my mind. I know that if I just keep pedalling, go out for another lap, making sure that the gap between myself and Katrin does not blow out, I will be ok come morning. Nighttime here we come.

NORM: John Claxton retired at 7:45 pm. Katrin has a 3 min gap on Jess; rain has slowed by 8 pm.

Jess: Norm is telling me the time gaps with Katrin. I ask him to go F—K himself about Katrin that I can only control my race, and let's focus on that, ok? I am prepared to stay steady during the night, follow the plan, eat and drink, stay awake and stay off the caffeine for as long as possible.

NORM: Change of batteries, a new attitude, chasing down Katrin. Katrin went straight through, so she must stop next lap. It's now 8:18 pm.

Jess: Nothing much has changed except I have lost track of counting laps now. I don't bother asking Norm either; I am sure he would have no idea either. Still happy, just going through the motions as planned. Nothing special is happening. Water is still running on course. The mud is sticky and the roots exposed. It feels like a hill that is much steeper for this reason.

NORM: Vanina Vergoz is now into 3rd, only 20 mins adrift of Jess, who is 4 mins back from Katrin at 8:30 pm.

Jess: Norm tells me about Vanina, and I pull my finger out instantly. Bugger that, I cannot have her be part of the game plan. I make sure I go a bit faster now and continue on my eating and hydration plan. I cannot afford to stuff up now.

NORM: Mark Fenner appears to have pulled the pin. However, the rain has now stopped. Katrin is now 9 mins up. Jess is still feeling good. Katrin has done the last two laps without a stop at 9 pm. Men's update. Jason English from Andrew fellows and Dan McKay.

Jess: Staying steady, in control. Time is passing, as are the laps.
NORM: Jess just put in a scorcher and pulled back Katrin by 2minutes and has put at least five into Vanina behind her. Woo hoo! It is nearly 10 pm.

Jess: I guess I am still concerned about Vanina catching me, so in turn, I have done a faster lap to ensure I put time into her. A couple more laps, and I am ½ way there.

NORM: Another strong lap by Jess. Put 15 mins into Vanina. Katrin and Jess are now lapping about the same, with Katrin just 5 mins up at 10:30 pm.

Jess: Nothing has changed; I am lapping, drinking and eating, having my chain lubed, changing the battery, doing what I need to do. Mindset is strong and focused on the bigger picture. The night will end, and the day will come.

NORM: Another 40 min lap by Katrin. She is in serious mode now, and it's nearly 11 pm.

Jess: Nearly ½ way there…starting to have fun now.

NORM: Woo Hoo! 40 min lap from Jess then. Bringing it back now. Katrin not stopping each lap to eat, whereas Jess is.

Jess: As I read Norms Twitter feed, I had no idea what I was thinking or doing; time has just become one big chunk; I am just lapping and being the best I can be. Focusing on reaching 6 am – daylight. However, it is good to hear the group of girls ringing cowbells still up and helping us get through the dead of night.

NORM: midnight and the race is about to start… Katrin had a long break then. Jess is still within 10mins. 30+mins now, back to Vanina.

Jess: I am pleased to be over the hump now. It's all a count down from here. I am starting to need to go to the toilet, wishing I had not worn bib knicks. Too close to stop and worry about it, see if I can hold it off.

NORM: Katrin is showing why she is world number 2… 39 min lap. Jess is still about 10mins back, and it's nearly 1 am.

Jess: I am still happy at this stage that no matter what Katrin dishes out, it really makes no difference to her position. Norm tells me that she is stopping, drinking coke, getting a little frustrated at the battle.

NORM: Anything you can do, Jess just smashed out a 39, her fastest night lap yet, and she had a minor fall that she laughed off.

Jess: My fall consisted of hitting a rock and being flung into the dirt and landing on my hip, thigh area. The guy behind me cannot believe I just get up and say it's all good. I get up and continue riding; no issues, bike works, and I am not sore at all. Just dirty.

NORM: Both Jess & Katrin are now a full lap up on the rest of the field at around 1 pm.

Jess: Norm tells me this; it spurs me to make sure I pass them some more. Excited as I started to do the sums. I tell myself that I most likely have about ten laps to go. Who knows if this is true, but it's a nice thought.

NORM: Katrin's last lap 40.50... Jess' 40.40

Jess: Norm is excited. I think I have just been given a No-Doze. I feel clear-headed, no caffeine jitters, and I am happy with this as I am scared of the drug's potential effect. But I smack out another good lap.

NORM: Katrin pulled into pits then and had a sit-down. She has done this three times now. Once again, 40 min laps each but Jess 2 mins quicker through at 2:30 am.

Jess: The trail landmarks keep popping up quickly; it's incredible how fast time is going. The need for a No.2 has not gone, starting to plan my toilet strategy. There is a port-a-loo on the trail, saving time and keeping my toilet stop a secret to all. I need to tell Norm that I will change helmet batteries so I don't have one in my pocket & change jerseys so I can unzip the entire way and not have to take my helmet off. Tummy is rumbling with gut-churning action going on.

NORM: Jess has put over 5 mins into Katrin's lead over the last two laps. She is catching her now.

Jess: I forget to tell Norm about my toilet plan this lap.

NORM: Jess has cut Katrin's lead to just 4 mins. Here we come at 4:30 am

Jess: Forget yet again to tell Norm about my toilet plan.

NORM: Just about through the night. This race is really starting to heat up. I hate the waiting between laps; it's nearly 5 am.

Jess: I remember to tell Norm about my toilet plan, oh one more lap, my guts are hurting, and I need to go!!!!!! That's all that consumes my mind now.

NORM: Another minute up that lap, but Jess needs a toilet stop out on course this lap; let's hope it's a quick one at 5:30 am.

Jess: This is a happy lap; I know that in about 15 minutes, I will be sitting on the port-a-loo, inviting a new lease on life! Oh, the relief. Now I can race. I am smiling from ear to ear & ready to smash Katrin, not to mention a few kilos lighter.

NORM: Jess lost 6 mins that lap. However, she is feeling better at 6 am

Jess: As I said, smiling from ear to ear. It's nearly sunrise, and I am a new woman.

NORM: Katrin just took a break, and Jess just did a flyer and got back 10minutes. The race is back on at 6:45 am.

Jess: It is incredible what you can do once you can concentrate again. The light is up, my helmet is free from the bounds of light and battery. The morning fog is like misty rain. It's beautiful. Sunlight is trying to sneak through the mist, and I am going to win. I just know it. Oh wow, 5 hrs to go.

NORM: Just 4 minutes now separates Jess from Katrin, Katrin leading. Just 3 minutes Jason to Dan at 7:24 am

Jess: The mist is lifting, the mood is growing, the crowd is very excited. Norm is ecstatic, holding back all he can; a nervous Richard, Katrin's husband, is looking at me as I ride past him out on the course. No doubt he is waiting to see how close behind I am.

NORM: Jess is back in the lead! 1.5 minutes up through transition, and it's nearly 8 am. 4 hrs to go.

Jess: I cannot believe it. I am feeling so strong, not at all tired. I vow to go hard on the sections that I am best at & stay conservative at the uphills and pinches. Katrin is now further behind as the single track winds around. Well, and truly up on her, I remind myself to go hard to break her NOW!

NORM: Jess is now with a 5-minute lead. Katrin continued to lap hard. Jason English leads by 3 mins, and it's 8:45 am.

Jess: Not deterred by Katrin's persistent efforts, a smile on my face, I believe I deserve this win. It is mine, just stay focused, keep lapping, drink up, have a gel, do what Norm says, there is no pain, just winning.

NORM: 12.5 minutes lead now, and we are inside 3 hours to go, 9:23 am.

Jess: I cannot see Katrin on the single-track sections now where I used to. Don't slow down yet, I tell myself. Just keep lapping as you were. Stay safe, smile, enjoy, stretch, eat and drink. You Deserve this, Jess!

NORM: Jess is now lapping almost as quick as many of the top 5 men. Katrin is still back some 13 mins. Jason English is holding Dan McKay at 9:50 am

Jess: I am loving my laps, doing the sums, maybe three laps to go!

NORM: 17 minutes now... Jess is still in the big ring, smashing!

Jess: Not long now...hang in there. Amazingly there is no pain from fatigue, just from holding my body on the bike for this long. Arms are starting to feel weak, not enjoying the bumpy bits. I find I am going a little slower in these sections and pushing it harder on the smooth bits. Still loving the Big Chain Ring.

NORM: Jason English still holding Dan McKay by 3 mins. Jess is now at least 19 mins up at 10:30 am

Jess: I now know that there is no way Katrin can catch me; I just need to keep lapping; new sums done; maybe I do have to do three more laps. Whatever it takes, I will do it. I am prepared to win.

NORM: I just heard Katrin say she was stopping. Jess is up by 23 mins now.

Jess: Norm tells me that I can lap Katrin now. So I try my hardest and keep smiling.

NORM: It's official. Katrin has stopped and is waiting for the 24 hours to tick by & roll through for second place. It is 11 am. Jess has now lapped Katrin and is on her final lap. Cross your fingers! She is very excited and still in great spirits. All she has to do is stay on, and she will win.

Jess: Norm tells me that Katrin is out on the course waiting for 12noon to tick by and will take on 2nd place. It is a bit of a letdown that I will not be racing her down to the final minutes. So now we take our time; I have a drink, lube chain etc. Norm tells me to do my slowest lap and enjoy. I leave transition, with the MC letting everyone know that I have won. It is a relief; I vow to myself to flow and enjoy. Stop at the Port–a–loo for one last toilet stop and cruise home. I get back to the finish 10 mins early, so wait with Jason English for time to tick by. I have won, and it's so surreal. Katrin congratulates me.

NORM: Jess is the 2009 Australian 24 hour solo champion

Jess: I need a shower, Norm has a tear, and he kisses me. I sit down, but my lower back is killing me. I eat chocolate because it's Easter, and I have a recovery shake. I collect my change of clothes and head off to the shower to get the last 24hrs of mud and sweat from my body returning renewed. I have won. I can relax now.

Katrin and I waiting it out to roll over the finish line at 12noon.
Adam McGrath

This was the race that changed my mindset and showed me what I was capable of. So many battles within the race. To come out at the end, the victor, when I would have so quickly decided that second place was a very credible position, given I was racing Australia's national champion. My respect was tremendous for Katrin and the other women I was racing; it was just that I wanted to make sure I gave it everything at this race. This was my first national championship and was an honest appraisal of where I was, what I had to do next, and perhaps my future in the sport. It wasn't until after I had won that it even occurred to me to consider attending the 24 hour World Solo Mountain bike championships in Canada. After a shower, a sit-down, something to eat while waiting for the podium call up, it started to sink in that as a team, Norm and I fought hard with a never give up approach. As opposed to last year's DNF, where I lacked motivation, today's win was a testament to how well we worked together. We had learnt from that race and applied all of those lessons.

Here we were, 24 hours later, on the other side, celebrating a National title, about to be presented a green and gold jersey and a gold medal. I was exhausted, my body was tired, and my brain was fried. I was not prepared for what came next. Nervous and excited, I was called up to the podium to accept the win, chat with the crowd, thank my sponsors, and congratulate the other women racing. Russ Baker, who was the representative of MTBA and 24hrs of Adrenaline World Champs, presented me with an envelope with instructions for the offer of a lifetime. I would never have considered this off my own back. All I had to do was pay the entry fee for the 24 hour World Championships in Canmore, and I would get my airfares paid. Norm and I didn't have any spare cash sitting around, but how could I say no? We made it happen with a government grant for high-performance regional sport and scraping the bank account down to our last $200 we were going to Canada.

April 2009, I am now the Australian National Champion; in July, we are heading to Canada to give the World 24 hour scene my best shot. Thirteen weeks to recover and get some climbing in my legs. I was preparing to peak again. The situation was a little crazy and totally off the schedule. The offer could not be rolled into 2010; I had to grab this chance now. Each race, each month, every year of my life revealed more and more opportunities for growth through racing. These experiences were so enriching, and each day was utilised in its entirety. The weeks consisted of training in the morning, up to 5 or 6 hours on the bike, shower, eat, 30-minute sleep, 3 hours of work for coaching, our MTBSkills business, housework, parenting, and general running around. That was your typical Monday Friday. On the weekends, skills courses to run, races to attend and training if I wasn't racing. Many weekends were double racing, with road and mountain bikes with other things piggybacked on either side. As a family, we relished doing nothing if we could find time for that.

I like to use the saying, *"There is always a price to be paid."*

We had been teetering between surviving and thriving for a while now. Every aspect of our lives relied on another to flourish; it was an ecosystem in itself. Cracks had started to appear many times over. Nothing catastrophic, though it revealed our weaknesses. Our family unit was reliant on each other; it took the whole team with it if someone was down.

> **Damn, these were stressful times, hell-bent on making stuff happen.**

Thankfully we weren't held back too long with each little setback, though the hard work was racking up interest, in both a positive and negative way. We had survived so far, and one thing we both knew well was that persistence and consistent effort was all we required; we had the resilience to keep showing up each day. My only hope was that eventually, we could start to breathe a little, enjoying the fruits of our labour, that tree I had planted; I was hoping it would be soon.

Scott 24hr with the MTBSkills crew 2008

Epic Rides with Epic People Forrest 2009

Loving the mud Forrest

Chapter 6 - Welcome to the World Stage young Padawan.

Say Yes now, and work out how later. What began as a fun way to learn new skills had now become a pathway to elite sport, and I was scrambling. Not in an unpleasant way, though this journey was all so unexpected. There was no particular goal, no pressure, only to keep learning and invest in those 1%'ers. At the time, I had no idea where this investment would take me; all I knew was that I had the most fun ever period. I knew, so long as I was having fun, I would see what I could achieve and where it would take me. The simplicity of improving my skills and fitness on the bike was so benign that I had lost all fear, enveloping myself in processes that were just so damn fun. And I knew then, even as I prepared for racing in Canada, if it's no longer fun, maybe it is time to reassess my priorities. It was the one thing that kept me going, then, and in the years to come. Keep it Fun, Race for Fun and Enjoy yourself. You chose to be here, now make sure you enjoy it!

Canada, we made it! Amazing

The opportunity to race my bike in Canada was unexpected. There was a lot to plan for, including getting a passport as I had never travelled overseas. It cost a fortune, the money I had to find, just scraping in enough to make it happen. The support from sponsors with all the bikes and equipment needed to race certainly helped, our airfares paid for, and thankfully we had family and friends to help out whilst we were away. My grandmother came and looked after the animals and Saskia. Winning the 2009 Australian National Championships has now changed the course of my life. A sliding door moment. I had just entered a space of elite sport; my body was ready; however, my mind was still playing catch up, but I knew I had to say yes to the opportunity. One minute striving to be my best at club races, then believing I could win a national title, and now about to represent my country in Canada.

Despite the achievements, my self-belief lagged.

With three months to prepare, I began some self-talk, working on the outcome of the national championship win, what it meant for me to go to Canada on a world stage, and shaping my thoughts to catch up with the reality of what was about to happen. It was time to prove I deserved to be going and it was time to live like a champion. But with such a short lead up, the transformation wasn't perfect, and Norm and I were under a lot of pressure in our working lives and financially making this trip happen. With a sigh of relief, a few spare dollars in the bank account, two bikes and a World Championship to race in a country I had never dreamed of visiting, we were off to Canada. Having never been overseas, the longest flight I had been on was four hours long from Melbourne to Darwin. Our flight was direct from Sydney to Vancouver and then onto Calgary. However long it took, it was too long. Our next and final mode of transport was a bus from the airport to Canmore, adding another hour. By the time we arrived, I was a mess. Alica Evans, who had lived in Geelong, picked us up and showed us around Canmore until we could check in. As soon as we got to our accommodation, I went to bed and slept; jet lag would become a real problem as the days wore on.

Meeting Anna Mei from Italy-riders from everywhere, this was truly a world stage

We arrived in Canmore on Sunday and would be racing the following Saturday. It was July, hot, and the sun was up for a good 15 hours of the day. We were sharing accommodation with friends, Adam Kelsall and Kirstin Honey, who were also racing. A large contingent of Aussies wanted to catch up for dinner and a ride and social stuff. It was exciting and overwhelming. I wanted to do it all. And we pretty much did. Though my jetlag never got any better.

Testing the racecourse was like nothing else I had ridden in Australia, using winter ski trails with many other single track links, walking tracks full of tree roots, and technical. I wondered if I had done enough to prepare my body for the battering it was going to endure. Then to find out that there was a mumma bear and her cub out on course, well, that changed things up a little.

I knew only too well that people visiting Australia feared snakes, spiders, crocodiles, sharks, and stingers, but as a visitor to Canada, I was keen to avoid encountering the mother bear looking after her cub.

Bears, cougars, mountain lions and moose bulls to watch out for, give me snakes any day! Canmore is a lovely town, nestled in amongst mountains and a fast-flowing river. Our days were busy, going to bed late in our pre-race week, sleeping in, eating, and exploring the outdoors whilst trying not to deplete much-needed energy. Trips to the supermarket for race food was a fun exploration of culture. This week leading up to the race lasted what seemed forever, and we met many Aussies here in Canmore, including Jade, at the local bike shop. He offered to help out with the race, supporting Adam, Kirstin, and Norm. This journey of becoming a world champion came with much sacrifice and anxiety, hoping somehow this would be worth all the time and effort. I had to make the most of this, and the pressure was building, not just about my race, as Norm and I were acutely aware of the lack of funds we had left in our bank account, and this left Norm working day and night on websites and fitting in a ride or two as well. The days flew by; race course practice was complete, as much sleep caught up as possible, group dinners, bike prep, food shopping and race plans. We shared our race set-up with two other riders, Adam and Kirstin. At the race sign-on and briefing the day before, it all started to become very real that I would be racing in Canmore for 24 hours at a World Championship.

I allowed myself to dream, what if I could come 2nd to Rebecca Rusch, the current world champion? I didn't know what it meant to race someone with such an extensive race resume. Rebecca was known as the Queen of Pain. Many years of adventure racing and now her imposing force on the scene of 24-hour mountain biking gifted her this accolade.

Yes, I allowed myself to dream, but mostly was excited, nervous and intimidated at the prospect of seeing where I fit in the world arena the next day.

For this to happen, I needed to be at my finest, my equipment needed to work, the required fueling to be perfect, and I had to have the right headspace, that's for sure. Perhaps I spent too much time preparing for perfection and not enough time sleeping and resting. Race night eve was so hot, and sleep was hard to get, waking up the next morning exhausted but equally drawn to do the best I could.

Could I mix it with the world's best 24-hour mountain bikers? What would it take for me to race at my best?

Mountains everywhere Canmore

Race Day.

We arrived at 9:00 am with plenty of time to test bikes out, prepare all the gear, stretch, rest, eat and chat about plans. The place was pumping, and it was easy to get caught up in the vibe, so instead, we hung low and stuck to our 3 x 3 marquee, but I was still struggling with fatigue. I found myself yawning with the heat of the morning. Maybe once the race started, I would perk up, my legs felt great, but this damn jetlag was leaving me in a haze.

> There was no delaying the inevitable now. Time will pass; the race will start at noon, and before you know it, it will be midday Sunday, and the results will be final.

At 11:30 am, we were corralled into our seeded numbers and set up for the start of the race. I was number 13. The race started off the bike, and we had to complete a 500 metre dusty, rocky and hilly run a Le Man's start. Get to my bike that Norm was holding, and then start riding and start the lap. Heart in throat, legs were burning with lactate and trying desperately to settle down for the long haul. It is time to race. The terrain was rocky, and we were running to our bikes along steep ski home trails, only a few hundred meters. It took a long time to get the heart rate down. The weather was hot and humid; it was July, Summer in Canada. Dark clouds were building on the horizon, with a chance of showers and thunderstorms later on. I hoped it wouldn't transpire; I saw photos of previous years with mud and rain; it looked like challenging work.

The start of the race, those first thirty minutes, are the pathway to the rest of the race. It is a good plan to drink, settle into a sustainable pace, and take stock of how you are feeling. It's a long way to the end, and all these small details are crucial. Perhaps I could have noted this, but I was fresh and had a point to prove, here in Canada, racing the world's best. It was lucky the course was dry; we had a lot of tree roots and slippery rocks to ride out there, and in the early stages of the race, everything was rideable. The price for riding everything was energy expended, and I was spending a lot. But right now, I love it. Concentration was intense, with not much downtime to catch up on eating or drinking. I was riding out of my skin and forgetting to refuel. Ahhh, the lessons of a young Padawan. My laps and time became a blur; I was in 3rd position on the first lap and progressed to 2nd place on the second lap, changing a few times with Jari Kirkland, an American rider. Rebecca was in first place, on the first lap, and already 4 minutes up.

Rebecca planned to lap the women's field. It took her 12 hrs to do this.

Darkness fell around 10:00 pm; I was now in 3rd place and started to feel very tired. Not the fatigue in my legs, but tired, as though I needed to sleep. The trails were becoming challenging, my brain was shutting down, and all I could think of was which parts of the course I would allow myself to walk on. When it gets to this stage, everything is a battle, eating, drinking, riding, thinking, being motivated and positive; you know you must, but you don't want to anymore. My mantra was, 'I didn't come all this way just to give up; I was here to finish.' I had my first caffeine fix at midnight, and then caffeine every lap. I found it hard to eat, getting my energy mainly through hydration. Norm told me that Carena Dean (in 4th place) was on fire and might want to speed up a bit if I could. But I couldn't, and it was some time in the early hours of the morning that Carena passed me. With my ego shrivelled up inside me, I hoped no one noticed or cheered me on, feeling like a fraud, embarrassed to relinquish that position so easily without a fight. I had reached my low point. Mentally this was a terrible feeling to cope with, knowing that I was now out of contention for a podium finish. All this way to Canada for 4th place, and there was nothing I could do to respond. This zombie state lasted for an hour, and then then the morning light started to appear.

Night riding at the World Champs

Morning always brings new hope and energy in 24-hour racing; at least you hope it does. I wasn't here to quit and decided to put on some new kit and kept racing. Four laps later, my race was over. I finished on the identical laps as 2nd and 3rd place, which was some consolation, and I felt like this was the biggest challenge I had ever completed in my life so far. No matter what positive spin I put on it, my ego was bruised; I was disappointed and left wondering what stones I'd left unturned. I needed this hardship of racing to take me to the next level. It had been an investment to see where I fitted in and what I needed to do next, to be the best in the world. Still so much to learn.

> I had leaned hard on this quote from T.S Elliot in getting me to Canada, and it gave me strength for what was to come, "Only those who will risk going too far can possibly find out how far one can go."

My energy, my hopes, my finances, everything invested so that I could have the chance to see how far I could go. To finish 4th best elite female 24hr mountain biker in the world was a good result for my first hit out on the world scene, and I returned home hungry and motivated to do better, especially knowing where the next World Championship was. It had my name written all over it. My heart lit up with hope, my stomach filled with excited butterflies. The next World Championships was to be at Mt Stromlo, Canberra, Australia. My favourite mountain biking racecourse. Motivation is massive now, and I have a plan with 18 months to make it happen and a 100% guarantee of zero jetlag.

"Norm, let's go home, rebuild that bank account and I am going to make sure I win next year."

We were both keen to get home, there was much to do now, and we also had some bills to pay. After such a considerable investment, I found myself struggling with training, motivation and tiredness for some time after returning home from the World Solo Champs in late July 2009. It had been two months since that weekend, and finally, things were starting to pick up again for me. It didn't help that we returned home to gloomy Victorian weather, some of the most prolonged bouts of rain and wind I can remember in some time. Cold, wet and windy. I was sleeping lots and training less. The training was hurting; sleeping was like a drug. Whilst I was in bed, I had no responsibilities, and time would go by without having to think or do anything. There were good days on the bike and some bad ones. I had to learn patience and give it time; it would be at least another eight weeks before I felt 100% again, and I was starting to have second thoughts about where I was heading next with my racing. Was I in or out of this 24hr racing business? Did it matter? Who cares anyway?

> Too much downtime, I had to get momentum going again, back to fun. As winter ended and days got warmer and more light, I got my mojo back.

I gave myself a couple of events to have fun and see where my form was, in mind and body. This second half of 2009 was busy. Norm and I were both self-employed. We had to re-earn some money to pay the bills. And I had a schedule, racing all over the state and a quick respite trip to the Gold Coast. Then my favourite race of the year, the Scott 24hr.

Racing the Scott 24h in Canberra 2009

It was October, in the Spring, with the capital at its finest with the annual flower show called Floriade going strong. I flew in, Norm drove up and arrived in Canberra late in the afternoon. We went for a practice ride before lunch, checking out the day lap. The course boasted a great climb of around 7kms to the top with a fantastic descent finishing off with some excellent flowing single track. After a quick bite to eat and a refill of the drink bottles, we headed out again. Now I was excited to be racing, feeling happy with the course and loving the flow; my "mojo" was back. Mentally I was so prepared, and physically I just had to do my best. Win or lose, I was ready to ride. Having learnt so much in Canada, today was the day to bring out the tools and start the campaign for the 2010 World Championships. The Scott 24hr was also at Mt Stromlo, the perfect race scenario, with precisely 12 months to go.

As the morning of the race came around, laying in bed, I thought how amazing it is that something you plan for and get excited about for so long eventually just pops its head up, and so quickly, it is over and done. Today, I took my time, savouring the lead-up. I spent more time and energy being grateful, immersing myself in each moment as it came along, and not worrying about much at all. I planned to hang low, stay seated, keep warm, talk little, relax and eat and drink small amounts until the race started. Today I felt good, so relaxed, and so prepared. Somehow I just knew I had it in me to pull off a win if only I could keep myself in this mental state. Waiting for the start, it's the part I dislike the most. Once I am on the bike and racing it, all just falls into place. Norm gave me a big kiss and told me he loved me. I chose to stay back in the second row to see what would happen at the start. With two minutes to go, I made sure I was in the right gear to start. Half a bum cheek on the seat, toe pointed to touch the ground, fingers on the brakes, eyes focused on the wheels in front of me, elbows out, heart rate relaxed and purposeful, smiling at the prospect of the 24hrs to come, and we are off. We were pushing up the fire road to enter the first bit of single track, one solo rider up 10 meters ahead and the rest of the bunch sitting on my wheel. I turned around to Jason English and said," mate, c'mon, get on the front, would you!" I started climbing the switchbacks with the rest of the crew, and these were happy times. I was getting a visual now and again on the climbs—glimpses of Trudy Nicholas, in second place.

Early on, many of us were riding together, enjoying the flow of the trails. The spirits were high. The tracks felt smooth, the rocks were easy, causing minimal dramas to my mental or physical state.

Lap one down; Craig Armour handed me a bottle as I threw the empty to the ground; Norm gave me a peanut butter sandwich as I rolled past. With lap two underway, up the first switchbacks, I could see Trudy maybe 800 meters back. I continued to dig deep, a simple plan to push 1% harder than I believed I could. I prepared ahead, politely asking to pass people in the most efficient way possible. I made sure to put in hard to get past each cluster of riders I approached, hoping that she took 20 seconds longer. Up the climb, I was having fun, down the descent, even more fun. Back to transition for more to eat and drink. The exact process as before, drink and food on the run, facts told by Norm is that Trudy is about 1 minute down. I decided to push hard on the next 5 minutes of lap 3, sneaking in another 20-second gap. Good, I say, a mental fist pump, and proceed with my 1% rule. It works. As I get to the switchbacks, there is no sight of Trudy. On my next lap, Norm has some good news. I was 5 minutes up on 2nd place.

The laps just merge, and that 'flow' state now exists. There is a point in a 24-hour race, or any endurance event for that matter, where the workload is a creative force, there is no pain, there is only action and a tremendous amount of drive. I don't know how people listen to music whilst riding as I like to hear my inside voice, my breathing and the riders around me. That flow state brings forth the night before too long, and this is the fun bit. The first proper night lap is always incredible. It's the start of the race, in my opinion. When it is dark, it's easy to lose track of riders in front or behind, so you just ride your race and rely purely on autopilot and support crew feedback. The heart rate starts to slow down, and somehow or another 12 hrs seems to disappear.

Always at night, I am a little scared of what is to come, but I tell myself that just as surely as night is here, the morning will come, time will pass, and before you know it, the race will be over, so just enjoy it now. It is also the time of the race where other people tone down; campsites become quiet, chatter on the course becomes less, making it a lonely time. Each lap brings you closer to the hint of a new day cusping the horizon, you hear a bird tweet, your stomach starts to want food again, and new hope is born, as well as the pain that comes with the sun up. Early in the morning, Norm told me that I was about 10 minutes off lapping Trudy. I would put in on this lap and make it my job to pass her. At around 4:30 am, I could finally relax a bit. I sat down, had a quiet chat with Norm about my plan for the next 6 hours or so and waited until Trudy came in before I headed off again.

It's incredible; once you have gone through all the hard work and get the chance to take a breather, how much it starts to hurt. Now, so close to the end, all I could think about was how many laps I would have to do before I could win the race. My body started to ache in all the spots where the impact of the course took the full brunt—arms, forearms especially and the lower back. My muscles felt shaken off the bone, fibre by fibre. I knew I was going to win and slowed right down, took my time, got off the bike and walked sections so that I could mentally have a break from the course. I got to meet people and chat and even have a meeting on the top of a climb with a bunch of solo riders keen for any excuse for their last lap to take as long as it needed to so they would not have to go out again. On my final lap, the most incredible thing happened. A planned Beer O'clock break! What happens next goes down in my best 24-hour racing memories.

The beer was offered to me by a group of boys at the top of a climb. Their names were James and James, and they were racing in a team of four, so they both shared the role of writing funny things on their whiteboard that was out on the track visible for everyone to read. On one particular lap, the whiteboard message said, "Hey Girls, call James on 0410 etc."

As I rode closer, my instant thought was, Hey Boys, so I yelled it out to them, wondering if they knew what angle I was coming from.

They responded, "Superstar DJ", and I yelled back, "Here we go!" We were on the same page of Hey Boy Hey Girl, a song by The Chemical Brothers. This small encounter uplifted my spirits so much, and the relationship grew after that with personal messages to me, wishing me well during the rest of the race.

Giving me high fives, shake and bakes, and then the beer on the last lap.

It was nice to stop and talk, drink half the beer, and proceed slightly tanked to the finish line. I would love to go back to that moment in time and savour it some more, and it's moments of humanity like this that remind me how special these times are.

I won this race for the 2nd year in a row, and I was starting to get good at the hurt and pacing myself to win; plus, it was a lot of fun. I crossed the finish line and attended to media requests with Norm waiting for me, fading quickly and in great pain, with my whole being shaking and shivering. My knees were throbbing, and I was sure I would not be able to make it to the presentations; by now, I was coughing up big chunks of green stuff from my lungs. Norm left me be, 30 minutes and three paracetamols later; I was up and ready to get up on the podium. Amazingly coming good, and was able to finish off my final task of the day.

You never sleep well after a 24-hour race; tonight would be no exception.

I had shown up, on the back end of a nasty cold, sniffling and coughing, unsure if it was the right thing to do. Eventually, I paid the price.

On the return home, there was always so much to do. The washing of clothes, cleaning of bikes, answering of emails, blog posts to write, planning and preparing of Mtb skills courses, camps, bills to pay, invoices to send out, coaching plans, a teenage daughter to look after, pets to love to and feed and of course training to keep striving towards that world championship goal in 2010. Thankfully I listened to my body and didn't race too much in the latter part of the year, and saved it up for the next. I had started to comprehend that achieving something grand and seemingly impossible only required a few main ingredients to dream, a desire and determination. It also became clear that I was just as qualified to want this as anyone else in the world, so why not ME, right? It has to be someone! 2009 finished on a high note with a renewed hunger and vision to become the 24hr World champion. I had begun working on the lagging self-belief, knowing that this was one of the most significant gains I could make in my pursuit of becoming a World Champion. These experiences I was investing in were helping me dream of what might be possible. Had I not gone to Canada and raced, I would never have known what I was capable of and never have come home with curiosity to explore more. I was starting to dream and visualise something that was never even in my vernacular.

Walt Disney had an excellent quote that resonated with me, "If you can dream it, you can do it."

I was now capable of dreaming, so now I started to believe I could do it.

Chapter 7 - Cracking the Code to Life

2010, this is my year. I know it; I have decided it to be.
My chance to shine, and I am not afraid of hard work.
I know this is one of the defining attributes of a champion.
I feel so calm and confident like I am close to cracking the code and that all I need to do now is refine my craft.
All the days of living, hurt, joy, hard work, lessons, and everything have brought me here, the present. It wasn't that the desire to win some mountain bike race was the be-all and end-all; it was what it represented to me, to the people looking on, to anyone who cared. Being the best version of myself was simply the culmination of years of apprenticing life, and I finally felt ready to put my best work forward.

That was how easy it felt, not that the work was easy, but the desire was the drive and commitment. Here's the short of it, there are no shortcuts in life, every experience adds to your resume, and it's up to you how you next use it. Cracking the Code to Life, I knew I was close to understanding this and couldn't wait to use this World Championship event to test my theories.

One big fat year of "all or nothing". With no fear of failure. Just lessons and a whole lot of time and money invested in anything that feels like it might lead to the path of enlightenment or at least a damn good journey.

To win, I have decided I must first believe I am worthy and get to this point; I must do what I say I will do. When it gets a little uncomfortable, this is the precise moment that I must continue and disable my thinking brain and just do. In the years thus far, I have learnt a few valuable and critical components of winning, and it's not just about being the best athlete, the fastest, or the strongest. Instead, it is my mind and how I use this, and I love that no one can see what I am thinking—this is my secret weapon.

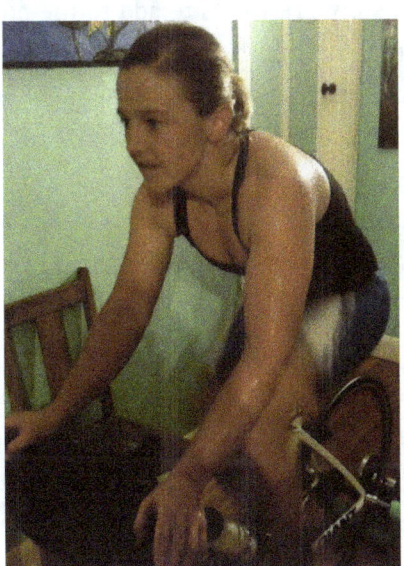

Lots of indoor training in the middle of winter

We have now been living in Forrest for two years, a quaint village town of around 200 residents, nestled in the foothills of the Victorian Otways, where agricultural farmland meets the Australian bush and temperate rain forest region. The region boasts mountain bike trails, endless back roads for riding, 4wd tracks and beautiful routes for cycling on. The winters are cold and wet, and it can still be cold and wet in summer, but it is lovely and quiet and easy to train. Norm and I spent the year working long and hard. Saskia turned 16. Each day is full of tasks to achieve, exhausting but also exhilarating for us both. At the start of this year, Norm suggested I focus more on the World Championship in October and less on paid work opportunities. So we worked out a strategy to make this happen immediately.

From here on, I am essentially a full-time athlete, and I like it. Rain hail or shine, my priority is to add to the pool of experiences with fitness, strength, health and mental resilience to win the World 24hr Solo Championship in October. The single focus is also easy to maintain; the routine and purpose are calming to my mind.

> 2010, here we go.
> I didn't realise anyone was watching.

Yet they were, spectating all my progress. It was a responsibility that I was unaware of. The impact of my actions would take a while for me to digest. I was a girl who wanted to get better at something and share all my learnings and knowledge with the mountain biking community. That was the simple recipe I was following, and I made it all up along the way. I had learned that to improve, I must do what I was not already doing and invest in what my competition was not—exploiting my competition's weaknesses and turning these into my strengths. Not rocket science at all. The concept was so simple. I was perplexed at why those I raced against seemed to miss this; either way, it gave me calm and a lot of confidence to stay focused on my processes. No matter the result on the day, in training, work or racing, I could gauge my success on accountability to my process goals rather than a result.

Fear and nerves were always there before a race; I took it to signify I wanted to do well. It was pretty easy to calm myself down with a plan of attack and focus. I was no longer wasting energy on my competition, or the course, the weather or whatever. Process-driven goals formed my entire year and subsequent years after that.

Small actions become strong habits, and I further extended my belief in my 1% rule.

My training sessions were full of intent. What I ate beforehand, the sleep I had that night, the thoughts I would digest and then allow myself to dream big whilst executing. The entire process was cyclic and one action fed into another and so on. The most enjoyable aspect of every training session was the practice of visualising. If I could play out movies in my head on scenarios, I could feel the pain, the suffering, and the excitement of the day or whatever race I wanted to play out in my training. I knew it would serve me well. I became less focused on Personal Bests or other metrics, spending most of my energy, physical and mental, on simple execution.

Each day I would front up and ask myself, what were my goals, what would I regret not doing, and what value could I add to today that would add to my tomorrow. What edge could I gain over my competition purely by being more engaged in the daily process of building a solid and robust habit system?

If I could construct an unbreakable resilience now, I would be well-rehearsed for almost any situation, from the best case to the unexpected show stoppers. This mindset, process-driven way of doing things was transferrable to everything in my life. This purpose to my training sessions made it so much easier to stay focused. I no longer had to rely on daily motivation as, of course, this would wane often.

> On the tough days, I often referred back to, "Do today what others won't, so you can do tomorrow what others can't." This always worked for me.

When it was raining hard all winter long, the rides outdoors became part of my armour construction. Forging on regardless of the weather taught me many lessons, which would come back when the time was right.

I cannot even begin to explain the hard work of 2010. Every week spent teaching skills courses on the mountain bike. Often the day before a critical event. We ran camps in Forrest and Mt Buller on long weekends, catering, administering and delivering pretty much everything. We attended the Easter National 24hr Solo mountain bike championships at Mt Majura, and I won. We raced in the Merida 24hr at Hidden Vale in South East Queensland in July, and I won. The challenge to ride as solid and fast as possible when the competition was not pushing me was tough. Could I finish in the top 5 or 10 in the elite men's field, or could I do a faster lap or a myriad of other measurables that had little to do with the win?

There were so many events throughout the year, road races, mountain bike marathons, multi-lap endurance races, cross country races, including the XCO national championships in Adelaide. If I wasn't racing, doing skills courses, or running camps, I was training in some form or another. using a large wall calendar and putting all my commitments on it, making it as straightforward as possible when I was busy and when I was free. Unscheduled time was gold, often resulting in illness, fatigue, burnout, or small bouts of depression, all needing a break from the world.

Forrest Jnr trip to Adelaide Nationals

I still find it hard to believe what I could sustain. My mental and physical workload, including parenting our daughter, was over the top.
If I procrastinated, I learnt not to.
If I said no, I would fill that time with another obligation.
If I said yes, I had to work out how to get that done then and there, or a week would go by before I knew it.

Norm looked after my bikes like a full-time mechanic; he needed to. My weekly training was around 30-40 hours, including mental rehearsal, stretching, core and strength work, and time on the bike. The monthly routine would often go like this—busy busy busy. Fall sick. Forge on. Win a race. Fall in a heap. Rest and recover. Repeat.

> My investment was massive in winning this World Championship in October, and nothing was going to stop me; this was a once-in-a-lifetime chance to see what I was capable of. I felt confident that becoming a world champion had more to do with my attitude and consistency than athletic ability, though influential all the same.

This was to be the year, the 'peak' for all the life lessons I had procured, and the year that I would unlock so many secrets to success.

Saturday 9th October 2010, the only date that mattered now. As the year pushed forward, I slowly honed my focus on the simple task of preparing to win. Every night, playing out the race from start to finish how I wanted it to go. I would see the start line and feel the nerves in my mind. It felt real, allowing me to feel the pain of pushing hard in the first hour. I would act out positive and negative outcomes and use every emotion, rehearsing how I could make them work best for me on the day—playing out the mind chatter that would come with not feeling good enough or having a mishap that changed my position in the race. What would I tell myself, and how would I get back in the right mental space? The mantra I always came back to was, "I deserve this; I have done all the work needed to be the world champion today." It was no lie, I had done the work, and I did deserve it. It was September, one month to go.

A long cold winter endured on the bike. I had practised my 1% rule day after day, did what others would not so I could do what others could not—believing I deserved success due to my work ethic and evidence of results. When I set out down this path to see what I could do with my mountain biking, the goal was self-improvement, and through this, I enjoyed the activity that I loved. This pathway happened over time, with the growth and enjoyment factor compounding almost every week.

> All my failures strengthened my mind and desire to win the next time. These setbacks were beautiful lessons for when things don't go to plan.

Possibly the most significant challenge was learning how to commit to success. It is scary and involves pain, in mind and body and a lot of planning and sacrifices. It is much easier only to go part way on the road to success and stop short of your potential. Success distanced me from friends and training buddies a lot. So much planning from day to day. Daily life must go on, but somehow I had to fit in that killer training session.

Success was never just athletic ability. It required going to bed early and getting up at 4 am to ensure it all got done. I let many social things go by the wayside, only participating in races or events that I considered relevant or close by to alleviate stress. Juggling it all was mentally exhausting. It was using every day to its potential, striving to do my best, always 1% more than my competitors and believing that success could be mine. Every night as I went to sleep, I read books to confirm my goals and self-belief.

Being the best, winning, coming through with the goods, what I can tell you is, if you want it, you can have it, but it's not easy. Success is a lot of hard work, crazy dedication, daily consistency, surrounding yourself with positive and like-minded people and doing whatever small thing you can, every waking moment, to move towards your goal. That simple 1% approach. One day at a time, one week at a time, one month at a time, one year at a time. There are no shortcuts, just consistency and the courage to believe it.

Road Trip to Canberra always fun

Race Day

If you read the first chapter, you already know what is about to happen. It's the day it all changed for me.
October 2010, final exam day arrived, World Championships on home soil, Canberra, ACT. 18 months of work done, but my self-doubt still appeared on the start line as I looked around me and wondered what on earth I was doing here, on a world stage with all these athletic, strong-looking cyclists.

> Who was I to win this event? I remember this feeling. It came, and I let it jump around in my head, popping off silly stories about why I should relinquish my dreams and settle for a minor place.

It would be far easier and less threatening and far less pressure. These thoughts were just that, thoughts. Ahah, I know what is happening; this is normal, and thank you for the reminder, crazy brain. I will remember this feeling, for it is sure to return throughout the race. I then put myself in the shoes of the other riders I feared; what were their thoughts and their most significant fears today as they embarked on this race? It occurred to me that they were possibly going through precisely the same turmoil as me right now, but none of us could see this; our minds held these secrets. My mind was my secret weapon, that's right! Ahhhh, the relief washed over me; I had control back again and knew this was my race to win. For the next 24 hours, I would need to tune into my mind, understand when it was trying to trick me, and be ready with strategies to get back on track. The physical ability to achieve exists only because the mental game is strong. I had developed this part of my race craft; now, I was ready, and I was excited to test it out.

When the start gun went off, I knew it was only a matter of time before I could enjoy the process of my race. That was what I was here to do, enjoy it, excel at it and be my best, so I could be the best.

The elite women's field was large and from all over the world. Who would be there at the end to fight it out? Every second, every minute, every pedal stroke, and thought focused on me being there for that chance. This opportunity was such a magnificent experience, and I wasn't going to stuff it up.

Dusty work at the world champs 2010
Greg Long

The race started incredibly well, finding myself at the front of the women's field. Straight up, I realise I am a contender. It doesn't last, and others pass me. Did I start too fast? Oh, that's it, I have stuffed up; there you go, you don't deserve it! Whoops, that self-sabotaging imposter is at it again. I almost believed her, as she told me that all I had to do was finish and come top five. I had to remind her that I deserved a chance to win today just as much as anyone else. I remembered that my mind was my secret weapon and that all I had to do was be patient and follow my processes. I was having a great time racing today, the trail was fun, and I was riding well. Norm and his brother Rick were doing a great job of looking after me in the pits, and spirits were high, we had hope, and we had a plan. We were all invested and onboard.

Then the night came. Then the race started.

It is like life, really, a metaphor. While it's early days, the sun is shining, the body is not so weary, resilience is high, and motivation is strong. Anyone can go that investment. Now bring on the hard slog, darkness, unknown, desire for rest, and comfort. Now see who keeps digging deep. Now is the time to pounce and make your mark. Close to midnight, I found myself in 4th position, not too far back, but enough to be out of sight; but it was dark, with only the lights on your bike and helmet. It's hard to know where you are in the race. As I slogged it out on a steep long fire road climb, I happened upon the women who were racing for the podium. Here I was, finally, what did I have now to pounce and make my move? Could now be the time to make my move? Did I dare, or should I wait it out a little longer? When I found myself slowly moving away from them up an even steeper section, I instinctively grabbed the chance to take control. I attacked silently into the night, leaving a deep dark void of time and space for them to contemplate the next move. It was everything I had ever planned for, total commitment and self-belief.

Norm understandably is getting excited; I can feel that, and I can feel the whole pit lane area buzzing with excitement and cheering me on. I don't want to let anyone down, but mostly I want to prove to myself that I deserve it. I can do it and can see it through to the end, with more determination and desire than anyone else. The laps pass by, and I put more time into that trio I passed some hours ago, but there is new competition nipping at my heels as the sun is rising. Katrin Van der Spiegal, the athlete I beat back in April last year at the National Championships, is slowly gaining time on me, and Norm reminds me of this. She is a half-hour back but stomping it in with six hours to go. It's not over, and I have to stay focused on everything. Mostly I have to know and believe I have what it takes to see this through; I have come this far. She is chasing me, I am already in the prime position, and I am not prepared to relinquish it.

Jason and I repping Australia for the win

The finish line
Adam McGrath

Sticking to the processes and kept my mind chattering in check. I eat, I drink, I lap around as I have for the past 20 or so hours. When the trail allows me, I coast when I can, braking smoothly for upcoming corners and pedalling out of them to maintain momentum. It's working, Katrin can't catch me now, and all I need to do is ride without incident, and I have won. In the final few minutes, before I won the 2010 World 24hr Solo Championships, I approached the '1km to go' sign on the course. Knowing that this was my last lap and my final 1000 meters to ride to achieve this dream, I felt ready for how my life would change. I had a vision of who I would be and how I would conquer the world with the next challenge.

Norm and I celebrated with friends; it was amazing to do this. There was a massive release of pressure: jubilation and an indescribable juxtaposition of disbelief and joy. For the next week, I allowed myself total disarray.

No expectations, no timelines, no training, just eat, sleep and bask in the glow of the hard work and winning result. Once we were home, the responsibilities of life returned in full force. Then came the people and the interest in my story, media, sponsorship responsibilities. It was only one week in from the most fantastic thing I had ever done, and I found myself in a deep hole. People wanted me to share my journey, and I had no energy or desire to do this and I couldn't work out why. The achievement felt so huge that energy had to go somewhere. I had set out to do something that only others dream about. In pursuit of a dream, for no other reason other than to see if I could. And now I was in the lowest of lows, the beginnings of a period of depression and withdrawal that had me wondering if I should or could ever reinvest this much of myself ever again.

It would be a good three months before I found my mojo again. There was no plan in place for this lengthy period of depression. I had no desire to train as I had previously; perhaps I knew all the hard work it took to be the best. So instead, I got back to having fun, social rides, team racing, solo rides with no real focus, and a bit of trail running as well. Slowly my joy returned, and 2011 turned out to be a cracker year off the back of my World Championship win. I bloody well did it. I had an opportunity. I grabbed it and said, yes, let's see what I can do. I fell short and chose to learn and grow. I gave it everything.

> It was just a mountain bike race; in essence, the process and the self-belief taught me so much more that would be transferable in so many areas of my life forever. The accolades of the win were pretty special though this life lesson was so much more profound and rewarding.

You may have seen the pictorial representations of 'success' as an iceberg seen above the waterline. Yet underneath is so much more. I now understand why I reached such a low point after such a massive high point in my athletic career when I look at it retrospectively. I have always told my coaching clients that motivation is not something you can just manufacture, wish, or hope for. Instead, you must have a fiery passion, with an impenetrable desire that gives you focus. Because of these elements, your actions are fueled with dedication, and you develop discipline. Through this, you start to see results, and with consistency, you realise that motivation comes from this, not the end goal of winning or whatever that might be. Yet to get all this, there is always a price to pay. One must hurt, suffer, sacrifice, give up and invest time. To be open to failure, rejection and ready to get back up again. You are actively seeking to be your most vulnerable and courageous as you experience loss. You are often feeling anxious, spending so much of your own money. Slogging through long days of hard work with unrelenting drive and determination, rail hail or shine to see it through, knowing that there is no guarantee that your dream will come to fruition. And that you would wake up every day and keep going anyway because you love it; it is what fills your heart with joy and provides you with a sense of purpose. When you can keep this day to day routine going, no matter what, then you have found your passion. I was keen to keep moving forward now that I had recognised this depression period as a side effect. It was to be expected, given my totality of self-investment.

Thanks Chris Ord for the opportunity to stretch myself!
Chris Ord

To replace such a grand goal of 2010, I sought about setting mini-goals throughout 2011. Races where all I had to do was turn up, have fun and engage in something different, and whatever the result, this did not matter. 2011 was a year of growth, expanding my horizons as an athlete and as a person. The year was filling up quickly with events that followed a new format than what I had been doing. Many were shorter but also multi-day stage races, with loads of interstate travel. I was still coming to terms with going back to defend my 2010 World Championship title, but this decision was removed from me anyway. The 2011 World Championships did not take place and sent the endurance mountain biking community into a bit of a spin; what would we strive for now? The smaller events had less meaning if you wanted to build your race resume to pursue the world scene.

In a sigh of relief, I welcomed this reprieve in the 24hr world. Each time I put myself out there, I was learning and growing. I learnt a lot about myself when I kept showing up. Aligning myself with passion and purpose kept my motivation high even on bad days. Being open to failure taught me how to own it and grow from it. Even when life gave me hard times, I was able to stay on track. After a great start to the year, I joined forces with Brad Davies as a mixed pair in a mountain bike stage race called Terra Australis, a magical six days of racing in the Victorian alpine region in March. It was a significant six-day event, with terrain like I had never ridden, let alone raced before. I would be tested and pushed beyond my limits; very blessed to have Brad pushing the pace and looking after me. We had a fun week of racing, coming 2nd in Mixed pairs and forming friendships and bonds with many riders. It was probably my best mountain bike racing experience, as hard as it was, and I am so grateful for memories like these.

Now I had two positive and rewarding experiences to start the year with. Getting ahead of myself, I decided why not; let's aim for a third win in the Australian national 24 solo mountain bike championships. I figured I was in great form, now was the time to take out number three. It was meant to be a year of simple race goals; to show up, try new things, enjoy myself, and focus on podium placings. I had forgotten this detail and allowed myself to get all excited again. Norm and I decided a few weeks out that we would turn up to the nationals in Canberra and go through the motions. A dangerous approach.

A good gauge for me to use to lead up to a big meaningful race was to ask myself how excited I was and what processes to follow. When I felt butterflies and started to write down my race plan, even on the back of an envelope, I knew I was invested. I didn't do any of that this time, hoping I could just wing it on the day.

This race gave me a wake-up call, and it sucked.

The endurance racing scene was watching, and I failed big time. Essentially I didn't care, and it was too soon; since winning the World Championship in 2010 in October, I wasn't ready to hurt again so soon, or ever. Perhaps I had fallen out of love with 24hr racing, and this was the end of it? Maybe I was going to retire from this discipline? The start went well. I rode strong; everything was hunky-dory. Norm was happy to support me. All I had to do was keep riding. With the pressure on and feeling my ego out in full exposure mode, I wanted to smash the field and go out hard to prove a point. I was a champion, and I can keep winning. It was a weird pressure that perhaps I put on myself more than others, but I felt it strong and didn't want to fail today. It's downright embarrassing to fail in front of your fans and those that might be hoping you do slip up. The national championship's of 2011 was just that for me.

Six hours in, holding an incredible pace but pushing a little harder than needed, with a target on my back, I had the women's field pursuing me to see when I would crack. I had been open about my uncertainty in continuing 24hr racing and how depression was holding me back. I have been on the other side, hoping to crack my competition, so it was no surprise. At a dark and lonely time of night, I started to flounder for energy, purpose, and strength to go on. Perhaps I had gone out too hard; I started making mistakes and hating the course, hating being there and desperate for it all to end. Self-talk confirmed that turning up today was a stupid decision and that it was time to retire from the scene. I continued with this dialogue until Jo Wall passed me. Thoughts entered my head, oh, you could just ride around and be happy with coming second, and be graceful in that, allow her to enjoy the fight for the win. But I just could not sell that concept of riding around for another twelve hours and accept 2nd place.

I look back now and can see it as clear as day. I kept racing because I felt it my responsibility to uphold this new identity; as a World Champion, I could no longer just turn up and enjoy finishing, thinking I had to win or not at all. I see this now, and it is no wonder I kept finding myself dipping in and out of depression for many years to come. Jo Wall won. I did not finish, we drove home, and the feeling of self-loathing was heavy and all-consuming. I had let everyone down, taken the shine off Jo's win, come across as a sore loser and wasted time and money to do so.

Norm was withdrawn and found it hard to trust me again for a long time as this was the second time I had pulled the pin on finishing a 24hr race.

It's hard to explain my motivations for returning to it. My challenge now was to get back to that space I had promised myself for 2011, to race for fun and new experiences for growth as a person and athlete.

But who was I if I was no longer a 24hr mountain bike champion? I had to find out; this was my job now. Everything I did pivoted around my cycling pursuits, and that's how I found out my purpose next. It was not about winning.

It was about being open, honest, vulnerable, giving it a go. Showing other people that you can keep reinventing yourself and that failure does hurt and offers growth. After working so hard to get to the top, I had lost the plot; I had forgotten my roots. Even more than this, I had to get back to basics and not forget my mantra, my philosophy—the simplicity of ticking along just 1% at a time. I would do this process many times over in the years to come. Racing had become my apprenticeship for life, for finding out what I was made of and what was possible. What was worth investing in, and what I could do with what was gifted to me via knowledge, relationships and privilege. I had begun to realise that the racing had only a small amount to do with me and so much more about what I was doing for others.

It became easier to get on the start line regardless of what I was expected to achieve. I knew I had to just turn up, be friendly, chat with people, be open and honest, and prove that if I could do it, then maybe others might be inspired to as well. It just so happened that racing bikes was the tool in which I had to express myself. Life is full of many uncomfortable and awkward moments, many I would have preferred to have avoided. However, as I already knew well, accepting this last failure and moving through it and accepting the learnings would allow change. On the other side, I would find new direction and hope. As always, I was not disappointed. Next in line was a wonderful trip I had booked when I won the World Champs in 2010. I had just won $5000 and treated myself to a race and a flight to Alice Springs to race a 5-day stage race with a friend, Claire Stevens. It was like a future-proofing event to strive towards for its fun and get out of the Victorian chill.

It was May, and as I sat on the plane, I wrote myself a blog post that showed promise and new hope.

As I was flying to Alice Springs on Sunday 15th May, I was filled with such inspiration. When I saw the green trickles of land winding their way to Lake Eyre, I felt new life. Overwhelmingly so, I was holding in tears of joy. You know the ones that when you cry, you are so happy, but you just can't stop crying anyway?

Here was my story that flowed from my heart. Maybe it is a story that inspires or gives you hope?

The purpose of life.

My life is incredible. So full of beautiful experiences and good people.

Loved ones and a blessed life surround me.

So why have I been floundering to find myself?

Often you hear people talk about spending so much time working towards a goal, such as "when I retire, I am going to do this and that...", or "when I lose 5kgs, and I fit in size 10, my life will be better", or..." I will work 80hrs this week on such and such a project so I can sit back and relax for a bit with an empty in-tray."

Do you ever really reach the pinnacle, the desired result? Or do you get to what you think is what you were searching for only to realise you had it all along?

The process of being driven to succeed is called LIFE.

I have been reminded of this many times and reminded again as I write this. Every little step along the way, every minute of every day, every tick box checked, every goal reached, is just a paving stone on my pathway of life. The path I pave is neither straight nor perfect, and sometimes there are gaps with weeds growing between; sometimes, the pavers fit neat and tight.

The only goal I need is to keep this path going forward. I have to live in it every day. Ensuring I take the time to plant some beautiful, inspiring scenery around me because this is a lifelong project.

I have been struggling for eight months now with a sense of purpose. I am not feeling connected to anything but moving forward anyhow, hoping that life would just "click" for me.

Surprise surprise! My life has been clicking all along.

I promised myself from this day forward to follow some guidelines to live my best life. Always live in the moment, breathe deep, let it fill my pores, my every being for what it is, good or bad. Do my best to love freely, build bridges and not walls. Find it in me to keep giving, keep caring for this will make a difference to someone somewhere. Just smile more and not worry about what people think; my life is good, why not enjoy it. Always remember to be grateful for every second on this earth I am given. Embrace all the adversity. Find forgiveness. Live honestly to the best of my ability.

> The process of living can be so overwhelming, earning enough to be comfortable, keeping people happy, reaching goals, feeling a purpose in life. All these things seem hard sometimes, but we are all the same. Exactly the same. How comforting is that?

This week away in Alice Springs was just what I needed, some space and a new environment with no expectations on my results other than to enjoy the experience. Well, funny how taking the pressure off can give you more than you bargained for. I unexpectedly won the event, and I went home refreshed, with a positive mindset and renewed self-belief. Who would have known that a 24hr solo champ could race seven short races over five days and win? These kinds of races were proving to be fun, and with each experience, I was gaining more enthusiasm to be my best on the bike again. It was an excellent strategy for my overall mental health and wellbeing. Thank goodness for moments of clarity, for when I got home again, it was full-on. So many skills courses to run and plan. Interstate race invites, logistics and budgets. Could we run classes and race? You see, every cent and every dollar we earned or spent was ours; there was no full-time job with holiday pay to use up. An insane use of October, with so much travel, racing and working, this is how it played out.

Drive from Forrest to Canberra, 800km.

9th -10th October, Scott 24hr in a four female team. Drive from Canberra to Nambucca Heads, 760km.

11th 13th October, Ride the MTB Trails at Nambucca Heads. Drive from Nambucca Heads to Brisbane, 430km.

14th 16th October, deliver MTBSkills courses with Rowan at Gap Creek and ride Mt Joyce.

Fly from Brisbane to Cairns.

16th 28th October, Race the Croc Trophy in FNQ for ten days. Fly from Cairns to Melbourne, then drive to Mt Buller from the airport.

28th October 1st November, MTBSkills MT Buller retreat weekend with 40 people.

My strategy to make it happen was to say yes, work out how later. The code that I cracked was nothing revolutionary, simply to invest that extra 1% that others were not—coupled with a mindset of why not me? Why can't I do amazing things? Other people in the world make stuff happen. The difference between actually making it come to life was simply 'doing'. Norm had an old business mentor tell him once, "Better done than perfect". Each day my goals were to achieve what I could, building on my wealth in every area possible. When I found myself procrastinating, I drew upon strength in knowing my 1% methodology works. Adhering to easy, achievable processes, building enjoyment, fulfilment, and a pattern of success, regardless of how small.

> 2011 would be a huge year, full of opportunities. I wondered if I would find an endpoint and say, "I have made it." Each day would finish with a sunset, and I knew I could put my head on a pillow and sleep. The gift of resetting and being able to have another crack at life with a new sunrise and a new day.

But it was not over yet; I had more racing to do! My experience of the Croc Trophy was so unique, yet so very hard. This event has changed slightly in its current format, but back in 2011, it was a 9-day mountain bike stage race, starting in Cairns and finishing in Cooktown. Long days of often riding in 40 degrees Celcius heat. Early starts, late finishes, extreme distances and culminating in rushing around getting your bike cleaned or fixed, food and drink consumed and preparing your gear for tomorrows stage. All whilst sleeping in a tent with a few hundred other people attempting to achieve similar daily goals.

so many water crossings Croc Trophy 2011

My Giant Bicycles teammate and coaching client, Brad Davies, was always going to do the Croc. We had been busily scheduling in training and life and trying to avoid illness for weeks leading up to this event. I was already well in deep with the whole scene of Croc Mania. Four weeks out from the start date, I got a phone call from Martin Wisata from Rocky Trail Entertainment to see if I would be keen to attend and fit into my schedule? It took me about 1 minute to scan through my diary and assess that this was indeed possible. I would be stupid to turn down this fantastic opportunity, so I said YES!

In the lead up to this crazy event, I had a tonne of things already, which often left me wondering if I was biting off more than I could chew? My schedule started with a friend, Eliza Eldridge Bassett, coming down to Forrest for some skills, training and a women's Liv/Giant ride in early October. Then the trip up to Canberra for the Scott 24hr in a team of 4 with the Giant girls, Eliza, Jo Hall, Niki Fisher and me. The road trip to Nambucca Heads was quickly followed to ride the trails with the great club and people for a couple of days, finally followed by the final leg to Brisbane for our MTBSkills 1st Birthday with Rowan Lamont, one of our instructors. Finally arriving in Cairns, this was not without further incident, including losing my purse on the plane. No cash, no card, lost wedding and engagement rings. I contacted Brad at midnight to ask for assistance. Thankfully, I went to the bank on Monday morning, got some cash, and decided to worry about the rest later when the race was over.

Cairns' first thing that struck me was the heavy humidity that took away the spring in my step. On the evening of Monday 17th October, we attended the race briefing for all involved in the event. A lot to take in, and we still needed to do the final cull of our gear to take with us, get some sleep and prepare for ten days of racing. I had concerns about my race preparation, having enough electrolytes and other nutritional products. I was worried. Did I have the legs and the mind to go through with so many days of racing?

Greeted with rain for the race start was a sign of things to come. The start was in Cairns in front of the lagoon swimming pool area. Lots of hellos to people we knew and those we grew to know. The first job of the day was to get our water bottles to the depot dropoffs that we would access throughout the day. The daily grind of a ten-day outback race started with clean, fresh bottles, new cycling kits and perfect bikes. Having stayed in a hotel last night, day 1 was a breeze. After dropping off bottles, a weigh-in was required to ensure we kept hydrated at every stage with a follow-up weigh-in post-race. When all the formalities were taken care of, we finally started the neutral part, a 12km ride through Cairns and our official start partway up a climb to Copperlode Dam. I mentioned the rain earlier, which threatened all morning. It had held off until the race started, but the humidity was unbelievable!

Eventually, we got off to the official race start. Being a long climb winding through the hills, I was happy to find a tempo and get day one underway. Somehow with the humidity and sweaty, the rain that started to fall arrived unnoticed for a while; in fact, I recall I was grateful for the coolness it brought with it. Then there was a distinct change from rain to a torrential downpour, and as serious as it was, the fun factor of riding in this was gratifying. Unable to ride with sunglasses on and only see 20 – 30 metres in front of you made the time go quickly as intense concentration was needed. The race became neutralised when support vehicles required could not get through the course intended. After a long break in a tourist shelter, we proceeded to ride again in a non-race fashion. Still, the rain fell, it was wet, and we were all wearing black garbage bags to stay warm.

I wish I could have raced this day; I love racing, riding in the rain and enjoying the slippery mud descents. It reminded me of Otway Odyssey and how often the steep Noonday Track, back home, is wet and almost unrideable. After a day of 105km of what I would call my "Croc Trophy" Warm-up ride, we arrived at Lake Tinaroo. We seemed to escape the rain for about 2hrs, then it started, and poor Brad got rained on with water dripping through the tent all night. The sign of things to come for the next two days!

On day two, it's still raining. Riding in this and wet from yesterdays jaunt, we prepared for a re-routed stage of 114km. I had a good day on the bike, loving the rain, enjoying some company with a crew I had picked up along the way. I finished 30th in 4hrs 20 mins to a very sombre campsite.

> Puddles, rain, wet tents, people scurrying to keep dry, garbage bags used as rain jackets, it was a shemozzle! Brad and I managed to secure a better tent and better beds tonight. The only thing stopping me from sleeping was listening to the rain on the tent ALL NIGHT LONG.

It was so wet we just left our wet kits and shoes at the tent door; what was the use in cleaning or keeping anything dry? By the third day, due to the rain, we rode to Irvinebank and started to feel some sunshine on our backs. Another good day in the saddle as I picked up a big group of 10 along the course, working together and getting into Irvinebank a bit faster and smoother. Today was better, finishing 26th in 3hrs 57 mins. Being here for two days was like arriving at a refugee camp being told we could make this our home now. Everyone scrambled for a make-do clothesline to dry out their gear and make their little patch of grass home. We found a park bench on a 3 x 3mt patch of concrete to use as our porch; surprisingly, no one else had snatched it up. We hung out next to our neighbours John and Sandra Boswell from Townsville. Another visitor, Peter, also from Townsville, brought Brad and me some pegs, rice creams and lollies. Irvinebank was an oasis, a pub, internet connection and a dry tent for two nights.

By the time day five arrived the routine was down pat. Bottles dropped off, food eaten, race early to avoid too much heat and suffer for the first hour at fast speeds, hoping that the field would slow down a bit. Described as a technical day, I was looking forward to it. Finishing 33rd in 4hrs and 5 mins, it was a better day than the day before; tomorrow, I will prosper. I felt the heat today, from the soles of my feet to the top of my head.

It's day 6, and there's 190km to race. Thankfully, the longer the days are, the better I do. Today's stage was full of hills and undulations, river crossings, creek crossings, rocks and fast dirt roads. Punctuated with hot, dusty double tracks cutting through barren cattle properties. The rocks here are full of ore, sharp and metallic; the theme of the day was puncturing.

> I spent 2hrs lying in the river after the race, one of the things that made this race so worthwhile. This marked the start of my loss of appetite, as eating was becoming a chore. My only wish was a cold can of coke, which was very hard to come by.

Yesterday's stage was long, and so was this one at 150km. Not only was it lengthy, but the heat was also turning up. We were racing at 8 am today and feeling the heat from 9 am onwards into the early '40s, with the most heat felt on the feet. There was a definite feeling of flatness from the get-go today. 30 Km in after such fun rolling undulations, I was smashed and just could not maintain any intensity. It was food, I know, so as I ate a meagre dinner and breakfast, it was hard to be enthusiastic about eating. Now I was paying for it. At the next feed zone, I ate a muesli bar. Not a fan of these at all, but in 20 mins I was perky. I would feel good all day long, then bonk, and when I got to the final feed zone, I was now on fire again.

The last 30 km should have been easy to comprehend. But 15 km of this was the most incredible corrugations I have ridden on. I just told myself, "1km at a time, just let it tick over, don't stress, it's going to take an hour, so be done with it!"

A lousy day, coming in 43rd, in 6hrs 46mins. I promised to eat and drink and eat some more tonight and to have a very substantial breakfast to make up for today's horrible sufferfest.

Eight days goes quick when you're having fun. A very short day today and only 200mts of climbing. Quick, sharp and fast. With two drink stations, 90km and decent roads, albeit corrugated in sections. It was essential to be part of a bunch and be 100% on your guard. Accidents happened all over the place, with wheels touching and bodies colliding. At the top end, funny games and angry athletes were messing with the race. Thankfully we all worked well, and I even had the presence of mind to get a good position for the end 1km and finished well in the bunch sprint. Today I finished 27th in 3hrs and 9 mins.

Kalpowar was a lovely spot with Saltwater crocodiles in the river down the bottom of the campsite. There were rock pools amongst the river, and a group of us decided our lives were safe and had a dip for a good hour whilst checking out potential wildlife action around us. I came out cold, which was awesome. Days like these were in their 40's and life was getting tough indeed!

Day nine was the most challenging day of the lot, a big day in the distance and a more extended day due to the terrain. It started with a river crossing; the field soon split up, and thankfully, I was able to stick with the crew from yesterday and find my race legs. And yet another hot day in the '40s, lots of sand awaited us; in fact, we raced through a section of at least 70km long with on and off areas of deep, nearly unrideable sand. Whilst we had many spots of the fast and flowy route, there were also many long sections of hot deep sand. Today's most memorable and challenging aspect was the sand. These sections just kept coming and coming; once again, I just had to look at riding 1km at a time, rationing my drinks to last until the next depot. I did not enjoy racing today, from about 100km to 120km, and I had to be conservative until I became good again. Finishing 29th in 6hrs 51mins, this was probably the most challenging day of racing yet. It was hot, scorching and relentless heat. Once again, my appetite was gone. Tonight I did not go to dinner. Instead, I ate nuts, lollies and pasta from Jeroen Boelen and added a boiled egg to it.

**With one more night to go, I did not care right now.
Food was food, and sleep was far more critical.**

I had made it to the final day, only 80km of racing and 50km of riding behind a police car to Cooktown. And like that, it was over, Cooktown was hot and humid as we finished on the steep climb of Grassy Hill and overlooked the ocean. I downed two cans of coke, about six slices of watermelon and then enjoyed the presentations. I had won the female category and came 29th overall with 43hrs of riding in 10 days.

Flying back to Melbourne the next day, I drove myself from the airport to Mt. Buller for our annual MTBSkills Camp. A three-hour drive into the late hours of the night; exhausted, I called Norm, who met me at Mansfield and drove me up the mountain. Four more days of work, a big five hour drive back home before the chance to have ample rest. There were still more commitments to tick off yet. A trip up to Townsville to race and do skills courses. Racing in our inaugural event, The Forrest Festival. And plenty of planning and training to see the year out.

> One year after becoming a world champion, I had indeed found my groove again. But what would the next year look like? Could I keep going at this intensity, would I still have the passion for succeeding and was I even capable of more? It seemed the more successful I became, the more I didn't believe I was worthy. It was like I had a constant case of 'imposter complex' going on; even when I knew it wasn't true, I had to spend a good chunk of time invested in proving myself wrong.

I still felt like I was an imposter in the elite world of my sport. Every day I worried about my body image. Was I too heavy and looked unsightly in lycra? And what could someone like me possibly teach anyone on the mountain bike? Was I that good to share my knowledge? Yet, I had all the proof that I was perfect just the way I was and that I had won on skill and talent, not luck or lack of competition. I had enjoyed the climb to the top, but I was scared shitless of the responsibility. This would continue to be a daily battle with my feelings of worth and purpose.

Otway Odyssey start line - 2011

Just when I wondered if I had any more to give, I experienced my best 100km mountain bike marathon race in March of 2012. It was the Otway Odyssey, an extremely tough event. 100km was a short distance for a 24hr endurance racer. My form was magnificent, lighter, stronger, and faster, with a hunger to prove myself in this format that was not yet my strength. This race started down in Apollo Bay, around 40km from Forrest. Up and over the Otways ranges, the race started on the main street, next to the ocean.

Taking the hard way back to Forrest, via access trails, 4wd roads, motorbike trails, mountain bike single tracks and connecting farm roads, culminating to one hundred kilometres of sufferfest racing.

The elite women commenced 30 minutes before the main field that also had the elite men, which gave us a head start and prevented us from being supported by the men's field. The first twenty kilometres of the race was an excellent qualifier for what form the field was in, with some big climbs to test the legs out. A French adventure racer, Myriam Guillot-Boisset, rode away on the first climb and the rest of the elite women's field let her go. Quickly I found myself riding alongside Peta Mullens as she pushed the pace for the first half of the race. Myriam was up front, nowhere to be seen, then it was Peta and me. I was in the top three. I was motivated to race hard. However, when Peta took a chance to attack mid-race, my brain was switched off. I honestly didn't think about what had just occurred until she was fifty meters up the road. It was a sharp shock to the system to get my mind into gear again. I wouldn't see Peta again until the finish but never gave up hope. I came through the race hub one last time, grabbed my final bottle, and knew I only had fifteen kilometres to go. I would be done in less than one hour.

The final section was on Thompsons Track, which went up and down many times over. At an overgrown moto track, I passed Myriam. She was a petite, high cadence mountain goat climber, whilst I was strong, out of the saddle grinder. I knew I needed a break on her now before the technical nasty 4wd track climb came up. This was affectionately known as the 'sledgehammer'. Attacking Myriam at the bottom of this, hoping to get a buffer and choose the correct uphill lines as there were many ruts to avoid. I willed myself to make it, to have a clean run and hurt hard. I did it; she was out of sight as I looked back. Getting closer to the finish, I was within a few minutes, and I will be 2nd today. I was stoked. Coming over the finish line, fifty seconds behind Peta, and I had no idea I was so close, putting five minutes into Myriam in that final section.

Today's result was the best yet for me in this form of racing. This year was to be a huge one. Norm and I put a lot of effort into growing our businesses, taking MTBSkills interstate to South Australia, Tasmania, Queensland, and more instructors in Victoria. We also needed to train our instructors and offer these courses to other people outside our organisation. We had camps and lessons held over many states, and we attended many of them this year to help establish our name. Not only were we invested in this significant project, but also our events were growing too. I was still racing in them and assisting in their running.

Then in April, we got a call from Russ Baker, who joined forces with BluBike in Italy and NoFuss Events in Scottland, to start WEMBO. This organisation made sure the World 24hr Solo Mountain bike championships continued after no events were held in 2011. Russ asked if Norm and I would come to Italy to defend my 24hr WC title with some funding from the ACT government. Meaning we would be looked after considerably. The catch was, I needed to make a decision pretty quickly as the WEMBO (World Endurance Mountain Bike Organisation) event was on 19th May.

> This concept freaked me out, and well, honestly, I needed to 'un-freak' myself before I said yes. I was honoured to be asked, especially by Russ Baker; it meant a lot. But I needed to find a reason for going, not just to defend my title.

When I was young, I was so shy and wanted to fit in, wanting to be sporty and accepted. Instead, I was an introvert who enjoyed her own company, inventing, dreaming, cooking, drawing, creating stuff. I see who I am as an adult, and these behaviour patterns still exist. I want to prove myself to the world, feel accepted and worthy, and show people that I can do things they think I can't. I love my own company; I love to create; think up great ideas and see what comes of them. Over the past year, my question has been – why did I need to feel this way? Why did I want to do great things? Why did it matter what I have done in the past? Who even cares what I do in the future? What was I meant to be doing in my life? What value could I bring to the world? How could I be the best me there is? These are the kind of things most people ask themselves from time to time, often after life-changing events. For me, it was after becoming the Solo 24hr World champion in Canberra in 2010.

It was not so much the title that had me questioning such "whys" but more so the whole process of what was before the result of winning. After spending 18 months inching towards a goal, focussing my energy and actions on it, the purpose can be easily forgotten. All I knew was that I wanted to be the best Jess Douglas I could be on the day, in every minute aspect of my being.

> I had simply forgotten to stop and enjoy it. I achieved my goal when I won, but did I feel anything about it? I had been creating this masterpiece for so long that I could no longer appreciate it. I only saw the hard work and layers underneath the glowing result. I know why I am ready to go to Italy in 5 weeks and race a 24hr again. It is simply my gift to work hard at what I do; I have to; I am on this earth to suffer a little and grow heaps. To show people that the hard stuff is possible. That our minds are silly and disabling if we let them rule us, and equally unique and boundless. I used to say a lot to myself, a quote from somewhere..." we have been born with a body that can do almost anything; it's our minds we have to convince."

I avoided hard work and was fearful of failure, afraid of what people may think or say. In late 2011, I had made the call that I was definitely out of the 24hr scene and would not want to defend my title in 2012. I considered and eventually turned this down too, and got on with life. Why? I didn't want to say yes just because there was an offer on the table. So I pushed on. I used my summer season for excellent base training, got some great rides in, some great intensity, and skilled up. In January 2012, I had some goals to attend, get fast, have fun and get stuck into some travelling. The 1%'ers were paying off with no actual plans for 2012 – just to get faster, work on skills, work on my speed and endurance in 100km races, do the events that I was not so good at to get better. There was no talk of doing 24hr solo again. However, I still had to work out in my own heart and head why I was resistant to doing another 24hr, let alone defending a world 24hr title. Then it started to happen without my trying, and it's often the way we stop worrying and let life talk for us. I received a few Facebook messages and emails from people who race

24 hr events. Conversations about how I had inspired them, that my "words of wisdom" helped them improve something in their racing, and then started to build inside me. Then, finally, I realised what I had known all along.

It was my job; I had quit what I had chosen to do. I had tried to avoid the hard work – avoid the pain and suffering of racing a 24hr; the whole ordeal of training, racing and recovering. This form of racing had taken its toll on me for the time. Mostly in my head, and I was also thinking about it far too much. In my heart, I was still keen, but I was blocking this out. After reading a message from a fellow racer, Rachel Edwards, just about something race-related and some advice I had given, I knew I was in. The moment I got my head to shut up and listen to my heart, the answer was yes, and it probably always was. Then an amazing thing happened, I was on a race list that I had withdrawn from. The race list got distributed to many people. Suddenly I was on the list to race the 24hrs of Finale in Italy, even though I thought I would have to register again now that I had decided to race.

> It was meant to be. Then it all flowed through from there, all the support I had ever had as a world champion; it was all still there and flowing freely. The decision that I deliberated over felt so right. My stomach got butterflies just thinking about it, the racing, the travel, the 1 am night lap, the first 6hrs of fast pace, the pain of the last 2 or 3 laps. I had made the right decision.

Again it was a reminder never to stop moving forward. To never stop believing in my dreams to listen to my heart. Invest in all my days on this earth; I may as well make the most of it. It was abundantly clear to me for the umpteenth time that to continue the growth in myself and this sport; I had to adjust my perspective. This became a daily reminder. My ego and expectations were well in check when I raced my bike, not to be the best in the world, not to win every race, not for the glory but for what this opportunity signifies. In my heart and how I see it, putting myself on the line, giving myself up for the suffering, opening myself up to these experiences parallels being an entrepreneur, an inventor, or an explorer. I was on a mission to give back to this world through my experience as a mountain biker, face my fears and show others that you can achieve your dreams.

Welcome Australia to Finale Ligure

Race Day

So I said yes to Russ Baker, and to the idea of defending my 24hr WEMBO world solo mountain bike championship, and mainly to the experience. We were heading to Finale Ligure, Italy. May 2012,

Italy. After arriving and a week of exploring, it was time to race. We arrived at the event village early enough to prepare. It was cold, with light drizzle, which I did not mind at all. I spent the next hour visiting the portaloos. The nerves only stop when the race starts. It was then time to start warming up the mind and preparing the body. Listening to my music mix on my iPod, I felt pretty relaxed. Not focussed at all on the next 24 hours or who my competition was, just me, the trails, the bike, my support, the nutrition, and then plan.

There is nothing more I can do at this stage to improve my chances; I've done it all. I took my bike for a spin, checked the gears out, brakes, ride and spin, and was happy and warmed up a bit. Amazed to be in Italy, Finale Ligure, about to race a World solo 24hr MTB championship, I believe I'm already the winner. I can see it, feel it, just need to ride it, but I don't want to rush it, enjoying the moment. It's like an aftertaste in my mouth from some fabulous meal that I want to have again and never finish. Promising myself that I would not take any moment for granted, that I would savour the experience, and I am; it's just too easy to feel this good.

The clouds are still covering the sun, but my back is warm with the glow of my inner peace and happiness.

It's 12:30 pm, the race briefing is given in English and Italian. There is no turning back; it's time to submit, time to hand it over, no longer do you have control. You've entered what you have signed up for, and getting the start over and done with is the thing you want to tick off. I settle my mind and body for what is to come; the nerves are there, butterflies in the pit of the stomach have me wishing for one last toilet stop. Twenty-four hours will pass regardless of how I manage my race; there is no turning back. We are all asked to line our bikes up and start for a short run before mounting our bikes. The countdown occurs in Italian, then the final countdown in English.

Go. Elbows out, trying to run fast to get on my bike.

Feeling comfortable, perhaps too comfortable, it was nearly impossible to pass with riders in front on the single track. Soon enough, the riders spread out, and it was now me and Ricky Cotter from the UK out front of the women's field, having a great time.

I am thinking of my game plan, watching, listening, tuning into any hints of weaknesses of my friendly opponent. I like Rickie, I admire her, we chat, riding like mates, but of course, she wants to win, and so do I. It's like a road race where you are the breakaway and help each other out, no attacking if the other mucks up but knowing the whole time that one of you is waiting for the pounce. The start is probably the most challenging part of the race; settling into a fast endurance race pace. Finding out who your competition is and watching their every move adds to the pure delight of racing these 24hr world solo champs.

Finale Ligure trails
Sportograf

After Ricky and I settled into our race, we lapped together; sometimes I would be at the front, sometimes she would. Patience. Coming through transition, I took a few moments to pick up food or drink; Ricky gained about 20 seconds in this time. I never worried about it, as I would be on her wheel before long. Conscious of expending more energy than I needed. Not worrying at all – letting Ricky do her thing, I had a plan to stick to. The course went through transition twice; the laps were over an hour-long. The first part was out on more challenging trails, with limestone cliffs overlooking the Ligurian Sea. The view had to be looked at, even if only momentarily each lap. The water, sapphire blue and still.

Many sections in this lap messed with your mind, and several gave you so much love that you forgot that the next bit coming up required 100% effort. It made for tough riding and was mentally taxing, but the brainwashing effect that occurred was just what was needed to smash a lap out. My climbing legs were protesting today. On the climbs, Ricky was pounding down on the pedals; she was really walloping them. I kept in contact with her back wheel as best I could. Then we'd hit the descents, and I was back on her wheel. It was perfect. Keeping my heart rate and efforts just off the limit, then recovering nicely on the downs instead of attacking. We would hit the bermed section on the return to transition, and if Ricky was ahead, it was the magic spot where I would have some fun and catch back up again, ready for the second half of the lap. Our transition area was challenging for a typical run through, too short, bumpy ground, straight into a down ramp where you needed both hands on the handlebars. I stopped to do safe bottle swap overs and grab some food. It was only twenty seconds, and it was a good plan this early in the race. Every moment I was resting, my opponent was riding.

> Patience and planning, and putting in effort only when it is needed.

I suggested that Norm may need to employ a second helper's services of a 2nd helper, which he eventually did in Sarah O'Callaghan. The next part of the lap started on fun, tight twisty singletrack, flow flow flow. I enjoyed this in the wet, at night, when I was tired, and even on my last two laps. The ground surface was loose dirt with roots that helped bring your back wheel around, tiny drops that you could launch off, the kind of fun any mountain biker looks for in a ride or race.

We rode a beautiful rocky outcrop, with a steep descent on the other side and a view to mask any discomfort momentarily. There was a nasty steep climb that was freshly whipper snipped into the hillside. This was rideable but very hard; as footsteps overtook tyre marks on the track, it became a challenge to ride. Ricky and I rode it every lap we did together.

Lap 1, Prologue lap. Jess 34:33. Ricky 34:36

Lap 2, Full lap. Ricky and I now settle in and find our place in the race, passing many who started ahead of us still, no one passing us as yet. Watching Ricky climb, I decide to settle behind her good form focusing on saving energy, looking for signs of weakness early, making mental notes constantly like a nurse checking vital signs on a patient every hour.

Tick boxes are being created. Looking for spots to drink every lap too.

Jess 1:05:26. Ricky 1:05:25

Lap 3, Still lapping well; I was enjoying myself now. Ricky is having a ball too. Life is good. The bike is good; the trails are fantastic.

Settled and feeling comfortable, watching for her strengths and weaknesses. Ricky was smashing out all climbs, me conservative but finding lots of recovery in descending. No sign of any fatigue in Ricky; she is still chirpy and a good talker too. I see that for no extra effort; I am catching her as the trail points down.

The massive efforts being put in on climbs by Ricky are incredible. If she can win it doing this, then well done, yet I am not sure it's possible for 24 hours.

Jess 1:07:33. Ricky 1:07:10

Lap 4. Repeat the same, but I see that Ricky only gains 2 meters on each long climb this time. No longer 10 or 15 as she was previously, I see lots of upper body movement, pulling on handlebars, and pulling on handlebars stomping on pedals. I am now braking behind her on descents; maybe it's time to get in front more. I am pulling away a little, so there is no need to put in on these climbs; let Ricky do her thing, and the time will come soon enough.

Jess 1:08:27. Ricky 1:08:27

Lap 5, Again, we lap around as before. No talking now. Just a few words, passing people who we are lapping already. I take the front a lot more this time. Making an effort to be in front before the final descent into the berms and ride on the rivet a bit here, really having a crack at the 30+ bermed corners to see what comes of it. I arrive at transition, no Ricky, where is she? I have dropped her.

Jess 1:09:14. Ricky 1:09:37

Lap 6, That renewed energy you get when you make a move in a race, the defining moment. Oh wow, did I just have a massive boost of energy? Smiling on the inside, finding the flow, riding strong. I had to be careful not to bust myself here, feeling the adrenaline rush of a subtle well-planned attack taking place. I am enjoying the control.

The easiest and most fun lap I did all race.

Jess 1:10:03 Ricky 1:12:02

We are nearly 6 hours into the race now; this is where I feel good, and I know I can win, for sure, 100%, and it's the part in the race that I live for. The mental images come flooding into my mind, the ones that I had rehearsed over and over. I can't wait until nighttime. I love the night.

Rickie and I continued to battle this time alone, knowing innately that we had to ride everything as the other person would be doing this too. Precious seconds turning into minutes would be lost or perhaps gained if we could ride everything on every part of the trail.

Sections such as the long grind with loose dirt on the hurty half of the lap where I promised myself to ride this beyond midnight, my first walking lap was 1:00 am. After that, I rode it the next three laps, angry that I gave in to my mind doing deals with me. By sunrise, it was a given, walk ¾ up and get back on, the hoof marks from people walking had churned up the soil, and my right knee was starting to hurt. And then it was night.

Nine hours of night riding is a long time managing your vision and taking on the extra weight of lights and batteries. Night laps always take a little longer; it feels different from asking the body to go at the same intensity. Fatigue sets in, and you can no longer see where the end of a climb finishes. I settle into an accountable meditative state. Completing a lap, astounded that it went so quickly. Pedal strokes turn into laps, which turn into battery changes and then into losing count of how many laps I had even done, or how many more do I have to do?

There were no hiccups for us during the night laps. I deliberately pulled up for every pit stop overnight. Norm checking my batteries, giving me some hot pasta or risotto, getting recovery shake into me, some caffeine, big teaspoons of Nutella right off the spoon. There is no rush for me in this race. I have patience, perfect riding, no crashes, no mishaps, and I ride as much as I can for as long as possible. I listened to what Norm told me each lap, "Ricky is 30 mins down, daylight to 3rd." No idea who was 3rd, 4th or otherwise.

The trails where I made my move to win
Sportograf

As time passes, I ride my bike, but my thoughts consume my time and keep me fighting to the end. Am I drinking enough? What gear am I riding in? Could I go harder? Should I go easier? How long is it taking to get to this section from the transition? Can I ride this section smoother? Get off the brakes! Ride this section and reward yourself with being a world champion at the end. That horrible rocky climb again. You can ride it. Your mind that wants to walk. You will do so with your head down; it will take longer, and you feel disappointed when you walk it. Just ride it. How many laps have I done? How many laps have I got to do before it's the end? Who believes in me, who wished me well? Norm loves me; I am so lucky. I have good bikes, good lights, good support; I am blessed. Winning this race is fantastic. But it can't beat the reality that I am riding this 24hr world championship; here in Italy, I am alive, and life is just unbelievably amazing. Oh no – not this hill again. Ok, get out of the saddle then and smash it quick. Hills hurt – yes, but if you do them faster, they hurt for a shorter time.

At 5:00 am, I started doing the deals with myself and my crew. How many more laps will I do, how many more times will I do that nasty climb, how many? There is one more lap to do with lights on, and then I can take them off. It feels like a fresh change of clothes. Now my knee is hurting; it's a tight ITB for sure; I can feel the nerve twinging, almost giving me a dead leg from ankle to knee now, I can feel pain, but I also can't feel any power.

> Day time, Day 2. It's time to win, which is so much easier said than done at the time.
> The devil on my shoulder is now strong. She is messing with my process-driven mind. She is trying so hard to sabotage my best efforts, so we start the internal battle – to finish.

With daylight comes renewed energy and excitement that the race is coming to a close. I still find it hard to believe that I keep pedalling, and here I am. Nearly 20 hours later, still riding. I always say to myself, "A day will pass regardless of how you manage it; the sun sets and rises with no thought about us and our actions. How we use this day is up to us, so use it with no regrets, savour every moment and be present in the moment. Use this day well, for it is a blessing!"

At 5:00 am I was praying for daylight, I could see the hint of sunshine on the horizon, but it was still dark. I was trying to work out how many more laps I had to do to win. The devil sometimes visits more than once in a race, and this time my alter ego devil wasn't leaving my side. She was looking for any opportunity to get me from doing another lap. Her nagging comments were doing me in, and I found it harder and harder to search my mind and heart for the happy places that keep me going. I started to talk aloud to hear myself over her ranting. I wanted to do three more laps; then, I told Norm and Sarah that I would stop for breakfast and work out the plan from there.

I was no longer racing my opponents; I was racing myself.

When I got those laps done, I told Norm and Sarah that I did not want to stop for anything now. I may as well just keep riding. Let's see how I am travelling next lap. On the next, I knew I would have to do it all over again, so no whinging, no procrastinating, just do. These last two were done with a smile; I was happy now; I could see the light at the end now and knew that I would be a World champ so long as I kept riding at this pace and kept myself from having a crash or a mechanical.

As I was completing my 2nd last lap, that knee niggle came back, and this time no drugs were going to help the pain. So I just got on with it. The power in my right leg was gone, and it scared me a bit; right now, at the 11th hour could I lose this race based on a knee problem? I caught up to Sylvia from Germany, who was also on her last lap; I told her to stay in front as I could not climb all the pinches; she was in the same situation.

It occurred to me it was just pain. If I put more effort into my left pedal stroke whilst pulling on my left upper body on the handlebars in a slightly harder gear, I could get my right to just roll over into the next revolution with minimal pain but the same output speed. I knew that there were many one-legged cyclists out there that I have seen at races and events. Even with a prosthesis, their power output would be less on that side. I was having fun now with this new game, and suddenly, I knew I was coming in to win this race. It was just the impetus I needed to find my positive mindset again, challenging myself on every climb.

It's always a magical feeling to get to this point in a race. I always want to savour it but get it over with equally.

When I came into transition before going through the finish line, I stopped at our pit to get the Australian flag from Norm and rode on into the finish.

It was over, and I had won, and I could relax now.

I could enjoy my holiday in Italy.

I could sleep and start recovering.

I thought of all the great things I could do now that I was no longer on my bike.

Thanking Ricky Cotter for a brilliant race

Before I could do this, there were interviews with the media, the race organisers, photos to be had, hugs and kisses, and congrats to everyone. After all the excitement of finishing and winning, there is reality. Shuffled off to do a drug test, I talked like a sleep-deprived 24hr racer to the lady about to watch me pee. The first priority is to get out of my gear, shower, and take some anti-inflammatory drugs. My knees, especially my right, were fat and puffy with fluid. This was the sorest part of my entire body.

As the adrenaline wore off, my actions slowed right down, and I really could not think or do anything with any urgency. I think it took me half an hour to shower and get dressed. Norm found some food, I had a chair to sit on and a chair for my legs to rest on, I wrapped myself up in a jacket and a scarf, put my iPod into my ears and closed my eyes. Finally, it was time to receive the reward, accept my win, and share the five minutes of glory with everyone.

> The proof is now there for me to fully realise. I have what it takes to pull off another one of these crazy World Championships. All the years of consistent and persistent effort, many mistakes, a few embarrassing failures, all the while digging deep to understand my motivations for this sport had paid off.

My success still did not sit well with me. I didn't think it was that special, and, honestly, anyone could do what I did if they wanted to. Preferring to lie low under the radar and align more closely with the laid back weekend cycling enthusiast and not the elite mountain biker. I had put a lot of energy into the one-percenters. I was capitalising on what my competition was not doing and ensuring that I executed the small things well over the 24 hours. Doing this made the most significant gains. Of course, I needed to have the body and bike to handle the challenge, but I still believed that what was in my head was my greatest asset in this sport.

So what on earth do I do with this epiphany now?

Am I back in the arena to battle our more 24-hour races? Or was this just a fluke?

I didn't have too much time to think because a week later, as soon as we were back in Australia, the rest of 2012 needed me and my energy.

Thanks Norm, it's your win too!
Sarah O'Callaghan

Chapter 8 - Hard Work

I remember the few weeks of being newly married, paying bills, cleaning my house, budgeting and all the rest of those adult responsibilities. I wondered how real-life adults coped with the external pressures of daily existence. I hoped I would learn this craft over time and that it would get easier. Now that I look back, it was just a layering process. Over time as one thing became regular and routine, I could invest time and energy in something new. Before long, I was doing more than before without even thinking about it.

Well, I am sure my experience is not unique. As the year opened up, I was about to tackle more than I ever thought possible. And you reckon 24-hour racing sounds tough.

Our time in Italy was life-changing. We fell in love with the country, its culture and its way of life. Bringing a renewed passion for being our best, racing, and business. It was more of a holiday than a racing opportunity and exactly what we needed to appreciate our lives more back home. The next six months would prove our biggest yet; say yes now, work out how later. It's just how we got by. The offerings were plentiful to be involved in almost everything bikes, and we were overwhelmed with decision fatigue.

The only way forward was to wake up each day. To be open to opportunity and embrace it all.

The list of my daily mantras reminded me many times to do today what others won't, so you can do tomorrow what others can't. To keep going when things get tough and when you feel like giving up, don't. This is precisely the moment you must go on. By persevering, you will find yourself a part of a small minority of "high achievers" or "big dreamers" or "doers". The more you do this; success is a normal part of life. A reminder that something is always better than nothing, stop procrastinating and do what you set out to do. It is better done than perfect, and you can learn along the way. Damn, it was so obvious; I needed to stop thinking so much.

It was due time to get on with it. Time and energy had been spent seeking purpose out of all my efforts. Yet, all I needed was to do the work. The results would reveal themselves in good time. This required letting go of some control, focusing on processes and small gains over time, continually learning through mistakes and failures, accepting that there was no endpoint. Only to live out each day for what it was.

> I had won another World Championship, executed the plan with a calm, process-driven approach and backed myself all the way. I knew the code; I now had proof it was not a fluke. I could apply this to anything I chose. To rise above the rest, it was all about the 1%'ers.

2012, the heavens opened up now, and it was time to work hard, more challenging than I had in the years before any racing success. Over the months from June to December, we visited Cairns, Hobart and Adelaide for our MTBSkills Launches. The Corner Store Forrest opened in November as well. Amongst all this, I kept racing, training and maintaining forward momentum. Norm and I made the most of our time in Cairns, running skills courses with William

Bird, then off to Atherton for more; I also got to race the Atherton 8 hour mountain bike event. If we had a day free, it was spent working or racing bikes.

Atherton 8hr so much dirt!

The Corner Store Forrest
Peter Monagle

In September, Norm and I drove to NSW to compete in the Jetblack Sydney 12hr. A different experience for us, a new course, new people, and an enjoyable event, in which we had a great win. Arriving home, we were straight into preparing for The Corner Store opening and the Forrest Festival planning. I woke up in the morning, got dressed, and did what it took to get it done. No one else was going to get it done. Life was full-on yet simple. Keep plugging away and do it to the best of my ability, every single day. Many days it felt like we would never get there. These big picture goals, the dreams, kept me striving in racing and business. Let me tell you a little about The Corner Store Forrest.

Norm and I had an excellent relationship with Giant bikes, namely Darren Rutherford, and we purchased a fleet of hire bikes but didn't have a retail space, just our home. Our businesses were all very complimentary. Teaching and coaching mountain bikers. Creating and running cycling events in our local region. Racing and promoting cycling to anyone who would listen and dream up crazy camps around Victoria to help people enjoy a supported weekend away on their bikes and teach instructors how to coach as well. Now we would put these under the umbrella of a retail shopfront. We hired bikes, sold coffee and food, promoted the Otways and got all our other work done when there were no customers in our store. It took Norm a while to get me on board. I didn't have the brain space to conceptualise fitting this into our lives with everything else we were already doing. Norm was juggling work. Building websites and hosting them, rustling up business, working in Geelong as well, plus taking courses on the bike, helping me run camps and classes and getting Saskia, our daughter, fully involved in our new shop.

>Opening The Corner Store Forrest filled our days more than we could have imagined. Anyone in retail or hospitality knows, once you open the doors, your time is no longer yours.

We moved our offices into the shop. And began the process of adding another ball to the juggling act of our business structure. As the shop grew, we found we needed staff, then systems, management, and time. I kept racing but allowed my form to slip a little and made the most of every skerrick of spare time to train or ride, even if it was an hour or less. Every cog in my life relied upon consistency.

Small efforts often, nudging each piece of my puzzle forward. It was fun and exciting to live this way, and because of this, the opportunities kept flowing in. What do we say yes to? Should we say no? Is this good for us? Often Norm said yes far more times than I did, but we both did our fair share, biting off more than we could chew. 2012 ended strong with the Forrest Festival mountain biking event in its second year. The vast number of people in town who frequented our small shop was insane but exciting. The Forrest Festival was a 2-day stage race, with four races spread out over the weekend. I was racing and returning to the shop, serving customers for a few hours before racing again, repeating this all weekend. Not much different to a 24hr race.

When the weekend was over, Norm and I were elated. The smiles on people's faces, the sharing of our town and trails with these mountain bikers was what we envisaged. It was a fun, carefree social race that allowed people to enjoy themselves and immerse themselves in the village with their families and friends. Norm and I had nailed it; we were so proud of what we had created. This year we had the added element of The Corner Store, like hosting people in our house all weekend long. The vibe was high. In fact, I loved that we had the scope to create something out of a simple dream.

It was 2004/05 when we both became self-employed. It was both scary and full of promise.

Together we were rearing a teenage daughter, with Norm building and hosting websites. We built our cycling events portfolio. Hired staff, delivered mountain bike skills courses Australia-wide, trained instructors to teach. Facilitated mountain bike camps and women-specific events. Opening our first retail business, The Corner Store Forrest, and speaking at high schools to deliver the message of the 1% rule.

And things were only getting started. The following year would keep producing more gold, so we kept working. We knew the formula; we had to keep believing it was worthwhile doing and not come up for air.

> In 2012, I achieved so much and crammed in so much more than I ever thought or dreamt that I could. Winning another World 24hr Solo championship in Italy, building on my business MTBSkills, opening up the Corner Store Forrest, employing and training staff.

It was now 2013, I also turned 40. I could not fathom how quickly this came around. What would the next 40 years bring? Life suddenly felt like it was moving by far too fast, and I hadn't done enough. The wrinkles on my face, the grey hairs sneaking out on show, it was a good reality check to be grateful and get cracking—time to enjoy the rewards of all these efforts. Time to start using my races and events to visit places I would like to go. To enjoy experiences and the people I meet. This was the part I loved most, the chance just to enjoy what the world has to offer because you're at a specific place at a particular time and avail yourself to the world. This year I began social rides with the local Forrest Primary School children over the school holidays. Introducing them to the mountain bike trails safely and with loads of fun. My sense of purpose was strong when I saw these children have so much fun, experiencing first-hand what it is to have strong role models around you, people who show you the way, provide options, and pave the way to whatever you decide to do in life.

Norm and I were delightfully exhausted from running The Corner Store in Forrest, leaving my training sporadic. Working on so many projects left me depleted. I had begun investing in massage, acupuncture, Chinese medicine and Bowen therapy to ease my stress and anxiety. Not eating properly, not sleeping well, feeling unsettled and anxious. Deep down, I knew what everyone expected of me, and it was starting to wear down my confidence in many of my races. So I kept searching for more significant reasons to turn up, be a role model for others, do my best, and enjoy the experience regardless of the result. Though it sucks to not be in your best form, I would always be pleased with myself for not quitting but inside devastated at how much it hurt to be off the pace.

> Having bad days bad races bad months bad years, it's all about that inner search on what is important to you, and I know that I loved racing my bike. When it stops being fun, I won't race. This is what I would tell myself to take the pressure off.

In 2013, I travelled to France, New Zealand and nearly every state in Australia. Racing as well as delivering mountain bike skills courses and keynote speaking. However, it was the first time I competed in a 24 hour road race, the Delirium 24hr in Western Australia. I had talked about it, planned for it, spent loads of money getting here. But what next? Twenty-four hours on the road bike, what's going to happen? We had no script, so we just let this one unfold. Having done many 24-hour mountain bike races, I was uncertain what concepts would be transferable, if any, other than nutrition, mindset and not sleeping. But 24 hours on a road bike? Am

I allowed to ride in bunches? How would we feed? Just what is my race plan? Would I be cold? How soon would I get tired, bored, unmotivated, zoning out?

Norm and I discussed everything we could think of, but I kept coming to the same conclusion. We knew I could race 24hrs; we knew I could stay awake 24hrs, we knew I was physically and mentally capable, so let's stop thinking and just do. Those who travel for racing know that there is little return on investment if you look at dollar for dollar. The return is hard to measure, and it's up to you to convert experience into something that money cannot buy. Yet, we are here. Invested. To set out to achieve something that we know little about. I also have a chance of winning.

This is my simple and methodical way of looking at too big things to fathom in one chunk. Devise a plan, a recipe, so to speak, tick the boxes, allow for ad-lib, have some fallback plans and let Norm know emotionally how I am doing.

Race day finally arrives. I took my time, two small breakfasts, preparing clothes, going through the process. It was casual, friendly and just like a mountain bike 24. We had plenty of people come and say hi; good luck. I had no idea how fast the race would start or what teams would do, but I understood it was my sole focus to find team riders that would keep my average speed up for the longest time possible. As I lapped around in the 2nd main bunch with an average speed of 37kmph, it soon became apparent I should have started with my back pockets full of food and extra water. Making the most of the daylight hours, the steady pace of each lap for as long as possible. When it finally came time to grab a bottle and food, I stuffed up, no musette either and going way too fast. Eventually, this cost me losing a bunch when I finally got it right. I was by myself for a very long time lapping around solo, trying to find a bunch that was my pace. Most were too slow or too fast; the initial bunch was probably the only bunch worth staying in. Most people in the solo category suffered this situation a few times throughout the night.

It was imperative to work with others, get them to sit up for you as you received a feed and repay the favour.

Eventually, all my hard work started to show through a knee niggle. Something I wondered about before the race, as it gave me grief at the Wembo 24hr champs in Italy last year. As the night arrived, I started to falter, getting out of the saddle. Leaving me seated for a heck of a long time, dealing with the niggle, trying my hardest to avoid acknowledging it, yet being as perfect as I could with my pedal stroke to extend my pain threshold. I had no idea there was a race between Joel Nicholson, the No.1 male solo and myself. My focus was on going as fast as possible for as long as possible and seeing what transpired. How I can race another 12hrs with this knee pain with any power or ability to put in?

> The ebb and flow of pain began. Voltaren tablets, Voltaren gel, tiger balm, mental strength, pedalling technique, bike stretching, off-bike resting for only 1 minute at a time, and sleep monsters from around 1 am – 5 am.

The following seven or so hours of darkness, I repeated to myself, "it's only pain, its only pain, its only pain"...for hours on end. Followed by a stretch, a bit of a tear, a big out a loud cry of pain, and then I would come good for an hour. I did have pain free laps when I could focus on my job of riding my bike. Yes, I told myself, welcome the pain; at least it's keeping you awake. The thought of giving up never occurred. It was just a constant challenge for Norm, how to get me going round and round until I reached 700km and to make sure I did so by the 24th hour of the race. We had great helpers from teams, solos that had more power than me, riders who

I was previously passing like they were standing still were helping me! Then there were chit chats about everything from childbirth to teenage daughters.

The most challenging thing was following a wheel at night, sitting behind a rider almost mesmerised by the speed of the road. Corners came up way too quick; bitumen passed underneath in the darkness giving a weird feeling of spatial awareness. Now and again, I relished a solo lap to snap myself out of the trance I was in. Hot chocolate in my bidon was like true heaven, and I asked for it a few times. We survived the night with zip lock bags with pumpkin risotto heated up in it, chewing a corner off and squeezing it in my mouth. Finally, at 6 am, I could see! No more sleep monsters, yet still 5hrs to go. I tried to do sums, but it's just impossible to get your brain to work, and I had to stop and talk it out with Norm. He told me that I had to keep lapping, averaging 27kmph, which was ok; it just hurt like crazy. I had some team riders helping me out, who kept me going by constantly talking to me. No matter what pain I was in, they didn't allow me to focus on it or try and solve it; they just kept me pedalling. The result 1st female. The longest distance travelled in the 3rd year of this event by a female. 2nd SOLO rider overall, and breaking the male record covered as well. 703km – 190 laps of 3.7km

What did I get from this race? Set the goal. Then, engage in the process. Follow the steps with planning and perseverance. Continue to proceed forth, no matter what obstacles pop up. Be open to the world and avail yourself of the opportunities. Strive to see the answers, not the problems. Finish what you set out to do; better done than perfect. Such succinct and straightforward concepts, and without fail, I get to meet amazing people and visit magical places along the way. I have nothing to fear ever.

On our way back to Perth to return home, we dropped off at Busselton, a beautiful north-facing town on the coastline of Western Australia. Typical sapphire blue water and a long jetty that runs 1.8km out into Geographe Bay. We spent about an hour here, enjoying the morning sun and some lunch. Our time was always rushed when we travelled. It was remarkable to be rewarded with even a small gift like this, using all my senses to inhale the beauty before going headlong into the next big gig.

> Right about now, the world was full of opportunities.
> It was hard to say no.

After the 24hr race, I was only home for a few days and then off to do a seven-day charity event, from Mansfield in Victoria to Port Macquarie in NSW. It was called K.I.D.S Ride, raising funds for the foundation's injury and trauma prevention programs and recovery. The event was supported by Giant Bicycles Australia, which is how I was involved. The next day was one of our events, the Forrest 6 hour, a mountain bike race. It was always such a relief to have a break in the schedule after having so much on. I am grateful for a quick vacation before my short coaching trip to Rotorua in New Zealand at the end of May. A fun interlude to enjoy riding bikes, teaching a group of girls and being away from home. Still working but also a lot of play.

Upon returning home, all systems go again to get my work done before heading off to France. I was going on holiday, with Top Bike tours to ride in France for ten days. A portion of June was spent in the French summer, which doubled as base training for me—leaving Norm at home holding the fort for the shop, skills courses, administration, parenting, and his I.T business. These were crazy times. Each week new opportunities presented themselves, and it was our mantra to say yes now and work out how later. The next trip away was to Darwin to teach more mountain bike skills for a solid three day weekend. Three sessions a day, for three days. Wake up early, morning session, midday and an afternoon class. Thank goodness it was winter up here; it was still warm for a Victorian. I went to Perth as a guest instructor for Rock and Roll mountain biking a few weeks later. All the while, Norm was working on expanding MTB-Skills into other states with our qualified instructors. Australia was very much in the early stages of skills coaching and development, even at a club level. It seemed we were riding the wave, and it was up to us where and when we wanted to get off.

I never had to search for events to do; they came to me.

When asked by the organisers to come and do the Mongolia Bike Challenge, a 6 stage mountain bike race, I was unsure if I could handle it with all the travel I had done already this year. Plus, it would only be a few weeks to recover before racing the WEMBO 24hr Solo Championships. As the reigning champion, I wanted to win again and have three titles to my name. This was always the underlying reason for any of my racing in 2013 to prepare myself for this. So making the right decision to race in Mongolia was a challenge. To take up the offer, all I had to do was pay for flights to Mongolia, and the rest would be covered. This opportunity came in July, with the event being in late August. The plan was to go alone, but Norm was keen to go too, so wrangled his own Media gig, and so it was, we were going. Mongolia, I would never have dreamed of travelling to this country.

Sight seeing on bike before racing - Ulaanbaatar

Turning up as part of a large organised race is similar to signing up to a tour group, except you have to race your bike, of course. For that reason, it was comforting to know that navigating this country would mostly be taken care of. I had no idea what I was in for. I didn't do much research other than look at what gear I needed, the weather for this time of year and what sort of terrain we might be riding.

Upon arrival, I instantly was confused by everything.

> Ulaanbaatar was so different to anything I had ever seen or visited.

Even at night, when we arrived, it was visible that roads were not all equal; what I first thought to be roadworks was just a regular road. The traffic was passing any which way, horns beeping, and everyone was perfectly organised despite what felt like mayhem to me. When we got to the hotel, which was quite Westernised, it had hot water pipes coming in from the steaming hot water pipes for the city, not its own hot water systems.

In the morning, when light revealed more, the views from our hotel window showed block concrete everywhere with a complete disregard for completing any works on landscape, buildings or roads. No drainage, as roads were covered in water from a couple of days of rain.

A short ride out of town Ulaanbaatar

I dug deep to crack some sort of code, to understand where I was. No matter where I looked, the mixed palette of trends was there. There was a distinct Russian vibe, with old USSR structure and regimented design, a mild Asian undertone with Western influence, all presented in a third-world backdrop. So I just accepted it. We had a whole day to prepare bikes and get our gear together before heading off to our race start location the next day. Norm and I needed a walk, and a few extras before we would be off in the wilderness, so we got a ground-level view and feel for the place.

Footpaths existed, but they randomly ended or fell away into the depths of the earth without prior notice. There was so much new construction mixed in with the old, with enormous piles of rubble everywhere.

Chinggis Khaan Statue Mongolia

I was looking forward to racing, nervous about my current form and of the terrain. Most days, we were racing at 1500mts abs amongst the Mongolian steppe, with the mountain tops peaked at 2000mts above sea level. The racing was hard, but I felt my legs and mindset improve, getting faster and stronger as each day went by. Still, I finished 4th overall in the women and put in a solid training block in my lead up to my World Championship title defence in October. Erin Green from New Zealand came 3rd, and I knew she would be at the World 24hr championships. Now I knew what form she would be bringing. Like many others on tour, I got sick on the final night, with all the symptoms. We were flying back home the next day; this was harder than racing feeling the way I did. Safely back in Melbourne, Norm helped me sort my bikes out as I stayed in a hotel and flew out to Townsville the next day. We had left my extra gear in the car and swapped a few things out.

Racing in Mongolia
Erik Peterson

As soon as I settled into my room, it was like my body could let go. I was losing energy, had the runs constantly, and, what's worse, had the period from hell as well. I hoped for a miracle that I would wake up renewed in the morning. I woke up worse, though at least I had been in a bed, resting. Back in these times, I was so very used to suffering; it was all just part of the process. Checking in with myself, can you keep going? Yes. Well, let's get going then. I was trying to eat, trying to drink, and focusing on mind control. But it was all coming out the other end. I knew I had to keep forcing nutrition into me, hoping my body could glean some of it for energy and wellbeing. This illness started Sunday night; it was now Wednesday when I finally arrived at the warm winter sunshine of Townsville and the hospitality of the Tilley family. Yet now I was shivering; I was cold. I needed to sleep for a bit, so I forced myself to put my bikes together, then had a nap. Having done many 24hr races that hurt like hell and have left me depleted, I knew I would be able to tell if I was sick or just fatigued if I rode my bike. The next day, I went for a ride with Brett Tilley and a few others on fun, easy trails. I was at the back dragging the chain. I was depleted, and things were not going to get better on their own. After this ride, I was still shivering, so I went and had a hot shower, made a doctor's appointment, and rode into town.

Catching up the Tilley's thank you Haydn for everything

The doctor ran some tests. He gave me an antibiotic that he suspected would help right now, avoiding ending up in hospital with a drip to rehydrate me. I felt hope now, went to the chemist for the prescription and got myself a bag of jelly beans for instant energy. It was now Thursday; I had been ill for four and a half days and had lost five kilos. I went back to my homestay, at the Tilley's, sleeping for two hours and instantly, that desire to go to the toilet was gone. I woke up hungry. Oh my goodness, I was back in business!

> My test results came back, and I had salmonella poisoning.

The respite in Townsville was a blessing. Time invested in connecting with the good people of Townsville, enjoying the sunshine and healing from illness and racing. I returned home ready to do the final hard work for my 2013 goal race, the WEMBO 24hr World Solo Championships. Finally, I was starting to feel like I had nailed my build into race fitness and, as a side bonus, improved my power to weight by losing 5 kilos. Upon my return, it was a short two and a half weeks before Norm and I headed off to Canberra for the 24hr World Championships. There were a few more key training rides to nail, massage appointments, business administration and staff, ramping up the promotion and planning for the Forrest Festival in December, and not to mention getting the race bikes up and ready for the big race. I was taking on a brand new bike, the Liv Lust 27.5. Lots of work was needed to ensure the bike was dialled in for racing, and I had two of them to work on.

Of course, in this mix, I was also doing my best to improve my health, get loads of sleep, healthy eating, and be strict about any junk food. I was motivated to keep these five kilos off, knowing it was an unexpected bonus increase in my power if I could do everything right in the lead-up.

Despite my growing confidence that everything was going to be just fine, that I was going to peak to be at my best on race day, there was that nagging thought disrupting my peace. What if this trip to Mongolia was the undoing of winning my third world championship? Depleting myself in every way possible was upon reflection, perhaps not the wisest of choices; only time would tell, thank you David Heatley(my coach at the time) for supporting me in these crazy decisions. We arrived in Canberra many days early. Norm worked remotely, as did I, but I would always head out and get some riding in, slow, steady miles just to get the mind and body having fun.

The weather was perfect Spring temperature with the ride along the bike paths to get to Mt Stromlo. I used the half-hour commute from the city to the course to imagine myself winning. The glow of joy permeated my entire being as I rode my favourite trails.

A few months ago, I was not even thinking about it, just ticking my process boxes to get to where I was today. Maybe being sick and being forced to recuperate in Townsville was a blessing after all, and everything was falling into place just as it should be.

> I felt so good; my mood was high, my motivation even greater.
> I wanted to win and knew that I could; I had to keep reminding myself of this.

There is no doubt that this race was won in my head. Focusing on building self-belief, creating visual imagery of the race. The start, the laps, the feelings, the challenges from other competitors, eating, drinking and even the conversations with Norm through the transition. I even focused on what songs I would allow to enter my head, what words, phrases, affirmations I would use. It was all well-rehearsed in every single training session. But this would be my fourth world championship event, attempting to win for the third time, and I was wiser, intending to approach it with some new tactics. Many of my races were simply executed by riding as hard and fast as possible to break my competitors. This allowed me to settle into a maintainable tempo for the next 18 hours or so of the race. It was 2013 now, I was getting a little older, and my rivals were wiser, so Norm and I hatched a new plan.

Start fast, but settle in behind the girls matching my pace, sit on their wheels and watch their moves. Watch how they rode, where their strengths were, where they ate or drank, where errors were made or when they pulled away from me—even watching how their support crew aided them as they rode through the transition. This perspective was different for me, for when you ride off the front, you miss out on this information. I was excited and felt it was a great plan, looking forward to executing it. My competition would be expecting me to go off hard, giving them a little boost of false hope that they were in better form than me. I knew that I could reel them in, watching them self implode as they would work hard to get a gap on early.

These thoughts flowed freely as I meditated on them constantly while riding my bike over the next few days. I sensed the same warmth on my back as I did back in 2010 when I won my first world championship. Feelings of peace, contentment, knowing I had done everything possible to be the best on race day.

This feeling gave me the confidence to believe I was still worthy of being a champion.

Race Day

October 2012, Mt Stromlo, ACT.
And now, it's time to hurt; it is race day. Don't fight it; invite it.
In some way, it was good to get called up last in the Elite field and take my spot where it suited. I got to sit in behind a bunch in the middle; I didn't want to be boxed in on the inside and made a conscious decision to search for gaps and get away from wheels that would hinder me.

The start was a quick prologue around the crit track, exiting up a fire road that took us to Cockatoo switchbacks entrance. I felt good, yet had no idea that I would feel so good for the race start. I passed people, other elite girls and I saw that I was in a good position. I aimed to get past the Ukrainian rider. Very quickly, it was me, Erin Greene and Kim Hurst in a group of three for the next few laps.

The first thing I noticed whilst I sat at the back of the group was the lack of drinking during the lap from them. I took a sip every fire trail crossing, but I couldn't see them doing it, also noticing a lot of energy being expended on the climbs. Even on the downhills, fast lines were smashed hard, with bikes and bodies battered very early in the race. Whilst I felt this would serve well in an XCO race or even a 100km marathon, perhaps not so well in a 24hr. I focused on my plan from the first lap and let my competition smash hard. Even on transitions, the anxiety to receive drinks and food was high. Yet, Norm and I were relaxed and methodical. I used the mild uphill into a headwind from the timing point to finish my bottle; as soon as I turned to go to our tent, it was slight downhill into a tailwind. The girls were always back on the trail before me, but I would soon catch them with food and drink taken in whilst on an easy surface.

WEMBO 24hr Champs Canberra

Around my 3rd or 4th lap, Eliza Kwan and Liz Smith caught our bunch. Eliza mentioned that it was a nice pace that we were doing, and I asked if they wanted to pass. They both declined. And so we kept moving up Mt Stromlo and descended altogether in a bunch of 5. The next transition was hectic. Liz and Eliza smashing their way through timing to get to their support first, I continued to be methodical and not get caught up in their race. Kim and Erin were just ahead of me, and we let the other two go. It was early days, and their pace was high.

The heat was in the day now, no shade on many parts of the trail. This was a crucial time to prepare for the night. In the lead-up, Norm and I had discussed that if the race plan was not clear by midnight, he could start telling me what to do. Now was the time to eat and drink and settle.

My experience allowed me not to worry, run my plan, and stick to it.

Erin and Kim were enjoying our lap, so I suggested that we work together in keeping our pace honest. Swapping the lead to up the average speed, stick together and use each other for good energy to be allies until the natural selection occurs. Not much talk, we continued along until the next lap. Sometime soon, Kim dropped off. Now it was just Erin and I chasing the other two girls upfront. I sat behind Erin to watch her race, focusing on my strengths and mentally noting how I faired up against her. It felt like I was cornering better on the uphill switchbacks on this lap, so I kept this in my memory bank. Then the downhill sections, whilst Erin was fast and fearless, I chose my lines and kept them smooth and flowing, maintaining a stress-free environment. There was an equation going on here in my head. I would use less energy and wear and tear on my bike and body, giving me the ability to dig deep when it hit midnight, the final 12hrs of the race. We came through transition together, and I was out front this time. I started to sense that out of each corner up Cockatoo Switchbacks; I was exiting 3-5 meters in front of Erin. So I didn't go any faster on the next couple of switchbacks; instead, I rode with total concentration and purpose, finding myself about 20 meters up on Erin.

Was this my breakaway chance? I gave it a shot. Corner, pedal hard out of it and repeat. By the time I reached Bluegums and then Bobbypin, I couldn't see Erin anymore. I was away, now I was racing in third, and it was still daylight. Time to swap bikes on the next lap so Norm could put a full complement of lights on my bike. Eat, drink, be methodical. Ride the smooth lines, drink on the fire road connecting trails. Be accountable, believe and follow-through, think positive thoughts, affirm the end result.

The night comes my time to shine
Sportograf

As the night fell, I felt myself gain energy. The flow built, and I was enjoying the ride. I had a natural rhythm going, and I began executing my plan to become a World champ for the 3rd time. With 18 hours to go, Eliza and Liz were battling it out. Eliza had pulled away for 1st place. It was 10 pm; Norm said I was now gaining on them both and that I would soon catch Liz, shortly after, Eliza. It was midnight that on the same lap I passed Liz, I also caught Eliza.

> The winning move occurred in transition. One moment I was 5 minutes down, riding through timing, and I was in 2nd place behind Eliza, exit from my support crew, and I was in 1st. Unbeknown to the rest of the world and those reporting the race, I was 8 minutes up just by exiting transition. A long way up the hill climb, before either of them, were even on the bike pedalling again.
> Now it was time to do what I came here to do, win and own the night.

During the night and early hours of the morning, I'd lose my appetite and my desire to drink. I was astounded that time had gone so quickly yet a little fearful of that moment that would be yet to come when I wished it was all over. This happens typically from around 3 am – 5 am. However, this year, at this race, I never got to feel this way at all. The laps just kept going, and so did I. Before I knew it, the sun was rising, and I was still in 1st place. At this point, it's certainly a little scary to imagine that there is another 6 hrs to go, six laps, six more climbs and six more bottles to drink. Rather than think, I just did. I arrived at transition, took my bottle, listened to Norm's instructions and rode another lap.

With 3 hours to go, the alarm bells went off. I had no idea it was coming. Absolutely no idea. The lap before Norm was cool and calm, and we were rolling along nicely. I came through this time, and there was an urgent request from Norm to put in a sub 1hr lap. Kim Hurst was killing it, that she had just done a 60 min lap and had gained 10 minutes.

> "Jess, Kim is stomping, you are going to have to do a sub 1hr lap if you want to win."
> His words were exact, factual with a sense of urgency. Norm knew not to get too emotional but I could feel his need to convey this message and I wanted to tell him where to stick his message, but chose to heed it as a real warning. I responded with a simple, "Ok, I will do my best."

What? After all this? Do I have to fight to win now? After all this time, it comes down to the final 3hrs? Really? I moved out of transition, went from flight to fight with this thought, "3hrs of hard work left. Ride in the big chainring and don't get out of it. Call for track early and win this race and show them who is worthy of being a world champion. It's only 3hrs, and that's about 50km; you can go at a hard race pace for 3hrs. Let's do this and thank you, Kim Hurst, for the pressure!" During the next three laps, I stayed in the big chainring. If it got too hard, I got out of the saddle and pedalled hard, keeping my descents smooth and off the brakes as much as possible, saving every second and gaining every meter, looking ahead and calling for track early, and I got it every time. It was like clockwork.

I came in after the call to action from Norm in a 59:13 lap. Sub 1hr! Norm was very, very excited. So excited, I didn't hear him give me any feedback. Did I need to do this again? Did I make an impact? How was the gap now? I assumed all was ok; he would have told me if it weren't. But what if he got it wrong? What if she had more in her? And so I pushed hard again and did another sub 1hr lap. Partway into the next lap, I came across a fellow rider, Kevin, who did me a big favour, rode ahead and told Norm I wanted coke, water and ice in my last bottle. My final lap was still done with some urgency, but I was more relaxed about passing on the track and came in with 2 minutes to spare before the 24hr mark.

I rode in with Norm, waiting outside of timing, telling me I could roll through and win. I was prepared to go out again if I needed to but being told that I had won now, well, I was pretty happy with that news. As I rode through timing and won the World Solo 24hr Championship for the 3rd time, I couldn't wait to give Norm a big hug.

This was my best race ever. We were a magnificent team. So much went on behind our win that I did not know about. Sam and Andrew helped Norm out, and my Dad gave some time splits. And of course, Norm and his fantastic ability to watch the race and know all the correct information at the right time. I won again, with integrity and won because I wanted it. It was my best win ever and was my third World 24hr Mountain bike Championship. I was 40 years old.

For the first time in my elite mountain biking career, I finally felt like I belonged. Though the field was smaller this year, the quality was top class, with many women fighting to take the top spot. Yet it was me, little old me, who wanted it most.

I won!

When you have worked so hard for so long and fought so many negative beliefs into oblivion, to conquer the world's best on one particular day feels like nothing else. I now knew that I had everything it took to be a world champion, there was a secret code, and I had access to it. But now that I had three titles, I wasn't keen to keep chasing more. So I parked the thought, celebrated our win, and got on with my To-Do list. As soon as the Forrest Festival was over in December 2013, Norm and I got The Corner Store at Mt Buller ready for summer 2013/14. That holiday period was intense. Norm spent most of it away at Mt. Buller, and I spent my time in Forrest; we made a good go at it, breathing a sigh of relief as the holiday season ended. The entire year, going from one thing to the next to the next. I created "Life Goals" to help keep me grounded and on track.

1. Remove all fear, instead believe it is possible.
2. Give sincere thanks to those who enter my life.
3. Set Goals, Plan, Execute, Reflect, Reward – often.
4. Love my family more often.
5. Continue to teach, provide hope, continue to add value to the world.

I needed to enjoy the experience, not just the results. This was how I started racing. Without continually realigning myself with the joy of riding my bike, I would have packed it in; racing was so far removed from who I really was. How on earth did I become a world champion three times? My rise in the sport and my professional life was reaching a saturation point. If it weren't for daily mantra's, sticking to my 1% rule, and just grinding it out, perhaps I would have just left it there. But it was time to evolve and offer more space to other opportunities. My energy was spent daily, working out what to say no to, or maybe next time, then getting on with what Norm and I had said yes to.

How much longer could we keep going like this? I was grateful, but I was also tired.

Chapter 9 - The Dark Side of Success

Gratitude - *no matter how challenging things got, there was much to be thankful for.* When days would melt into each other with a never-ending workload, there was always time to pause, and I took it. A simple bike ride to clear the head. A walk with the dogs. Any minor disruption to the routine slowed down the mind and allowed time to experience the simple gifts in my life. Each day I was grateful for my sleep; as I laid my head on the pillow, slumber would come easy, and a warm feeling of 'everything is going to be ok' would envelop me, and the promise of a brand new day was waiting for me on the other side.

Grit - Each new day required constant reframing of words, thoughts and goals. Requiring perseverance with daily reminders of why we were even doing what we were. It was simple for me; the essence of my efforts was to add value to the world in the ways that best suited my skills and abilities and aligned with our goals. It was exhausting to do this, daily and often. Even the grittiest of them all needs a break to restore the passion. Thankfully I found racing the perfect time out a distraction but also complementary to the process.

This too shall pass, the Yin and Yang - moments of glory, matched with failure or a poorly executed decision. Pushing through adversity and hard times to do what seemed impossible. The light and the dark of life, not always experienced in equal measure. Rest assured, this wouldn't last forever, everything comes and goes, and you always get another chance, so long as you keep believing in yourself.

Staying true to self - simply doing something positive, no matter how small today, to ensure it added towards my tomorrow, was all I could do—chipping away in achievable chunks. Little 1%'ers. Using simple strategies to manage huge tasks, making them less impossible and doable. Every single day. Even a rest day, of nothing, was a day that added towards tomorrow, as it was an opportunity to regenerate energy. All I had to do was keep believing anything was possible; it's ok to fail, so long as I learn and grow and it will be uncomfortable. Not all actions were perfect, and I wasn't always the best custodian of humanity, so forgiveness of self and trying again tomorrow was the only way forward. Just press reset now and try again now.

So long as I was aligned, mostly having fun, hard work was easy, staying aligned was the most challenging component of my day to day life.

By 2014, Norm and I were overflowing, blessed with an endless supply of work and opportunities.

> The saying goes, with great success comes great responsibility.

It was no longer just about keeping up appearances; we had two cafes, with staff, stock, bills and customers to keep happy. MTB-Skills was booming with instructors in numerous states, including our hub in Victoria, with camps, courses, planning permits, insurance, advertising, administration and staff training to manage. Norm and I were heading off many times a year to various parts of the country to run skill classes in Alice Springs, Darwin and Townsville.

Skills courses at Alice Springs Stunning!

Then we had two successful cycling events, the Forrest 6 hour and Forrest Festival. Offers to attend races far and wide were woven in to incorporate some sort of work-related exercise often to make it worth our while. Norm was building websites, hosting and managing his staff, 24/7 - busy. I had increased my coaching services as well. Then there was so much more we were involved in, the Forrest MTB club, Keynote speaking, talking at schools, junior development with other clubs, amongst other advocacy work. What had begun as a tiny spark of excitement to race my bike had turned into this. I never dreamt that I would be part of a movement, a small cog in the Australian mountain biking community, helping bolster experiences on so many levels. But there was only one me and only one Norm, and we were stretched. We were both beginning to feel overwhelmed by the success and expectations, yet found it hard to say no. We were in deep, staff and bills to pay, events to run, shops to open, sponsors to nurture, cogs to keep turning, no matter how we felt on the day.

> We had to keep reminding ourselves that this was what we had dreamt of. So each day, we would wake up and get going again.

Norm had been on antidepressants for a couple of years now, and for the longest time, I had felt the burden of keeping him happy. When I say 'happy', I mean shielding him from confrontation. Whatever it took, I was there to keep him on the straight and narrow path to some sort of daily fulfilment and not let him self-destruct and derail the plan. It was a daily ritual for me to wake him up as the drugs gave him a good 10-12 hours of sleep a night. Making sure he had a coffee and offering him reasons why life was good. *My mantra was, 'A happy Norm is a good Norm'.*

There was also the weight of expectation. To not let people down. Perhaps it was all self-imposed, but the pressure was there, and it was starting to build. Each day was an opportunity to chip away at the workload ahead, daily investment of 1%'ers, achieving something, anything to move forward.

In 2014, my racing slowed down, sticking to local road events, club racing, spattered with a few interstate trips, interwoven with work opportunities. We had to work and needed to earn money. There was no plan B. It's just what we had to do. By now, I knew things were getting out of hand, but we just kept saying yes, dreaming of a day when we would break through and find that happy place between work, play and making enough money to enjoy life a little more. I was not averse to grinding out long days, but we were starting to lose our way and align with what others wanted from us instead of narrowing our focus to enjoy and nurture what we had already built and doing well.

> It sure was an exciting space to be in, wanted, needed, overextended, overworked, yet so sought after, we just couldn't say no. What if we missed out, and that was it, our opportunity to the next best thing, gone?

A growing business, inspirational ideas, and making good things happen is terrific, and we kept reminding ourselves how blessed we were. And so we pushed on, even if we were both reaching breaking point. My days looked like this; wake up and have a strong coffee hoping that magic would happen. Sit down on the computer and start on all the administrative work for all our business, answer emails, work on projects, delegate tasks to staff, pay bills, pay staff, update websites, put on courses, market our events. Have another coffee in the hope to stay motivated and make more magic happen. Have a glass of water to clear the fog from my head. Wake Norm up as he is in a deep sleep from antidepressants; it's around 9 am by now. Drop into the Forrest shop, check in on staff, grab another coffee. Banking, shopping, post in Colac. Drop back into the shop, plan for tomorrow's trading, place orders. Take dogs for a walk. Go for an afternoon bike ride.

Meditation rides bliss

These rides were my meditation. I would head out, knowing my brain was fried with thoughts crashing around in my head, like an out of control pinball machine. My only goal was to ride, and then the next goal was to quieten my mind, let the thoughts in, let the thoughts out, no processing, no bright ideas, no answers to the meaning of life, just in and out. Sometimes it was 10 minutes, but often it took at least one hour when I would find myself in the flow zone, seeking a series of good lines in the trail, smelling the wildflowers, listening to the birds, hearing the noise of my tyres on the gritty earth.

Often I would just stop right there, to breathe in every tiny detail of who I was right there in that same space, and I would cry, with joy and with a lot of pain, and I would let this go, releasing it to the world. Then suddenly, I would realise I am here, in the quiet zone, and now I can go home and live another day. Without this ability to manage my stress, I am not sure I would have coped so well for so long.

Ten minutes later, I would ride home, with a smile on my face, warmth in my heart and new hope, only to be greeted by Norm, who was overworked and overwhelmed. He was in pain, and he would make a note to project that onto me and others around him, like a wall that said, leave me alone. I never gave up on him; I knew he was a good person underneath; I just wished he would take off his armour and share his pain with me.

Despite the pressure and the slow unravelling of our mental health, we stayed strong and focused together. Running events was so much fun. Managing the shops and all that came with it was rewarding. Devising new skills courses and meeting new people brought so much joy. Honestly, every aspect of the hard work that went with these opportunities was such a gift. We never begrudged it or the people; we were simply getting tired, and the successes spread our energies thin.

The Corner Stores and Mt Buller and Forrest ran hot and busy until Easter of 2014, so I enjoyed racing less and went back to riding for the love of it. My race schedule was still happening, but it had to fit in with what we were doing at the time. Our Victorian winter was always quieter due to the rain and cold. Fewer people wanted to ride bikes, which made for some opportunities to travel north.

Redback MTB Race Alice Springs

In May, the offer came for Norm and me to travel to Alice Springs for The Red Back MTB Stage race and managed to link this in with the planned trip to Townsville to run skills courses for a week. The changeover was super tight. Play, teach and race for a week, then on the final day of racing, our flight to Townsville was leaving Alice Springs at 1:00 pm, which was a massive motivation for me to ride fast and hard. We made the flight and then onto the warmth of Townsville, staying with Brett and Sue Tilley. A solid week of holding skills courses on the mountain bike before flying home. This is how we rolled, race, work, play and go home to get working again. Travel was funded by working, so these fantastic experiences never cost anything, only time and energy. My goodness, we met some beautiful people who opened their homes to us, friends from far away that gave us more than we could give back.

Not long after we returned home, more crazy concepts appeared in my inbox from Chris at Ride Whitsundays. Why not go to Airlie Beach and teach for a few days, get away from the Victorian winter and someplace new. I knew Norm would recoil from such an offer and had to work in a creative way to enjoy the whole experience. But firstly, how could I make this work, so I could also race the Paluma Push back in Townsville. The two locations are close, around 300km, but not conducive to accessible air travel. That's it, let's drive!

> Normie boy loves a road trip, and I knew I could get this concept over the line with the promise of a drive up and back. It worked; he got excited, and so we planned the next working, racing holiday.

When July came around, we were off in the car, taking three days to get to Airlie Beach. So much alone time, space to think, talk and dream. We talked about how far we had come, how much our lives had changed, what we had to look forward to and how blessed we were doing it together. Moments like these were treasured. A whirlwind five days at Airlie Beach presented more opportunities to enjoy meeting new people and riding new places. Being up north in the sun during the Victorian winter was very welcomed—time to enjoy more of this and more good people, skills courses and social times in Townsville. Norm drove home all by himself at the end of the week, and I stayed on to race the Paluma Push before flying home.

To be honest, living like this was a lot of hard work. Very grateful to have the assistance of our friend and team member, Kylie, who worked for us across many areas of our business to assist. This kind of investment was so rewarding, but the comedown was always huge. I always tried to give myself a couple of days of freedom when I got home to allow the brain and body to rest. Using this time wisely, I would plan the next six months, revise where to put my energy, and focus on racing and work. I came home so energised to get back into racing and improve the fitness I had let go of.

It was time for me to get fit and strong again. I found it a challenge to get the same motivation I had back in 2010, but I always drew upon my 1% rule to keep moving forward 1% at a time, to get started, and the interest will compound.

It was at a mountain bike race at the You Yangs, actually on the car trip afterwards, onto a road race at Meredith, that a shift in our lives started to occur. It was a massive jolt, threatening parts of our livelihood, and we would struggle for a while to come.

Norm had spent a few days driving back from Townsville to Forrest by himself after our trip away. What had struck him hard was when he would stop to refuel, he would hear the cattle or sheep or pigs in the livestock trucks, stomping hooves, making uncomfortable noises; after a few days of this, it's like a light was being turned on in his head, a view he had never even considered before. The real turning point was sitting behind a truck and seeing a sheep look ing out over the top tier, open section, with fear in its eyes, perhaps searching for an escape route.

Norm must have stewed over these thoughts and visions for days, as he never discussed any of this with me. He waited until the day at the You Yangs.

I was returning to race form and wanted to look after myself. I had prepared some food to eat, so we didn't have to rely on takeaway. Loads of good healthy food, including a salad made with chicken.
To which Norm responded uncharacteristically, "this would have been so much better with chickpeas."

Wow, where did that come from?
I agreed with him, as I preferred plant-based meals all the time, though I wasn't vegetarian. Norm always joked around with friends that drank soy or almond milk. We explored this topic in the car. What did this look like? Did he want to go vego or vegan? I suggested that he needed just to do it all, no animal products. And so that was it, Norm immersed himself into every video, film or story on animal agriculture, and we just gave up meat and dairy, just like that.

> This was the beginning of the struggle, how could we align these values with our mainstream cafe that served egg and bacon rolls? It would take a while to get there, but choosing the vegan lifestyle brought many internal conflicts.

So we did what we could, baby steps, choosing to focus on ourselves, minimising harm, making better choices over time. It was the start of many evolving thoughts and beliefs; we were changing. But most importantly, I felt I was back. I wanted to be back. I still loved racing my bike and the past 12 months seemed to have taken me in a new direction that was more work, less racing. I was not done and needed to get back on track over the quieter winter months and better manage our businesses' other pressures. August, September and October were full of fun, planning and getting race fit. Many shorter mountain bike events, road races, and a big twoweek trip away teaching again, at Alice Springs and then straight onto Perth. Honestly, could it get any better?

It was November. The daily grind of life had inundated us, and there was more to come, a lot more. It was a Monday; I was driving into Colac, a quiet countryside trip with beautiful rolling hills, farm animals and vistas to enjoy. We had just enjoyed a massive weekend at the shop and needed to prepare for the Forrest Festival next weekend. So I was off to the bank and a few other places by myself on a sunny Monday morning. There was quiet chatter going on inside my head, a mental checklist on what else I needed to get done today. I was grateful for the time alone.

Now two-thirds of my way into Colac, I had just passed the sweeping left-hand turn where the Colac-Lorne Road intersected when I heard my chatter say something that scared me to the bone.

> "Why don't you drive in front of the next oncoming truck and end this Jess?" It was a matter of fact and so clear, like I had a person next to me in the car having a conversation. My heart was racing, blood pumping fast akin to hot ants crawling over my skin, leaving me breathless and in that fight or flight response mode. The anxiety permeated my entire body, and I didn't know what to do next.

I did know, however, that I was not about to act out this crazy talk inside my head and continued into Colac to get the jobs done.

But I called Norm and shared with him what just happened. I made a doctor's appointment for the next day. I had run myself down and needed a plan from someone else. My GP in Birregurra was helpful, listening to everything and getting some blood tests then and there. I was low on all the good things needed to produce energy and repair cells; after years of endurance racing, it's often hard to differentiate real fatigue or not. It wasn't too long, about one week of focus, that I started to feel alive again. But I was still working on my mental health. Thankfully it was only the hide under the doona all-day variety, not the drive in front of a truck one.

We had both been suffering on and off for a long time. Experiencing depression, compounded with the isolation of living in a small country town and hard work. Norm and I both knew deep down that we had it good, that we knew how to find hope and get well again, yet still, with each day, sometimes each hour, we struggled to keep our black dogs at bay. We would often force ourselves to be social, get out and do things with other people, stop worrying, and start living. Because we didn't have enough going on and loved to share where we lived and the causes we stood for, Norm and I conjured up a 'participation event called Chase the Dog.

It is the very reason we started Chase the Dog; we knew we were not the only ones who needed a good excuse to get out and live our best lives—scheduled for the start of Spring, bringing new hope and a promise of brighter days. It was a hit and resonated with those that entered.

To be wholly and solely responsible for creating new and exciting events was a heap of fun. Our small team was growing, and we were having fun along the way. Chase the Dog was now on the calendar for 2015, and now it was time to ramp up the Forrest Festival planning, ready for December. We were concurrently preparing for the Summer season at The Corner Store Forrest, Mt Buller and now Derby. Norm and I had a good team working with us; we could not have done it alone.

After Chase the Dog, my mid-year training block finished strong, as in October, we were off to my favourite race location, Mt Stromlo, in Canberra. It was the Scott 24hr, 2014, and I loved it. I would race solo, and I wanted to win, but after the year we had been through, to be out racing and away from any other pressures was a win too. I always found that amongst the pain and suffering of these kinds of endurance races was also a quiet space and solitude. I got to ride, be looked after, and no one asked me to answer an email, plan a course, say yes to a business offer, pay a bill, or even simply cook a meal. The simplicity of racing for 24 hours was the perfect distraction from life, and it was one of the hidden pleasures I got from it.

Many people I raced loved the social side of it, and many a time, I remember other riders hoping to chat with me as we rode along the trail together for a moment. I had to do my best to be polite; all I wanted was to be alone in my mind, concentrating on the simple task of riding my bike the best I could.

But before we left, there was one decision we had to make that would tear our hearts apart.

As the days progressed through the week, it was getting to both Norm and me; we both did not want to make any decision. Soxy, our dearest elderly dog of 15 years, was not well. Every week I was visiting the vet trying out a new drug and seeing it have zero effect on his well being. Not even the Tramadol was calming him enough to be out of pain. I was starting to wonder, was it me desperately trying to give him quality and not wanting to let him go?

Was this the right thing to do?. It was busy like any typical week; we had work to do, planning for events, admin work, shop work, web work, emails, planning, and everything. And try and get some training in for the 24hr as well as pack and plan for it. Two complete bike overhauls, nutrition, some sleep, deciding whether to camp or motel it, what day to leave, and organising my brother to look after Max and Soxy.

Soxy Douglas bestest boy ever

It was not until the week before that I realised how bad Soxy had gotten, and I didn't want my brother to give him respite care for four days and maybe have him die without us being there. I couldn't handle that. Norm and I had a conversation. We called the vet with the same conversation. It was true; it was time for Soxy to go. Now we had to say goodbye to Soxy. We rang Saskia, planned for a 4:30 pm vet appointment, and spent the day with Soxy. We cuddled him, held him, kissed him and then drove him to the beach, which made him so happy. The 1hr long drive back to Colac was filled with tears and lots of silence. It was a countdown that was inevitable; we knew we were now saying our last goodbyes.

Our vet was so good; she gave us the time we needed not to turn it into a process but a proper goodbye. Here we were, feeling our hearts ripped to pieces, unsure of what to do ever again, like life no longer matters, who even cares about a 24hr race on the weekend.

> We had just lost our best mate Soxy Boy Douglas. We gave thanks to him for all the love he gave us and for that final day he spent with us. With his passing, we all took a huge breath; we had to get on with life.
> Norm and I were leaving at 5 am the next day to drive to Canberra.

Scott 24hr 2014 Me with Kate Penglase(L)
2nd & Sophie Clement(R) 3rd Female Solo

This day in October, Race Day, was a warm one, and at this time of the year, you could get anything in Canberra, from snow to rain to a heatwave. I overheated a bit early on, which always causes a bit of nausea, forcing me to slow down until around 6 pm, when it cools down enough to start feeling good again. When it's like this, and my body couldn't respond as well as I would like, I would choose to focus on skills or execution of processes. Simple tasks like a drink at this spot where it's flat, push hard out of this corner, count to ten out of the saddle up this rise, don't change gears here just push harder, get off the brakes, smooth, flow, breathe, grab another drink.

Night came, and so did my mojo, finding a faster groove. I was rewarded for looking after my body in the heat of the day. I increased my lead on Kate Penglas and lapped her early in the morning. Perhaps my lack of racing this year was attributed to this, but I was shattered, my whole body so sore, and as the sun rose, I had to find a new will to keep pushing hard.

Despite not wanting to be social on the racecourse, after winning this race, I relaxed and spent loads of time with others, like Kate Penglase and Sophie Clement, and other people who just wanted to say hi. The low key nature of the event gave me that space and energy, and for that, I was grateful I didn't brush off this opportunity to enjoy the company of others.

The MTBSkills crew at Buller

The rest of the year flew by, events, shops, and finally, moving up to Mt Buller to manage and work in our shop on the mountain. Bike hire, coffees, snacks, bike gear and more, staff to manage, hours to work, cooking, cleaning, serving, servicing and all the other things that come with customer service. I would get home at night and enter all the invoices, pay invoices, do wages, tax, superannuation, reconcile bank accounts, daily takings, go to the bank, order more food and bike gear. There would often be a trip into Mansfield to make a few of these things happen, too, when I would make sure to get a race in with the local cycling club. Summer Season 2014/2015 was insane and life-changing.

Often though, before it turned dark, I would go for a ride, or a walk or a run. Many sunset walks up to the Summit or descents down to Mirimbah to ride back up at dusk. Whatever it took, I made sure to keep myself sane by getting out in the beautiful alpine environment. As soon as it was dark, I would work, often until midnight, shower then sleep. Up at 5:00 am, ready to go again. It was so lucky that I would fall asleep quickly and soundly. Despite the build of this never-ending workload, I was doing good in the sleep department.

During this time, Norm would come up on Friday night, work with me all weekend. On Sunday night, we would do a bike ride together, and he would then head home. It was always an emotional time for me to be left alone again. Monday's were always quiet, with mountain staff and a few holidaymakers to chat to, but mostly just dead. The feeling I would have would be pure emptiness, so I would find plenty of other things to busy my mind with. From Forrest to Mt Buller, it's a 400km trip one way, around 5 hours drive. It was taxing on Norm. He still had websites to work on, constantly as well as help me at the shop, as well as help out at the Forrest shop, and making trips to Tasmania to help out the Derby shop. Little did I know, for I was consumed with my busyness, that he was slowly falling into a dark hole.

Mexican at TCS Buller with Norm and Wally

    We had some fantastic times, running Mexican nights, getting a licence to serve alcohol on these nights, finding time to do Summit sunset walks, lots of mountain bike rides, and so much fun with all our staff working together on busy weekends. Such a great team too. There was so much to love about it. Even though I would fall in a heap at least once a week, I was in a good space. I had options for my downtime, sleep or get out in nature, and both were lifesavers to keep my sanity. But Norm decided not to come up to the mountain over time, happening more often. He wasn't coping. I hated this; I remember telling him that being here without him meant nothing. We enjoy working so hard because we are best friends, business partners, and soul mates who are in this together.

Too busy to worry for long, and if he came or not, the show had to go on.

    It was a weekday in early January. Brodie Chapman, who worked for us at the shop, and I rode our bikes on the trails. We were just cruising around, and it was early, about 7:00 am. We were about to come down one of my favourite trails, Clancy's Run and in approximately 20 minutes, we would be back and working by 8:00 am. Brodie was an excellent mountain bike rider, fearless, fit and fast, but I went first down the trail today. My focus was always to be smooth, not fast, looking for the lines that ironed out the corners and enjoying the process, and today was no different.

In I went, over a rock launch, landed softly, high into the next left-hand corner feeling so relaxed and happy.

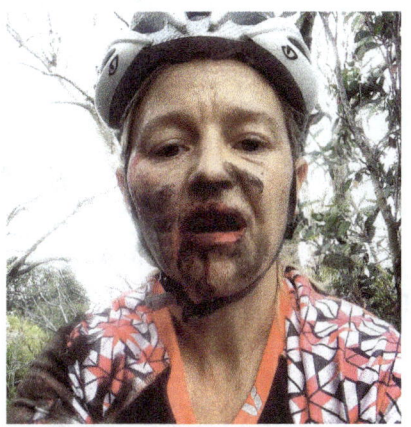

Not ideal at all teeth smashed in

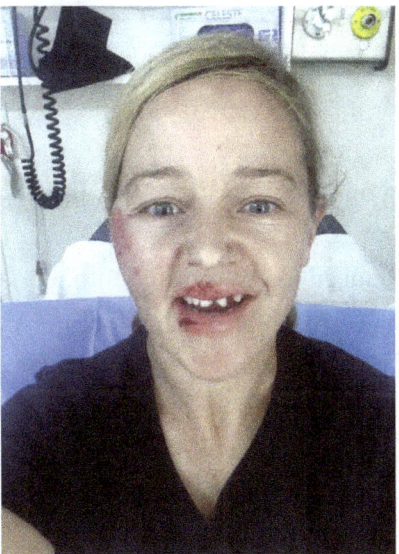

Same day hours later

What happened next felt like a minute but was over in a second. I heard a noise; it sounded like my tyre burped from hitting a rock, a very aggressive release of air. At that moment, I thought to myself, shit, I have not brought any spares with me, I can't even pump up my tyre, I am going to have to walk up the mountain and get Brodie to open up for me.

> In the next moment, I am on the ground, knowing that the feeling I have in my front teeth will require major dental work, and that's it; my day has changed, just like that. I had taken the full brunt of the landing in my face and predominantly my teeth.

There was no pain yet. I was pumped with adrenaline but also shock. Brodie came in quickly from behind me and went into help mode straight away.

Firstly I wanted to know why this happened. We worked out that my front wheel hit a rogue rock, which was now displaced. I hit it at the wrong angle, which stopped me in my tracks, and possibly due to being out of the saddle pedalling out of the corner, put more weight on my front wheel. The next thing I wanted to know was what this all looked like? I took a photo. Oh wow, right, I look bad, and my teeth are not good, one missing and a badly broken one. My face has taken a good hit, too; my cheekbone already swollen. I found it hard to talk with blood with the lost and broken teeth in my mouth, but I was not in pain.

I knew that I was now out of action but needed to get back and find my way to a hospital.

Brodie rode back to alert Andy Railton to the situation, and he came down on the road to get me and my bike, so I started to walk my bike down, which was clunky, so eventually I just hopped on my bike and rode it, slowly. Amazingly, I never felt shaky with post-crash adrenaline and realised I could have ridden back to home another 20 minutes away. When Andy arrived, it was time to work out what on earth to do now. We decided it best to get me to Mansfield hospital, at least they could triage me, and I could always get an ambulance ride from there, and Andy could go back to work on the mountain.

Back at my apartment, it was my first real chance to inspect my teeth, lip, and face in general as I stood in front of the mirror. I had been holding my tooth in my hand, hoping it was redeemable, but now I had realised that this tooth had no chance for any repair. I could see now my two front teeth were pushed back from the force, with one badly chipped. But there was a bit of a shock as I looked closer, the chipped tooth embedded in my bottom lip, and I was going to have to pull it out myself. I counted, one, two, three and released the tooth. The realisation of all the work that was needed was starting to become apparent.

With enough gear to last me overnight, delegating tasks to Brodie to open up the shop, I was off down the mountain for the drive to the hospital. On the way, I called Norm and started to plan how we would manage the situation. He was in Forrest, building websites, with staff and the shop to handle. The doctor on duty at Mansfield tried to help but said he would not fix me up as he thought I needed a plastic surgeon with how badly my bottom lip was from the impact. He and the nurses helped clean me up, getting rid of all the dirt, which gave me a fresh look at my position.

I had ambulance cover, but their job was to take me to the nearest suitable hospital, Wangaratta, and I wanted to get back somewhere closer so that Norm could be there.

The next decision was how to get there. I was considering going back to my place and driving. Could I, should I drive myself? I felt fine, but Andy would have none of it and drove me to Dandenong hospital. I was still holding onto that tooth, but I knew it was not redeemable. There was nothing I could do now to change what had happened; I was now in the processing phase, handing over control to health professionals in the hope to get the proper treatment. As I was about to find out, hospital emergency departments are not the place for my injury.

Andy took me into the emergency department; I handed over my referral and hoped. After an hour, I suggested to Andy that I would be fine and he could go. It would be many hours before, and it was the most confusing time where I felt I had no control over what was best for me, only that I was a patient with a presentation of x, y, z. Such a confronting situation to be in, Norm was on his way, but hours to drive yet, four hours from my home at Mt Buller, four hours from my home in Forrest, and I was not an emergency, but I kind of was.

> I slowly built up anger but didn't want to make a fuss. I just wanted to escape, but now I was in the system. Do I just go and lose what help might be coming my way? Or should I just sit it out, like what else can I do right now?

Sometime much later that day, Norm finally turned up and started asking for answers, I was having a hard time talking as I was emotional, embarrassed for making a fuss, and I could barely speak anyway. Eventually, being told that no more action would happen today and that I needed to go home and come back tomorrow. Norm had to explain where I had come from, why we were at Dandenong and why we couldn't just go home and come back tomorrow. He asked if it would be ok to get transferred to Geelong, in which they said no, you are already in our system.

This was so frustrating; eventually, we could access some assistance, which afforded us a hotel room for the night so we would come back tomorrow. It was so good to have Norm in my corner. But we had also started to ask our friends on social media about dental referrals to fix my teeth. All we wanted now was someone to sew up my lip, and it was starting to get ridiculous. Did I need a plastic surgeon? We were on the waitlist; we promised that tomorrow would be the day, so we turned up and got through to the next level, the waiting room for surgery. This now means no eating, no food, just in case you make it on the list.

It is easy to see how the staff in a public hospital managing so many patients with varying needs have to focus on details only, not the person. Keeping their emotions out of it, the nursing staff want the best for each person but are at the mercy of the doctors and surgeons, who can only attend to one person at a time. What struck me on the second day of being in the system is that you will get left alone if you are the quiet one. It pays to be pushy, which was not in my nature, so Norm did it for me. The problem is that everyone is waiting, nothing to eat, nowhere to go, and there is no honest answer about what will come next.

Eventually, but much later in the day, we got through to the next level of waiting, still no breakfast or lunch. It's time to change into a gown, and I'm in a ward on a bed, which feels hopeful. Now Norm gets to talk one-on-one with the nurses on the ward and finds out they have not much more information about patients than we do ourselves. You can see this by the lack of eye contact, hoping they won't get asked anything if they don't lock eyes—what a shocking place to work day in day out. Despite our progress to the ward, with a bed and fasting all day long, we still have no progress report. Have I made it up the list at all? Norm keeps suggesting we can go to another hospital; in fact, that is what we want to do. The only way I can do this is to leave and start again from scratch.

The day progresses into night, the surgeons have done their last procedure, but I can stay the night and get some sandwiches if I like and start fasting again tomorrow. There was no way I was going through this again, Norm agreed, and at 9:00 pm, we checked ourselves out and drove home. I was so angry at the system. I had just wasted two days when I could have just drove home, made my enquiries and got the job done locally. I was lucky; I had the finances and the know-how.

The next day, a local dentist, Jason Gray, saw me. Straight away, he rang up his maxillofacial surgeon, who bulk-billed me and took out my broken tooth, sewed up my lip all so swiftly in his rooms then and there. Norm and I went back to the dentists, and now we could map out a plan. Just like that, in around two hours, I was comfortably negotiating my recovery in Geelong with professionals that told me how it was and the processes required. I was lucky to have sought out alternate ways to fix my problem.

Unfortunately, this wouldn't be the last time I found myself in the emergency department. When I smashed my teeth in on January 6th, it stopped me in my tracks. Weeks turned into months, thousands turned into tens of thousands ($14 000 to be exact) and eventually, my smile returned. Not just with new teeth and my lips healing but the reconstruction of my life to bring me back to base.

Most moments of hardship in our lives are lessons, bolts of lightning to strike us down and force us to look at what's going on and make changes.

> I knew I needed to slow down, to get back to my purpose, but I didn't know how just yet. If I thought last year was hectic, this year was going to outshine it. The teeth incident gave me a moment that I would never have availed myself of.

January was our peak month to make it all work; all three Corner Store cafes were busy, cycling events and tourist summer season meant staff were overworked, and Norm and I were also spreading ourselves thin, with loads of travel too.

Being home for that short time gave me time to help Saskia plan her 21st, and I was able to make her birthday cake and enjoy the night. The next day it was all systems go again, as Norm and I headed off to Launceston for the Derby Mountain Bike Trails official launch and, of course, help our with our new cafe in the town as well. When we weren't riding, we were working; we were planning when we weren't working.

The time away was needed, even if we stretched our resources thin. We headed back to Mt Buller on our return as we needed more staff at another busy event weekend. At the same time, reports were starting to filter through the ranks that our Forrest staff were not in great shape, overworked and feeling forgotten. We just had to get through January, and then it would quieten down.

Each morning I woke, knowing that bedtime would come again, and I could sleep. This was what I lived for. Somehow I stayed focused, happy and giving. I damaged friendships and tested many relationships, but I was in survival mode. Running the Corner Stores in Forrest and Derby from afar and living, breathing and working at the Corner Store at Buller was slowly breaking my spirit. The only saviour was to ride my bike, and maybe it was the altitude I was living at, but somehow I stayed kinda fit despite the extra "5 stress kilos" I had piled on.

I woke each morning hoping a miracle would occur and alleviate my responsibilities. Many afternoons I should have been riding, I went to sleep and made my bedroom dark, waiting for slumber to consume my worries.

The last weekend of January went off at Mt Buller; everyone was on such a high, exhausted but stoked. Working so hard and soaking in the vibe of the big event weekends was very fun. We spent most of our energy preparing for it; then, it was full-on all day long only to prepare for the next day. It was party time in our stores, I loved the vibe, and we shared that with our customers. But on Sunday afternoon, after everyone disappeared back home, it was just me, left on my own to come down off that high.

> This hit me hard, and I never saw it coming. It was like I had been holding in my breath, knowing there was no time for anything else yet, only to get through a month of tasks and critical dates to fulfil. I had done it, survived, but now what? And what was it all for anyway?
> The storm clouds were coming. I had been doing my best, holding them off, and now I was inundated with all the emotions coming at me like a tsunami.

Depression was not new to me, and I had developed many strategies to find purpose in pushing on and finding joy again. But on Sunday night, after everyone had left the mountain, I was depleted. Empty of any reason to go on, the feeling seeping into every part of my body. Deep grief, I started crying, and I couldn't stop. I walked up to the Mt Buller Summit, as this always snapped me out of my thoughts, seeing the expanse and beauty of nature. Today, it magnified all my grief even more so, showing me how insignificant I was and that all the effort I was investing meant nothing against this beautiful backdrop. I had hit rock bottom, and I needed help.

That night I reached out on social media; I needed to release the pain; the pressure was hurting badly. I rang Norm, we agreed, we were both near the end of coping and decided that we would spend time planning some relief next weekend. Once I asked for help, I felt the load lift. The tears and grief still flowed, but I was happy to go to bed that night, knowing tomorrow I would have the chance to find my way out of this.

A friend shared a post about depression; it described everything about me perfectly and helped me understand I did need to seek help and it was ok to be vulnerable.

"People who are depressed live in a thick, murky soup of confusion over their truth, anger that has been so stuffed down they don't even know it is there, pain that they don't have language for, grief that has not been allowed to evolve to a healed state of acceptance and gratitude, a loss that is not so straightforward, trauma that is often complicated and psychological (if not physical), the feeling of a higher calling with no visible path or understanding of their abilities to arrive at those destinations, personality traits that have been overdeveloped while others that are necessary to support the weight of that are underdeveloped, gifts that feel like burdens because they don't have the tools to manage them, and tremendous sensitivities all sealed inside a pressure cooker of the body with a hefty sprinkling of shame."

The show needed to go on; the shop was open, orders placed, and customers served, and it was a quiet day. I made a doctors appointment in Mansfield to get the ball rolling on any sort of help I could get, taking the first one available that afternoon.

I was so nervous to talk to the GP; where would I start? I was experiencing depression and anxiety, and I needed to relieve some of the pressure on myself and find time to enjoy my life; otherwise, what it was all for? But my fears were alleviated when I met with the most compassionate doctor, who listened and told me what I needed to hear. We made a follow-up appointment; I felt hope and was grateful for his time and honest opinion, he was right, and now I had a plan.

Today was my 42nd birthday. Norm arrived Friday night, and we discussed our options. We needed to make the call; it was time to pull the pin on Mt Buller. Working up here, running the shop, adding to the experience of the summer vibe on the mountain was taking its toll on every aspect of our life, despite how much fun it was. We had spread ourselves too thin, and this was the pin we had to pull. The final trading day decided, and then I ended leases and provided as much notice to everyone as possible. We had about six weeks to go; everything was possible now.

> Once we made this decision, Norm revealed something even more significant; he wanted to finish up on everything, events, cafes, bike hire, MTBSkills, everything, now. Plus, he wanted to leave Forrest and move to Geelong and not wait a moment longer.

He had held his suffering closer to his heart than I had, and he told me that he did not want any of this anymore. So now it was up to me to find an answer to this, finally suggesting that we needed to rip one bandaid off at a time; let's finish up Mt Buller and get home and breathe for a moment. He offered his version that we would finish up Buller and move house by the end of March and that he would find us a place to live whilst I was working up here on the mountain.

So that was it; our lives would be changing in a big way. We both needed to look after each other now.

At the end of March, we moved everything out of the shop, moved out of Mt Buller, dropped off a lot of gear at our new house in Geelong on the way home, drove home to Forrest and spent the weekend packing up. On Monday, we moved in. After seven years, we were back in Geelong with a promise of a new life. We just needed to work out the next step in relieving the pressure.

Norm was doing more and more contract work with a Geelong design company, less and less with the shops and skills coaching. This is where I took over, and together we worked on our events. Kylie Hayles came into Geelong to work with us one day a week, and for the first time in a very long while, we had a spare weekend coming up. It was the weirdest feeling, not planning or being anywhere for anybody.

Now we had some space to think without any pressure; it was time to plan what to do next. We decided to sell The Corner Store Forrest or shut it down entirely if we didn't have a buyer. Eventually, we sold the shop to Cathy, who had worked for us. Now we could relax a little more as we transitioned out of this responsibility.

Enjoying life with Norm in Italy

With time up our sleeves to live a little, other opportunities came our way. I headed off to be a cycle guide for TopBike Tours in a European summer. Spending six weeks away riding in Corsica, Northern Italy and Sicily, I couldn't believe my luck to spend this time working in such beautiful locations. Norm came over for a short holiday, too, riding on the final tour with me. It was hard to imagine how we had gotten to this space where we could enjoy life again, but we were there, and it felt great.

The extra time I had now spent catching up with people I had missed, looking after my health, riding bikes, hiking and of course, racing. I was still building our events portfolio to include a new race called the Otway 300. My coaching clientele was building, and I was still running skills courses. But most importantly, on my return from the European summer, I felt reinvigorated to contest my 3rd National 24hr title and was excited to get fit and strong and do it all again.

Norm and I had planned to go back to Canberra to do the Scott 24hr. By sheer luck and surprise, it was announced that it would also be doubling up as the Australian 24hr National Mountain Bike Championships. When I heard this news, I didn't feel the pressure of the title's prestige, but rather an excitement. That's when I knew I would be racing to win and get one more National Title.

I engaged a coach, Greg Meyland, to get me there in around 16 weeks. I was not in my finest form, had put on weight, and lacked some speed in my legs, but I knew in this time, with a bit of help, I could get back to some semblance of race-winning form. Mainly because I was excited, and my stomach had butterflies about the prospect of racing. This was always a good sign. Now it was time to even up the numbers and go for three championship wins, albeit a few years apart. I lost a few extra kilos, gained a few extra watts in performance and rebuilt the winning mindset. I was so ready to race again. Norm and I were hugely motivated to crush this year's National 24hr Mountain bike championships at Mt Stromlo.

The week before, the start lists were up for viewing, and it was good to find out that I would be racing Liz. It scared me and excited me at the same time. October came around so quickly, and here I was, on the start line. I knew I had good form but wondered what Liz had brought along today, so I had many plans of attack in my mind. The first plan was to lead from the start.

Coming through transition at the National Champs

As we raced off around the bottom of the criterium track to enter the long fire road climb, I was up there with about 5 or 6 of the men. The pace felt comfortable. Within an instant, I knew I could win. All I needed to do was stay calm, focused, no crashes, no mechanicals, and all would be fine. The first few laps were warmer than I was used to. I needed to back off, my legs felt empty, and my stomach felt queasy. This feeling won't last, looking forward to the evening to give me back the energy I need to win.

Within the first two laps, Liz Smith caught me; I knew I had backed off the pace, but what I also knew was how hard work she would have put in to catch me, passing other riders and digging in that little bit more to reel me in. I cached that knowledge for later. I lost count of how many times we lapped around together, but very few words were exchanged. Instead, I listened to her gear selections, the sound of her freewheel and braking, just to make a plan in my mind on how I could win. What if we lapped around together for the rest of the race?

I noted every passing spot, every part of the track where she was on my wheel or where she would lose it.
Thinking this stuff whilst racing is a challenge, but I had about four or so scenarios that I was willing to play out after one lap. Around dusk, about 6hrs into the race, I made the move that resulted in my win.

Aussie Champs again. My last win

Norm and I had made notes of particular spots from the beginning of the descent at Wedgetail on how to milk it for all its worth. Engaging a focused mindset from the very top to the very bottom. So I tested it out, and each little flat bit, I pedalled, 1, 2. Each little roller, I would hit the top and pedal on the downside, 1, 2. Down Wedgetail, Skyline, Luge and into Slant 6. I made it up to the roundabout hill descending into Breakout with no visual of Liz, and so my mind rehearsal came into play, 'focus, engage, rail that corner, tip that bike in, get off that brake, pedal.' That lap, I put in a 2-minute gap. The night was just about to begin.

For me, the night laps are my happy place, the time of the race that flies by. By 10 pm, I was only 5 minutes up on Liz. Slowly and methodically, I just did what I could, stayed accountable and did quick transitions, purposeful climbing, deliberate descending, and before I knew it, I was out on another lap. At midnight I was 16 minutes up; I had forgotten about the race for 1st and became so engrossed in the journey of riding each lap in darkness. At 2 am that morning, I was now 22 minutes up, next lap 27 minutes, next lap 32 minutes, and by 6 am, Norm gave me the green light to see how long it would take to catch Liz and lap her.

Just after 7 am it happened. I started to work out what I needed to do to finish off this race. I had no more lights on the next lap around, a weight off the bike and body. This time of day is when actual pain starts to set in. Perhaps it's the knowledge that it is nearly over, and the mind signals this to the body to start recovering. Maybe it is in the light of day that the last 20 hours of hard work sinks in. I just want to fast forward this part, but it is the most critical part of the race, of anything in life, finishing off what you started. I knew I had lapped Liz, but still, it's not over until it is over, and so I was mentally prepared to race until after midday to secure a win, even though I did not want to. Now the climb hurt, the descents hurt, and my hands and feet were in agony.

The once fun 13km loop had become a battle zone. Each pinch on the climb burned my legs; each brake rut on the descents rattled my entire body, especially my arms and feet. Pain only hurts, right? I am going to be ok.

> My mantras were, "Pain only hurts, pretend the pain is not real, imagine you are fresh, like on the first lap, and the pain will disappear," and whilst it didn't vanish, it gave me something positive to focus on instead of crying.

Norm sent me out after completing lap 29 and said that it might be my last. I wished it would be true. I knew I had to finish after 11 am for my lap to count, but what if Liz went out again? I just wouldn't want to chance it; I still didn't believe it.

The final lap was slow, enjoying a few vistas without the intensity. Teeth gritted down the Luge and Breakout with all my might, seeing the 1km to go sign. I had no idea if one more lap awaited me, and then I came up over the rise on the bridge and dropped onto the bitumen to find Liz there waiting for 11 am to come. Knowing that I didn't have to do another lap, that elation was indescribable.

Norm came up, and we chatted briefly before it hit 11 am, and then I rolled over the finish line, and we won. I found it hard to accept that I could come back to win this event after such a tumultuous year. It was difficult to acknowledge that I had any talent, yet I still felt like I had unlocked a code to winning these kinds of races that others had not discovered yet. But the questions remained. Did I want to do this again? Was I done? Was three world titles and three national titles enough? Did I finally feel like I belonged, not an imposter in the world of the elite? And now that I had all these results, what next? What did any of it matter?

I didn't bother answering any of these just yet; instead, I enjoyed this win with Norm. Reminding myself; I now had the time to do this.

Chapter 10 - Ego is a dirty word

There was once a time when I was much younger; the summer school holidays would come around, meaning at least 6-8 weeks off school.
Summer holidays meant all-day cricket matches in the park. Catching tadpoles in the ditches that were like mini dams.
Riding my bike all day long with a backpack and a bottle of water.
Day trips on the bike to the local pool, swimming and diving and bombing all day long, buying 5 cent Redskins and Sunny Boys.
No shoes - ever! Hard as rock feet, prickles, rocks, glass, whatevs!
Up at 5 am, watching Thunderbirds. Morning television until I got kicked outside. Getting home at 6 pm, eating dinner and going to bed eventually to do it all again.
That time away from the school felt like a whole year in itself, returning in the new year to see everyone had changed, new haircuts, grown, etc.
Time stood still.
A year felt like a decade.
I remember elders recalling how quickly the year had flown. I had no concept or ability to understand what that meant.
Now I do.

Only a short ten years ago, back in 2006, I started the journey proper, on the bike. Pushing boundaries to improve my skills and fitness, so intrinsically motivated. However, I did not know that people were looking on and taking an interest. I was just an ordinary person that used my hard times and made them good times. I chose to succeed despite my genetics, age or circumstances. I represented the people, not the elite.

Loving local racing with the cool chicks - Kate

It was amazing to reflect on the flurry of opportunities and hard work that had been a part of my life. Norm and I owned and ran our Corner Stores in Forrest, Derby Tasmania and Mt Buller. I had smashed my teeth in a mountain bike accident and since had them fixed.

We had owned and ran a very successful MTBSkills.com.au with contractors helping us teach and share the love of mountain biking across Australia and even Singapore. I will always be able to say that I raced and won 3 x Aussie solo 24hr championships and 3 x World solo 24hr Championships.

As a female mountain biker, cycling coach, and skills coach, I had the opportunity to travel to places far and wide in Australia to teach, inspire, mentor, and even make a magazine's front cover.

I have bolstered strong ties with many people through my cycle coaching and my group of athletes.

New trails and locations around Australia ask me to ride, enjoy the local tourism and spend a week with the media to help promote mountain biking.

I have worked for an Aussie cycle touring company in Corsica, Italy, and France for the last 2 European summers.

Forming friendships with amazing legends in their own rights, trail builders, world champion cyclists from all disciplines. More importantly, I've had the opportunity to meet people who have become my friends. Through our mountain biking events, I allowed myself to slowly open up to amazing people on my level, who have also become my good friends. The energy that comes from delivering fun events fueled me for another year.

I didn't need a holiday, nor did I need to 'escape' from my day to day craziness of life. I am astounded by all that I have done and survived. In fact, I have flourished. Times have been tough; money has been challenging, relationships have been tested. Vulnerability to failure has been at the forefront, and the relentless day after day workload has worn me down.

But still, the sun kept rising each day with new hope and new opportunities.

In February 2016, I raced my personal best time at the Otway Odyssey in Forrest. This was my 10th time racing the event, at 43, despite all the stress I had been through.

We ran our inaugural Otway 300 event; despite the bushfires raging through parts of the Otways we were planning to use, working with authorities to change the course. Riders came on board, as did our army of super volunteers. The vulnerability of putting on such an event, financial & emotional investment was huge.

The event was a success, and I had the BEST time ever being a co-event director rather than racing.

As the year progressed, I felt uncomfortable, unsure of my direction, almost sad that I felt the desire to race slowly leaving me.

No longer feeling energised or excited about winning or training or travelling to race but fighting to ignore these feelings hoping I would find the passion again.

The Oppy Crew - Sarah Hammond, Jackie Bernardi, Rachel Edwards and Me!
Jess Varey

GDT500 start in Bendigo

I did a few crazy things like the Oppy 24hr Audax ride with Sarah Hammond, Rachel Edwards and Jackie Bernardi and a 400km Gold Diggings Trail Bike packing 29hr non-stop self-supported race.

People would ask, "What race do you have coming up next?" and I had no idea.

In April, we ran our inaugural Otway 300 - 2 day, 300km mountain biking event in the Otways.

It was the first time I was 100% involved in helping Norm run an event, as I had raced in all of them. It proved far more enjoyable to immerse myself in assisting other people in having fun, becoming involved in our volunteers and their jobs provided a more significant high than racing it.

In May, it was time to run our annual Forrest 6hr event, and this time Kylie Hayles was about to give birth to Toby, so it was just Norm and I. I was his co-event director, and I felt that same high I had experienced at the O300.

This got me thinking, "Did I even need to race anymore? " and the answer was starting to reveal itself. Over June and July, Norm and I were in Europe assisting Dave Olle and Emma Colson of Top Bike Tours. We finished off with a week in Paris; I got a chance to get some base training in and quality time with Norm.

Before we headed off to Europe, we had been working on restructuring MTBSkills. We no longer managed instructors and allowed them to continue separately or not at all; it was up to them. We had sold our Corner Stores in Forrest and Derby Tasmania. Kylie was now on maternity leave for 16 weeks or so, which left me wondering, what's next for me?

At the Louvre in Paris - it wasn't open today!

It wasn't until the downtime in Paris that I considered the concept of me returning to full-time work. I pursued it, and within a few weeks of returning home in August, I was working 9-5 pm, five days a week. Still coaching and fulfilling my MTBSkills coaching engagements in Darwin; this included 3-weekend trips over three months. Plus, Chase the Dog and Forrest Festival to deliver. Kylie returned from maternity leave shortly after we got back home.

Returning to the paid work felt weird, and it never quite sat right with me; however, I thought it might be a thing I had to get used to again. But no matter what I tried to convince myself of, my mind kept reminding me that this was 9 am - 5 pm, five days a week, with four weeks annual leave a year, and it felt like a life sentence. I needed to give it three months and reassess.

I trained and rode and started relying on indoor training at Crank & Grind studio in Geelong to get my sessions done. Barely put a pedal turned outside on the bike. I felt fit and strong, yet a part of me had lost the passion to transfer this in a race result.

Each day was a 5 am wake up. 30mins of emails. 6 am indoor cycling session. 7:30 am shower and breakfast. 8 am breakfast, quick house tidy up, put the washing on etc. 8:30 am get to work. 9 am - 5 pm work. 5:30 pm indoor cycling session. 6:30 pm dinner and housework. 7:30-9:30 pm work on coaching and events and emails—10 pm Bed. Repeat.

By the time the Scott 24hr, the Australian 24hr solo mountain bike champs, I had no idea if I was ready. I relied on my knowledge of following the process to see what would happen. These investments are never easy, food, accommodation, travel, bikes, mental prep, physical prep, support person. It was an expensive exercise, emotionally and financially. This time, I was not excited about being in Canberra, and I was busy using my time off work to get other stuff done, even on the morning of the race.

The race started on Saturday, I went out hard as I would normally, and I was in front and having fun for a bit. I knew I would slow down and that Liz Smith would reel me in after a few laps, and she did at about the 4hr mark. It was early days. I let her ride ahead and saw her race off, still in sight but moving fast. I was in no mood to play.

Descending back to transition, Norm made me swap bikes and said lights on the next lap. That's when I realised I didn't want to continue. Liz was in fine form and wanted to win, and whilst I desperately tried to convince myself to race for 2nd or 3rd place, I was mentally exhausted. There was no way I wanted to ride around for 18 more hours regardless of a podium or not; my time was over. The very moment I thought that I pulled off the course, did a lap around the roads of Stromlo, ripped my number plate off and felt the weight of expectation leave me. It was the best feeling I had experienced all year long.

I was done, not pretend done, not just today, but really well and indeed done with 24hr racing. I was tired, and I knew too much of the pain and suffering that would follow, and I wanted no part of that anymore. The hardest part was convincing Norm of my decision. It was horrible telling him, but eventually, he understood. It wasn't pleasant, but as I found out, each decision I was making to improve my happiness was uncomfortable.

I pulled out of the 24hr, Liz won, I had zero regrets and moved on quickly.

The life of Jess Douglas 24hr Solo racer had finished. Just like that. And I felt fantastic about this prospect.

We returned home on Sunday and back to work on Monday.

What the heck was I doing going back again? I had kept doing what I had always done and forgotten about the hell of last year. It was such an awkward and lousy feeling to retire this way, but here was another bandaid about to be ripped off, like a public shaming. Worst of all, I had brought Norm into the spotlight as well. It was awful.

Work colleagues don't care if you won or lost; they didn't talk about beyond, "how did you go?"

And so life went on; the sun rose and set each day. Unfortunately, the very next week, I was doing the Melbourne to Warrnambool road race. Upon reflection, for a good reason, there went the waste of another day, where I should have just stayed home, but these uncomfortable moments were coming thick and fast now.

The call went out to like-minded women to come and race the Melbourne to Warrnambool to significantly impact the female entries this year. I should have said no, but I said yes.

My start of the Melb to Warrny was horrible, slow and with sore, tired legs, but I managed to stay with a group that was quickly behind the pace. This bunch had a nasty and self-centred female in it that barked orders, and most of us hated her from the get-go, but it took more energy to bitch back at her; most just pulled out, as I did at 110km. I wanted my bike riding to be fun, and if I was going to be at the back working in a bunch for 277km, it needed to be with people I respected. My head and my heart couldn't deal with this person. So when I pulled the pin, I felt a sense of wastefulness of my day but also a relief.

And just like that, I had DNF'ed 2 races in 2 weekends.

I stopped training and ceased caring for just a week; I needed to regroup.

What did all this mean?

I didn't spend much time searching; we had our event Chase the Dog, on the very next weekend.

The fun I had facilitating this was exhilarating.

After Chase the Dog and my return to regular work for a bit, I realised I needed to ride again. I started to commute most days to and from work. Inventing ways to ride my bike before or after work whilst still juggling all my other responsibilities.

It felt so good to ride without a care in the world. Flushing my mind of negative thoughts and preparing myself for my 9-5 gig each day.

There was an engagement party, a wedding, numerous skills courses, a Skills piece for Bike Exchange in the Otways for Rapid Ascent, some road racing and preparing for the Forrest Festival on the 3rd & 4th of December.

I felt obligated to fulfil my promise but unhappy in my full-time job. I took Max for walks; I imagined life in a year should I continue down this path. All I wanted to do was keep walking and not return home.

It was simple. In this life, I am gifted; there are many times I will struggle, many times I will not be happy, many more times where I must suffer and be uncomfortable. Life is never a series of happy snaps linked together on a constant upward trending slide. No, life is undulating, and the periods of uncomfortableness are there for reflection, growth, understanding what is important to us, and an opportunity for consolidating our purpose.

It all culminated in quitting my job and delivering the Forrest festival all in the same week. It was liberating, gave me energy and thanks for the tough times. Allowing me to deliver the event with 100% passion and focus on our participants. I knew this was what I was meant to be doing within an instant.

However, if I was going to keep riding bikes as my vehicle to happiness and fulfilment, I had to start changing how I went about it. Time moved fast, opportunities came forth, and I barely said no. I was reaching out to the world in different ways, hoping to get a sign that said, here is your change in direction, take this way.

2017 was like every other; it filled up with engagements; I said yes, I was doing everything for everybody, and I was sure I was living my best life.

But ultimately, I was scrambling in an identity crisis, trying to create new pathways but still caught up in my reputation of past results.

I had already reached the top of my game in business and my sport. I was trying hard to put that to bed. Now I was expanding my repertoire horizontally. Exploring variations of what I was already good at—dabbling in different racing styles, road, long-distance bike packing, ironman triathlon, trail marathons and other fun multi-day rides.

Still busy with ambassador work for Liv and Giant, turning up to events, teaching skills courses, advocating for women's cycling, keynote speaking, and demo days. My coaching business was booming, with many clients over Australia and a few in New Zealand.

Norm and I had also added a new event to the schedule, The Otway 300. The concept was based on my training rides in the Otways and meant to be a weekend away in the hurt box. 175km on day one, 125km on day two, on a mountain bike, with support and loads of climbing. The extra addition was it needed to be done in pairs.

The lead men - Otway 300 day 2
Adam Kelsall

The saving grace was that we no longer had our cafes; we were no longer in charge of many things, just running events and my coaching business. But somehow, the days and weeks filled up again; I was not very good at keeping space for nothing, always preparing for the next thing.

I really couldn't believe it; I was a keynote speaker for the opening breakfast for the inaugural Cadels Women's race. Volunteering as a rider at Peaks Challenge Falls Creek, assisting the Otway Odyssey with women's skills courses to bolster numbers in the event, attending a women's weekend at Falls Creek as a female rider, representing my sponsor, Liv bikes. These were just a few of the engagements I was involved in. I could do more with my knowledge and experience rather than always racing.

March was flat out, riding at Falls Creek for Peaks Challenge, then the following weekend riding 600km over 24hrs with a group of women for the Oppy 24hr Audax challenge. The following weekend I drove to Canberra for a 3-day coaching course, and then the next weekend, we delivered the Otway 300 race. The event was so much fun to co-direct with Norm, and our volunteers were incredible, with the riders having a ball. There are pivotal times in your life that change how you think because you cannot unknow once you know. This weekend hit us with an unexpected event that was closer to home than we wanted to think about.

There was an ultra bike-packing race, known as the Indian Pacific Wheel Race. Starting in Western Australia and finishing in Sydney. The race leaders were well past southwest Victoria, where part of the course would intersect with a small section of the Otway 300 course.

Norm was out doing some early morning marking on Friday, getting ahead of schedule for the next day. He knew a friend of ours, Claire, was due to ride through Cape Otway in the next day or so and spray-painted a message on the road, 'Go, Claire!'

I called him not moments later, as Kylie had called to let me know of the news.

Mike Hall, who was coming 2nd, was hit by a car and died on the Monaro Highway, bound for Canberra.

This hit us hard. As event organisers, you know that someone can die or at least get hurt and need an ambulance. So, of course, you have a Risk Management plan and pray like hell that your riders make good choices throughout the race.

But you can't control everything.

The more time you spend out on the bike, the greater the chances of bad stuff happening to you are.

After a good hour of just sitting with what we had found out, Norm and I decided to go on. We would openly remember Mike in our race briefing and have a minute of silence for him.

The riders enjoyed their time in the Otways. The weather was a perfect display of Autumnal glow. We went home elated with renewed energy to go on.

Running events always did this to us; there would be worry and stress in the lead up. Then we would deliver the goods, interact with the riders, be in full adrenaline mode and finish up, super motivated to do bigger and better at the next one.

But Mike Hall's death was still at the forefront of our thoughts for a long time to come.

Signing on at the start of the Cloudride

Despite Mike's tragic death, I had signed up to do the Monaro Cloudride, a 1000km bikepacking race. Starting and finishing in Canberra, circumnavigating the surrounding mountains into NSW and Victoria and back into the ACT.

The race was over the Easter long weekend, and it was going to take at least four days to complete, and that's all I had.

I didn't know what to expect. It was easy to do research on, with prior knowledge via blogs and posts on social media and made an eclectic decision on bringing essentials but going lightweight.

The plan was simply to eat, drink, ride, and sleep if needed and get the ride done as quickly as possible. That way, I could get back to Canberra, have a sleep and drive home as swiftly as possible, like it never happened.

Just like in the heyday of my 24hr racing, the moment I started riding and got the first hour out of the way, I found my happy place. The sheer joy of being out riding with nothing else to do except move forward and self-preservation was precisely what I loved. However, I had no idea it would feel so euphoric.

I was so excited for what was to come.
Even though I had poured over the maps, my knowledge of the area was non-existent. Each new kilometre brought me a visual explosion of countryside, views, terrain, roads, trails, paths, towns and wildlife that kept my mind in overdrive. I longed to stop and take it in, to take photos and share my journey. But I had this overriding voice in my head telling me to push on, keep riding, go faster, don't stop, make up time here and there.

Damn, this incredible journey I had signed up for suddenly turned into a race, and it seems I was doing ok at it.
The race started in the morning, not too early, but the sun was up. We rode through Canberra, and before long had fragmented into smaller groups, I found myself in the second group of riders. We made our way out towards Wee Jasper. Rolling hills, undulating countryside, that went on for most of the day. After the glorious descent into Wee Jasper, there was a long, arduous and fully exposed climb. This went on for a long time; it was hot now as we were in the afternoon sun. I found it fun to finally be alone, no longer riding with anyone and following my route line on my Garmin.

The quick refuel at Tumut was needed, as I was keen to get to Batlow before the pub closed and knew it would be tough to do so. So many hours passed, and it was dark now, so many tricky parts of trails to get through, though this would prove easy compared with what was to come. I caught a couple of riders in the Blackberry maze, and we managed to get salt and vinegar chips and a ginger beer at the pub. That was it.

The night wore on, riding well into the dark, the other two boys decided to camp, and I kept riding. This was the most memorable night for me, with mobs of wild brumbies making their way through the dense bush, sometimes alongside me, crossing the roads I was on. This kept me on my toes and filled me with great joy to be part of their journey.

There was a lot of climbing overnight. With the sunrise, I crested the top arriving at the descent down to the Tumut Pond Reservoir. Tarmac and a new day, I decided not to refuel at Cabramurra, pushing on into some very harsh terrain.

I probably should have refuelled. Dropping into Mt Selwyn ski fields was a lumpy rocky tufted alpine landscape, mainly riding, sometimes walking, but not very fast. It took 11 hours to ride 100km, and I used the mountain streams often. I was grateful for the food I had, but this was a limited supply.

Refuelling at Jindabyne, I decided at 38 hours and 436km later to have a 2hr sleep on the side of the road; I woke up shivering.

The following 50km took 3 hours despite it being mostly downhill. It was dark, and wildlife was out in force, so taking it easy was vital. Crossing the Snowy River into Victoria took a good half hour, then shit got real. I realised now, hike-a-bike was not in my skill set. The route took some epic 4wd tracks up and over rugged ridgelines to reach the peak of 1000mt abs. Over 10km, the average gradient was 9%, but that doesn't give an accurate indication of the severity of the track. I paused often; this was tough. My resting time was 2 hours, and the total time elapsed was 6 hours. The other side of this massive climb was a descent that was just as crazy.

Thanks Peter and Alison for saying hi.
Alison Makin

The chase was on to get some more food and drink at Delegate before the store shut. By the time I scoffed down my next meal, I was 57 hours and 575km into the race. Over halfway with the worst over, but I was getting tired and knew I would need to sleep tonight to get the job done.

But it was just on dusk; I had just eaten and was over the hump. I hoped to get to Bombala and sleep somewhere there. All was good until it got proper dark; that's when my eyes just wouldn't stay open. I took a few micro naps on the side of the road for 20 minutes to see if this helped, but I was now in need of actual sleep.

Arriving at Bombala, I found somewhere to sleep and hit the hay. I didn't get going again for 9 hours. Seventy-one hours and 637km down, hot cross buns on board, I was a new woman. Let me get this job done. So much sleep under my belt now, I knew I could go non stop to Canberra.

The next refuel was at Nimmatabel via some vast wilderness and farmland. I ate and drank everything possible at two bakeries to ensure I didn't miss out on anything. Food and drink onboard and 735km down. Bring on the night.

It was nearing dusk as I found my way into the rolling hills that slowly turned into bushland and subalpine scrub. I was now in Badja forest, and it was beautiful.

I stopped and messaged Norm; I told him how amazing it was, that there were so many wombats, everywhere, like I had never seen and that I would need to slow down, but wow, what a sight.

I kept riding, putting myself into the middle of the road. Those wombats were crazy, darting across the road at the last minute; I needed to keep my wits about me.

I slowed down considerably, hugging the middle of the road to avoid any wombat altercations, using my brakes a lot to ease off speed on the slight downhill gradients.

Then, nothing.

With 180km to go until the finish, I was knocked out. Unconscious for over 20 minutes. I did not know this at the time.

I picked myself off the ground, realised I had landed on my shoulder because my jacket was all torn and dirty. This led me to see I had a few scratches on the right side of my handlebars.

I thought nothing of it, didn't even ask myself why and attempted to get riding again.

The first thing I did was check my Garmin; how many kilometres did I have to go?

Then the pieces of information started to leak back into my brain; I was racing; I had to get to Canberra. What was I doing on the dirt? How did that happen? Oh well, just keep riding.

Hang on; I can't ride; the bike is wobbly. I must have buckled the wheel—a quick look and attempt to readjust. Ride again; nope, it's still wobbly; I can't ride this. Actually, I can't ride the bike straight at all. What on earth is going on?

Oh, I think I might have hit a wombat? Maybe? I quickly deduced the likelihood that this would be the answer to why I had such an impact on my upper right-hand side and no grazing on my leg. The wombat must have scuttled along as my front wheel passed. Ramming into my bike and landing me straight onto my right shoulder. Resulting in a final head slam on the ground, delivering the concussion injury. This would be why I have no recollection of the fall and why I feel drunk and can't keep my eyes open.

Of course, now I knew what might have happened, it still didn't alter the fact that there would be no way I was riding 180km in this condition at night, back to Canberra. No freaking way.

I had to find a farmhouse with lights on and just ask for help. The lights were on; this would have to be the house; fingers crossed, they were friendly people.

I knocked on the door and did my best to explain the situation. It would have been challenging to describe what was going on to the average person, let alone why I knocked at their door. Eventually, after they sat me down, I found my phone to give them Norm's number; I couldn't even remember this.

They called Norm on their landline, "Hello, you don't know me, I am with your wife Jessica, and she's ok, but...",

I tried my best to help explain everything sitting on the couch, listening to the call go on between Norm and the property owner. So much to tell, so little brain capacity to do so.

I could hear them muttering concepts about why I was so spaced out and what must have happened, and every now and again, I would pipe in with the facts and then almost fall asleep again.

The concussion was taking its toll.

It was agreed that I would be driven to Cooma Hospital. The property owner had to go to work in Canberra the next day, he would take the bike, and Norm would fly there in the morning from Melbourne. I had a screenshot of where I had left my car, Norm had a spare key, and he would drive. That would happen tomorrow.

Now I could relax. On the way out, we saw Matt Turner, another rider and explained what happened, and apparently, there was a dead wombat on the road not far from the house I stopped at.

I rested at Cooma whilst explaining what happened, finally having a shower and something to eat. Sometime the following day, Norm arrived, and I was able to leave.

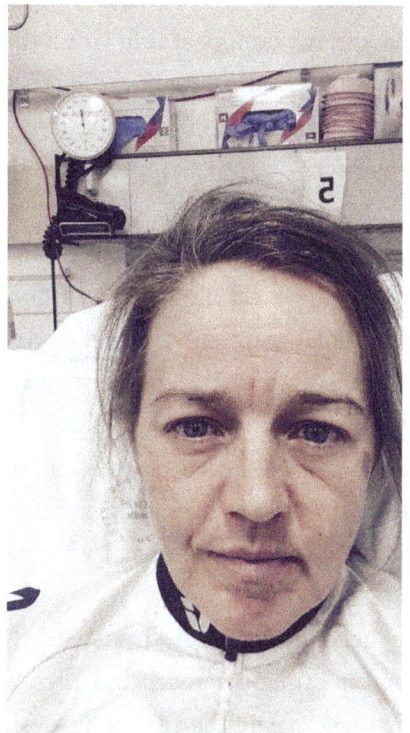

Selfie at Cooma hospital - stinky and tired

We had something to eat in Cooma, I was starving, but it was now that I truly realised the extent of my injuries. I lacked balance, could not use words or concentrate, and could not walk without dragging my left foot. These things would take time to heal, and I didn't have a great deal of it.

Norm drove all day long, and I took up all of the back seats, in and out of sleep. Then it was the simple recipe of rest, but first of all, I needed to let everyone know I was ok, but I would have to cancel anything I had planned, at least for the next seven days.

After that, I slept and desperately tried to explain things to Norm. This was the first time I noticed that my anger was quick to surface; it would take me more than a few seconds to respond to a question as I searched for the words to explain. This frustrated Norm, and in turn, got me cranky at him being this way.

All sorts of advice filtered in, keep the light low, stay off electronics, tv, computers, low noise, low stimulation of anything. Of course, I did my research (on the computer), and the consensus was, let the brain heal. Shut it down.

Words were hard to come by; sleep was often, but not at night, where I would wake up every hour on the hour. Walking Max slowly each day was exhausting, but I persevered.

By the end of the week, I had the energy to make an appointment with a sports GP that was a concussion expert with footballers in Geelong. She was great, we did all the tests as benchmarks, and I went home exhausted. Every brain injury is different, but the same advice was to back off using my brain as I was used to and ease my way back.

I had to get my head into order in three weeks, we were running the Forrest 6hr mountain bike race, and then we were moving house the very next week. And then I was housesitting for Phil Anderson down at Grey River for three weeks.

The wombat incident was mid-April, and two and a half months later, I was back racing and did my first trail marathon on foot. Physically I felt great, but all my words and memories were scattered. I knew the answer to so many questions but no longer could recall quickly. It was as though the accident had knocked my neat filing cabinet over. All my documents were now on the floor and out of order.

My memories and knowledge were not lost, but it would take a long time to sort them back into order again. By the end of July, I was back racing and felt super confident on the bike again.

This was when I started training for an Ironman Triathlon. Ironman had always intrigued me. If it hadn't been for Stephane Vander Bruggen, a triathlon coach, approaching me after a race, I probably would never have bothered. Running and riding, no drama, but open water swimming was a big task I would be mastering along the way.

Say Yes now, work out how later.

I was back racing mountain bikes and travelling to do skills courses.

Long rides and long runs were a staple, as were afternoon naps.

Norm was working hard and doing loads of overseas travel to the US.

We were back in the groove, and I loved it.

Soon after, as I was recovering from the traumatic brain injury, I ceased menstruating. I was waking up in a bed soaking sweat every night. My hair became brittle, and I saw a lot more in my brush every day. Was I perimenopausal? I had tests to measure my hormones, and they confirmed I was. Was I ever going to get my sleep back? The one thing that kept me sane? I remained grateful for the afternoon naps.

Even with my hormones wreaking havoc, I was strong and motivated. The training routine gave me peace and purpose. I wasn't sure if I fit the triathlete mould; however, I enjoyed the solo aspect of the sport.

The flat lay pre race

The critical race I was working towards was Ironman WA, in Busselton, Western Australia.

A 3.8km swim, 180km bike ride and finishing off with a 42.2km run. The swim leg was going to set me back, but I knew by now I could finish this, so long as I hung to the side of the back to avoid the starting flurry.

The day started early. It was going to be a warm one, around 30 degrees Celcius.

I was setting up my bike in the transition area, not yet dressed in my wetsuit. I knew I needed to go to the toilet after this, so I was waiting until then. I told Norm I would meet him outside of the compound in around 10 minutes.

An announcement came over for all racers to move into the bike compound with their bikes. To stay there for further news.

I was in the 40-45 year age group, and all the women around me were the same, and we were loud in chatter about the possibility of why? I thought straight away that there must be a shark in Geographe Bay; there always is. They are trying to usher it out, maybe? Are they trying to work out what to do and how to run this race today?

It was a good forty minutes before we were told. The sun was up, and it was warm.

The news was this, there would be no swim today, and the race would simply be a 180km bike leg followed by the marathon. People would be going off in intervals, two at a time, and this would continue until everyone had started.

We had thirty minutes to get ready and line up.

So now, the race had turned into an individual time trial; there was no way of knowing where you were placed until the end. Only the elites got to start first.

My dreaded leg, the open water swim, was cancelled. I dared not smile too much, though I had been looking forward to the considerable challenge.

The 180km bike leg Norm

I had a great ride, finishing 180km in 4:59; I had no words in my head, no songs, nothing, just the processes of cadence, speed, hydration, nutrition—5hrs of that.

And now onto the run. It was hot, stinking hot. I managed leg cramps for 90km on and off and knew that I had salt-encrusted all over me from sweating. I wondered how this would transpire in the marathon.

Instantly I focused on keeping my spine tall, sucking my belly button in, hips in bum under, elbows back, shoulders relaxed and breathing with a calm face. Straight into hydration and boom - cramping in the diaphragm instantly.

On and off the pain for the next 8km, which meant I had to walk a bit and then run, forcing my brain to hone in on running instead of cramping.

The cramps eventually went, and I was able to sustain forward movement again. Every 2km were Aid Stations with water, ice, coke, endura, water, ice in that order; I took everything except Endura pretty much every time. Ice in the bra and down my back, water over my head, water & coke in my mouth.

I wasted an extra 15 mins in aid stations throughout the marathon, slowing my average down to 6:09 pace.

It was so hot; locals said it was hot, 200+ racers DNF'ed and many were sick on the side of the road, even on the bike leg.

Maybe I didn't need as much hydration, but perhaps I might not have finished? Either way, I said yes to having water thrown on me and at me and run under every hose sprayed along the way. Consequently, my feet were wet, and I knew this would cause blisters, but I can run on sore feet. Blisters are manageable - heat not.

The run course was four laps, and it was kind of nice to watch the ocean on the left-hand side. I kept a conversation going: simply run tall, fall forward and push-off, elbows back, let them swing freely and add to forward momentum. Oh, look, next aid station - yay.

The marathon became a series of messages to my brain to keep going, don't stop, don't quit, don't think of quitting, 42.2km will pass if you just keep moving forward. And it did.

Each time we'd go through a finish chute, you were given a wristband that reminded you had completed 1, then I was excited. Before long, I collected a 2nd, then a 3rd, and then I was done on my 4th.

Norm was there watching me, trying hard to give me something positive, but I didn't want anything. I had to internalise the pain, the heat and the job at hand.

At the end of the marathon, 42.2km, I was in the final finish chute, and in my head, I was sprinting as I channelled Usain Bolt into my light feet. No doubt I looked nothing like him.

Finally, I was done. I couldn't speak; I was so relieved. I came 7th in my age group, 30 mins behind the winner.

With the Ironman under my belt, I had to wonder, would I do another?

It was early December, an entire month left of 2017, and there was so much opportunity and fun to get involved in before the year was over.

Bike is ready for the 800km ride to Adelaide

Not a few weeks later, I rode to Adelaide with Simon Wile; minimal gear, quick naps en route, loads of food and arriving hot and exhausted. 800km over 40 hours, with 30 hours ride time. Over the whole duration, there were around 60 mins of sleep, with loads of resting at cafes and roadside stops for food.

It was probably the craziest thing I have ever experienced, but I'm glad we did it. That night, we slept, and the following day, I caught a plane back to Melbourne, where Norm picked me up.

Nearly there, finish line is Mt Gambier

The following week, I rode on a 3-day bike packing holiday with friends, Corinne Rice and Tina Stenos, from Geelong to Mount Gambier. A total of 500km. That trip was a load of fun, eating, riding, trying to sleep and up again to go the next day.

We arrived at Mount Gambier, where Tina's husband John was meeting us. He was driving Tina and Corinne back to Geelong the following day, whilst I had a route planned to ride back to Geelong in one hit over 370km.

You can never count on this happening, but I had a tailwind most of the way, and whilst I was tired towards the end, the experience was gratifying. Time alone, riding at whatever pace I felt like, eating at food stops, enjoying life at its simplest.

Just me and my bike. My happy place. What a year. What a bunch of experiences I had been having. I had no idea what to expect, and my goals were simple. Be ready and able to do anything that might come my way.

The following year, 2018, I carried over some freaking exceptional fitness, and I could do it all, except for travel. I was not keen on too much of that.

So I competed in some local Victorian mountain bike races, club road races, trail running events, and longer rides, just for fun.

Racing XCO in masters

Then I decided to go back and attempt to finish Cloudride, the bikepacking race with the wombat clash. A weekend away, doing something extraordinary, and finally racking up a finish time, regardless of the result.

Easter was at the end of March, legs were tired from all the summer racing, but I didn't need to be fast, so I rocked up in a bit of a rush, it seems.

Again, I was under pressure to make decisions when things went wrong, and again, I let my damn ego get in the way. This time I was meant to be having fun.

I arrived at Cabramurra at 9:30 am Easter Monday. The course was in the opposite direction —700 km in with 300 km to go until Canberra.

I departed Jindabyne around 2 pm on Sunday after attempting to get my dynamo hub working again with the mechanic's help at the bike shop.

It was a long hard 100km slog ahead from Jindabyne to Cabramurra.

At around 10 hours in, I found myself not thinking about anything else but where to sleep. I was scanning everywhere that would make an excellent spot to rest and settled on a bunch of knee-high springy bushes—laying my bivvy and sleeping bag on without even inflating my mattress.

Sleep came quick, and around 2 hrs later, I awoke and got underway. Progress was painfully slow. Much of the darkness was spent selling the idea to myself to keep going, don't think, just do, get the job done.

It was now that I decided on a second sleep; I wasn't making much sense. I was dead tired and totally over it, so I pulled over, put the bike down, and once in my sleeping bag, and bivy was out to it instantly.

I was riding this section which was very slow anyway in daylight with a crappy $40 battery-powered commuter light and an Energizer head torch from Woollies. I had great light for my helmet, but it needed too much charge/battery power, and my wonderful K Lite mega truck light was not working as my dynamo hub was no longer working. I could see, the full moon was so helpful, but the concentration was intense and increasing the tiredness that I was already experiencing.

Common sense suggests I should have stayed in Jindabyne, charged up everything, got a good night's sleep and some food. But hindsight is a beautiful thing. Common sense suggests I should have accepted that this was the only way to finish; however, I was too fixated on a fast ride and toughing it out.

This is how it started. The Cloudride 1000; 2018.

Arriving at Canberra Thursday, I was in a total fluster, not enough time, too much to do. I left my Garmin at home and had only used my Garmin etrex once around the river, including my KLite front light at the same time. Testing was minimal. I was comfy with the set-up but did not give much time to ensure everything was 'good to go'.

I got a new Garmin, sorted my nutrition out, the bike out, the bags, the battery power banks, and the gear.

I even got to dinner late and had to wait for 50 minutes for a bowl of rice—what a hectic start.

We started at 8 am with my Spot Tracker not working. Peter helped me get it working, but then it wasn't tracking on the website, but I was riding with Scotty Preston by then with Seb, Callum and Lewis upfront. Scotty and I are following next.

It was stinking hot already, and we had a quick water refill at Hoskinstown and then rationed water to Jerangle Primary School. The temperature was very high in the 30's and hot.

I had pulled away from Scotty and was on my own. I saw a rider coming from behind after Numeralla; Lewis; he had to stop there and refuel after a hot dehydrated start. Seb pulled out and headed back to Canberra, and Callum had made a significant break.

Lewis pushed on, with me about 30 minutes behind by the time we reached Nimmitabel. Many dead wombats along the way, which I was very, very aware of.

Stopping at Nimmitabel, I ordered all the drinks and a bowl of mashed potato at the pub. Refilling drinks, toilet stop, reapplied chamois cream and got going.

My lights were working, and life was good.

Heading to Cathcart, there was quite a lot of national park to get through with some steep hike a bike to exit back out to farmland. I took my time here as there were many loose sticks and debris and quite a bit of low lying fog. It was around midnight that my lights started to flicker. I suspected a loose contact point with the pins on the hub and the cord attached to the lights. I had a look, and it had moved forward, so I moved them back and tightened the thru-axle skewer. Ten minutes later, it happened again, and this is where one of the pins came out, and I was without my front lights. I secretly shit myself as now I was not even 24 hours in and had a significant malfunction that would upset my plans to ride during the night and sleep in the day whilst it is warm.

My helmet light was excellent but used a lot of power, so I put it on low and got to Cathcart around 3 am. I found the toilet blocks, looked at the mechanical and decided I could do nothing. I had a hot shower and slept warm with as much stuff charging as possible with my one wall charger unit piggybacking all my power banks and devices.

Callum was at Cathcart, and I heard him leave at 6 am; I planned to go at 6:30 am for Bombala. Only about 1 hour away.

As I got going, I called Norm; he asked how I was and how everything was going and was everything on the bike going ok? I left a bit of silence and didn't answer straight away. Norm suspected something was wrong. I never told him.

I got to Bombala, bought some food, coffee and an extra power bank. I was hoping to charge everything at Tubbut that night at the community hall, and I needed to buy more wall chargers.

The terrain from Bombala started with a lot of big climbing but oh so beautiful. With the countryside's surrounds, rolling hills, and some big descents. And then, into some brutal rough, dry and rocky bushland with a bike and never-ending heat, dry and barrenness. The terrain opened up into dry sheep grazing farmland with a welcome cooling crossing of the Delegate River. This is when I saw the property owners and some welcoming hellos, cold water and a banana. Getting out of this farmland was no easy task, with much climbing to be done.

The temperature was hot, and now it was onto Delegate for food.

I bought many drinks and some potato cakes with salt and a veggie burger to take away for dinner at Tubbut.

Time spent at Delegate was mostly charging my gear again, making the most of power points.

Tubbut had a community hall with water, toilets, tea and coffee, and power points. I slept for 3 hours. James Garrick and Trevor turned up as I was leaving, so we had a quick chat, and I got up the worst part of the course. Some hectic hike a bike up and down. At night, I didn't want to see what I knew was there as I saw it all last year, and it was horrible, in the other direction—nothing fun about this section. Hours later, I could finally hear the river, and it was so easy to cross with low water.

I was nearly 48 hrs into the race. Next was Barry Way, a long and gradual gravel road climb and a rolling bitumen section into Jindabyne.

I arrived in Jindabyne around midday and left two hours later, and this is where things started unravelling.

I got to Cabramurra, and everything had turned to shit. By now, my resolve had dissolved.

Hours were spent telling myself to finish, keep going, not give up, and stay in the game no matter what it took.

And then, BOOM, just like that, I said no more, this is no longer serving me, I need to get home, I am no longer having fun. I was not proud of this mental attitude, but it was there, and I took it on as my reality then and there.

Heading towards Tumut - a DNF but happy to be pointing downhill

Getting food and sitting in the Bistro at Cabramurra, I was zoned out to 99% of my capacity to think. I forgot to tell Norm my plans but eventually worked out with Peter Makin, who had pulled out earlier to pick me up at Tumut. Quitting now still presented a nasty repercussion of a 110 km road ride to get my pick up. So at noon, I left the bistro and crossed paths with James. I told him I was out, and he wanted to know where to eat and what terrain awaited him. I promised him it was much better than what he had just done. The 110km back on bitumen to Tumut was another world I had never seen before up on the high plains of Kosciuszko National Park. It reminded me of the steppes of Mongolia. I was up at 1400-1500 mt above sea level, streams with wild horses drinking from them and not a lot of traffic for Easter Monday. I knew that I had to drop down to 300 meters above sea level over the 100km and started to realise this was not going to come until I dropped down to Blowering dam.

I stopped once in the shade, took my helmet off, rubbed my eyes and had a little sook.

I was halfway to Tumut, so exhausted and feeling sorry for myself.

And then finally the reward I had been waiting for, the massive descent down to the dam.

I mean massive. There was a beautiful viewing platform I bypassed and more awesome vistas in the afternoon sun as I just made forward progress and cached the Instagram posts in my head, not on my phone. I was nearly there. Losing about 1000 mt of vert in 20km was a pure delight, and I wasn't stopping for anyone and only waved one car past—what a way to end my Cloudride experience.

Eventually, getting to Canberra, I considered ordering room service but opted for a long hot shower and a long deep sleep instead. The drive home the next day was tough with 3 x 30 min naps and many cans of Red Bull.

I had to question myself, "Why did you pull out, and what does this mean to you?"

I wanted to ride at a steady pace with planned breaks and finish in around four days. Last year I did it and hit a wombat and ended up in hospital at the 800km mark.

When things started to blow out due to the power issue with a dynamo hub, I stayed upbeat until I had to get to Cabramurra with crappy lights and fatigue and stress. This is where I allowed myself to ask if this journey was serving me any longer? It was a struggle to let myself think of quitting, yet the idea of pulling out felt so right.

What does it matter anyway? If you plug on and take an extra day and get there in 5 days instead of 4, that's an extra day of recovery, an extra day you are away from your work and life responsibilities. Does this ride mean that much to you?

I then sold myself the idea that I would gain more out of adversity than success. This would allow me to have a good hard look at myself and what the hell I wanted out of riding my bike now.

Nothing matters, win, lose or otherwise; it's how you digest the journey and how you relate to others as they undergo their own individual journeys.

Out of my failure, I realised that I love training and seeing improvements in my mindset and physical adaptation. In fact, I do enjoy adversity and finding my limits.

Exploring new places is fun; I will always love this. But times have changed because I also love being home with my dog, cats and Normie boy.

I accepted any unfinished business or failures as Big Fat Lessons in Life. Understanding that taught me more about where I needed to invest my time, energy, and passion.

That was my great start to 2018, time to get on with it.

But then I found out that my grandmother was dying, the day I had dreaded all my life had arrived. I was well and truly devastated. She meant so much to me.

I was grateful to see her, to hug her and hold her hand and say goodbye at the hospital before finally leaving to return home. She passed away soon after, and now we could grieve.

The past two years, I had lost both grandmothers, with both grandfathers long passed, how lucky I was to have known and loved them all. It was a sure sign I was getting older.

Not soon after, we found out that our daughter, Saskia was pregnant. Norm and I would be grandparents in 2019. It felt like a gift; with death comes new life.

My daily grind was more of the same, coaching, training, racing and other crazy things like a virtual Everesting and moving house - again. I experienced my first stalker on social media, who harassed me; unsettling and certainly fed the inner self-loathing side of my personality. However, it turns out that he was a fine example of a psychopath.

But generally, it was a cruisy kind of year. Saying yes to great fun opportunities, travelling and doing a few adventures and enjoying the bike on a more local stage.

In September, we finally bought back into the Geelong housing market, downsizing to afford our way in.

At the end of the year, I gathered a few troops from my coaching group, and we met in Forrest, in the Otways, to enjoy a social riding weekend. A few longer rides, road and mountain bike, for fitness and fun. To revisit this region, stay for a few days, enjoy riding and eating and socialising without work stressors was turning out to be precisely what I needed.

On the final day, a few of us headed out to do a big circuit of the old Chase the Dog loop, which used the Beechy Rail Trail. I led the group down a descent that used part of a gravel road to bypass a closed section of the trail. A dog ran out of a farm driveway quite fast, I missed it, but Peter Makin didn't. The dog must have hit his wheel, but Peter was on the ground and hard, whatever the case.

The short of it was that Peter went to the hospital, amazingly no broken bones but a very broken brain.

He sustained a life-changing Traumatic Brain Injury. This was devastating for everyone, especially Peter.

I had experienced a few times like this in my life, being involved in cycling, including situations that I was the casualty. Being somewhat responsible for people as a coach weighed on me heavily more and more.

But I needed to keep moving forward and focus on what I could control.

I had signed up for the Alpine Quest Adventure Race. Trevor Mullens had contacted me asking if I wanted to; I said yes, and I was put in a Tiger Adventure team.

I had been training for a few months to be ready for January 2019; I was in a mixed team of four, getting prepared to race in Falls Creek. Yes, there would be mountain biking, but also running, hiking, navigating and kayaking, as well as no sleep.

I was a rookie. There was so much I didn't know, but I trusted that so long as I looked after myself and was able to keep moving forward, I could learn from the others along the way.

The experience was addictive, and I can understand how teams base their life around chasing these races—such a perfect blend of adventure and support.

It is a weekend away to selfishly immerse yourself in nature, move through it, and engage in every aspect of it. It mixed in with survival and using your brain, not just brawn.

I loved it. I would do it again...and again!

But it had a downside, a few, actually. It was expensive to do, the travel, the accommodation, the entry fees, the equipment, the training, and being away from home, returning exhausted. Norm wasn't a fan either. In fact, Norm wasn't a fan of much of my sporting pursuits these days, but he supported me all the same.

It was February 2019, and I felt like I was on the other side of all the turmoil I had been experiencing in recent years. However, I was still floating along, searching for an identity. All the various activities I was doing were fun but didn't have the same wow factor that mountain biking had in my first race.

The plus side was that I was as fit as I had ever been, if not more so.

Since retiring from 24hr mountain biking, I was obviously struggling to move on.

Hung up in my own ego, knowing that I was a formidable athlete who did things that many could only dream of.

I enjoyed being that person, some of it was for the wow factor, but most of it was because I too loved to be scared shitless of big goals. The journey of executing many small hurdles, the training, the lessons were possibly more enjoyable than the end game.

On the day, turning up to see what I could do was always more important than my position.

I am never afraid of what I would learn from myself and others, often choosing to go in a little underprepared, physically and mentally, to learn even more.

My failures have been many. This is where I have found my gold and had my ego broken apart, clarifying what is important to me in life.

These next twelve months were some of my finest, as far as experiences and race results.

I could also sense the emotional toll building again, increasing resentment towards those wanting a piece of me.

It was a cyclic trend, the giving of self and needing to recover in quiet.

As I enjoyed the process of discovery, seeking out challenges and sharing the experience with others, I would find myself being sought after for advice, for coaching, for volunteer work and anything else in-between.

This is how things started in the first place; I went out and rode my bike, wanted to get better and was oblivious to the fact that anyone cared or was even watching.

But I was getting worn down by my role as coach and mentor. I chose to say no more often and take a stance on gaining back some of my time. The energy I once had to help others be their best was starting to wane, but it had nothing to do with those people; it was to do with me.

The many years of saying yes, jumping at opportunities, feeling obligated to deliver value and taking things far too personally had finally started to wear me down.

But I didn't truly recognise this yet, only feeling more uncomfortable with the responsibility I had. Creating a solid wall that was slowly creeping on my joy for life.

Even with my mental health slowly deteriorating, I found myself hooked on trail running, not for the glory but for the learning and the journey it gave me. The act of running quietened down my busy brain and gave me a similar focus that mountain biking did. Forcing me to move slower, enjoying every moment, smell and sight.

My reputation did not proceed me either; I was a nobody in this scene of ultra trail running.

Running with Tiffo on a trail event - so much fun

I had been dominating in my road racing, age group especially. Years of solo endurance training were showing up in solid results, especially in individual time trials.

And I also became a grandmother; Finley, my grandson, was born in late April.

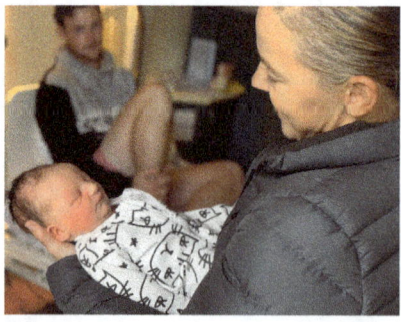

New born Finley - smitten

Norm and I had no idea what we were in for after Finley was born. We had been empty nesters for a good eight years, and apart from helping Saskia out with car issues, we had been free agents. We were cautious of James's and Saskia's space as new parents but quickly found they loved having us around, as did Finley.

With them living in Birregurra and us in Geelong, we often spent time, daily, on a video call with Saskia and Finley from a very young age. Playing games, puppeteering, playing with Max, our dog and playing Finley's favourite songs as well. It was safe to say, we were slowly falling deeply in love with our grandson and started a weekly regime of having him over once a week to give Saskia and James a 24hr break.

Our life was changing, and my goal posts were not just about training and racing.

It was the best thing to happen to both of us as we embraced this gradual transition into midlife. We constantly conversed about how lucky we were to have built up our small family together and now have our grandson to love and watch grow up.

For me, this certainly consolidated some of the unsettling feelings I was having more and more about what to do next. Motivation came from a different place, yet I was still caught in my past, but why? And how on earth could I change this? Was this all I was good at?

These questions were not answered yet, and the seeds had been planted.

Change was in the air and I barely rode my mountain bike anymore; it was my first love and used to be the primary source of enjoyment.

The other consistently present issue was this crazed energy and desire I had to achieve, only to get to the other end and be lost. What now? What was all that for anyway? Why bother? I am going to die in the end anyway? Is all this effort making any difference? This striving is ridiculous; who cares anyway? What matters in the end?

I was starting to experience the beginnings of burnout, with my lack of care, a large helping of apathy and many deep breaths every day to just get on with it.

My resolve was to stop thinking about me, to see the joy in the world through other people's experiences, and watch them smile and be happy in their journeys. Feeling lesser than by lowering my benchmarks, though I still felt bound by my reputation.

Of course, all these thoughts were my inner critic telling me I was no good anymore; seeking events, huge scary ones, was my way of shutting it up. So I kept searching for the same motivation I had when I was invested in winning world championships. Perhaps I would land on the pot of gold that would spark me back into the unstoppable Jess.

I liked her; I missed her and probably grieved for her. They were good times.

I had a great year; who would have known I thought I sucked?

I raced in a few long trail runs, including a 100km ultra marathon, finishing the year off with a 100 miler. I didn't finish that one, but I still achieved 100km; I had no regrets and loved it to pieces. I won many road races, including a national championship in the league I was racing.

Saskia and James got married in October; it was the most beautiful day for Norm and me.

Their wedding, the birth of their child all outshone any of my accolades.

The Individual Time Trial in Adelaide
Norm

Shortly into the new year, Norm and I travelled to Adelaide, where I possibly spent my last bit of energy. It was the Australian Veteran Cycling Championships, and I was there to win my age group again. I had smashed my training, feeling unstoppable, and I was. It was a clean sweep of the three road racing events. I won't deny, orchestrating such a convincing win was a lot of fun, and the holiday was great too.

> But on my return, I never quite found the same oomph again.
> As it turns out, it didn't matter anyway.
> By the end of March 2020, Australia was deep in the 'pandemic' of COVID-19.

I had also started a University degree; I was now doing it online and finding this part hard.

The past few months, I'd focused on my coaching business, my professional development and enjoying being a grandmother.

Racing on my mountain bike had long lost its shine; I hadn't touched it for a good six months.

Riding bikes and racing were not happening with the shutdown, so I invested in a smart trainer doing indoor workouts.

The last time I had these life direction challenges, it occurred to me that all I had to do was add value to the world.

It had been a significant challenge to understand who I was now, what was I striving towards, and what value am I to the world now? Change is uncomfortable, and it's definitely what I am experiencing now.

I was still a cyclist, yet I did not want that to go; what would I do if I didn't ride and race bikes?

But I also realised that my story is precisely what people resonated with its various hardships and vulnerabilities. It is also what helped me.

To avoid the limelight, I always found myself downplaying the wealth of experiences I've created throughout my life. The gift that comes with age. The wisdom gained from surviving the highs and all the lows. Every skill I now had, the past 47 years, brought me here. I was ready for change. I had the tools.

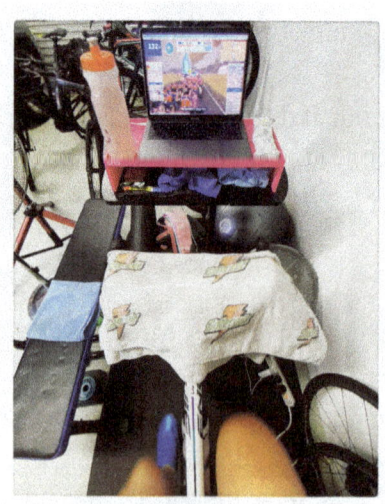

Pandemic? No sweat...bring on ZWIFT.

And so I took on 2020 - and the COVID 19 pandemic with gusto. I was born for this. Time to hunker down, nurture my introverted self and use this period to embrace a time to alter my direction. Re-energised by the prospect of no social expectations and the gift of time alone to achieve whatever I wanted was the most exciting thing in years. There were many not so enjoyable elements about the lockdown, but both Norm and I were secretly looking forward to days of immersing ourselves in our projects with little distraction.

Perhaps this was finally that time out needed to change direction and let go of the past?

I had been tuning into change for quite a few years, unsure of what was coming up next for me.

I used to know what I wanted and how to get it. Life is easy when you know your why; perhaps this forced time out would give me space to find that out again - I hoped.

Chapter 11 - Kintsugi; healing with Gold.

Kintsugi, the Japanese art of repairing pottery with gold to enhance the brokenness and make it more beautiful. The art relates well to us as imperfect beings, our healing and vulnerability, allowing the imperfections to reveal our fractured past. It is this that creates our uniqueness.

I was about to be broken; no longer could I hold my shit together.

By March of 2020, I began University, studying Bachelor of Exercise and Sport Science. Believing this was the next leap—age-proofing and upskilling as a coach. The commuter bike sorted, pannier bags, a lock, change of shoes and my pass for the bike room at uni. The stress-free 15 km bike path route meant I also got to ride. Uni life was exciting. I loved learning the nuts and bolts of human anatomy and physiology studies. I was in heaven. Then the beginning of COVID 19 hit Australia, uni life shut down, and online learning at home took place. I put the commuter bike away in the garage.

One day I was in the university courtyard, finding a spot to open my laptop and enjoy some pre-lecture study whilst eating lunch, and the next, I was at home, online, learning a new platform to exchange knowledge. I was sharing a small living room office setup with Norm; he General Managed away all day on Zoom calls. Living and working together from morning 'til night, day in day out, under lockdown and restrictions due to the pandemic, proved claustrophobic. We bought some expensive noise-cancelling headphones to aid in extra tolerance to do our work. Our daily life had become vastly different.

It seemed the world was scrambling to remain relevant in this climate; I began to feel myself, a nagging underlying anxiety. What would tomorrow's COVID updates say, and how many more days in lockdown? Would life ever resume as it was before? This anxiety was building in everyone.

Pressure and stress can force you to consider your choices that you might ignore if everything is hunky-dory. But things weren't the latter. I started to contemplate what the heck I was doing, my silly brain conjuring up scenarios of working in four years with the degree. Would I enjoy working in this sector later? Did it even matter? Who cares about elite performance anyway? I pushed on, reminding myself that I didn't have to be perfect; I just had to keep turning up. But the apathy was building; as I would sit in on the Zoom calls, I disengaged and spent time on other things unrelated to my studies. My ability to concentrate waned, as I often found myself daydreaming instead.

Out of the blue, the University sent out an email to inform the date that people could withdraw or defer from a course without penalty had been extended. This email was just what I needed; I postponed my studies until 2021. As soon as I made that decision, I was relieved. My views had changed; I knew it but dared not think about life without it. All this time alone, in amongst a pandemic, was the beginning of much change to come. Previous lessons in life had shown me that change was uncomfortable and often wrought with questionable actions; I was confident that I'd soon know where

I was heading, so long as I hung in there. Cycling, coaching, high performance, it was all intertwined with my identity. What would I do if not for this? What value was I?

Too much noise - Too little space. Iso life.

There was little time to think as my online coaching business grew during COVID. So much time at home, little or no socialising in person, I jumped into the world of virtual training with loads of enthusiasm. With my bike set up in the garage, using an online platform, Zwift. This platform became a large part of my social riding, allowing me to race my bike without being outdoors. I could train for hours if I wanted to. I rode virtual kilometres to rack up virtual sweat points spent on virtual bikes, wheels and other gear.

None of it mattered, but nothing seemed to matter at this time. As the months wore on, lockdowns were getting harder. But I continued, it is what I had always done—toughing it out, doing the hard work to reap the rewards. But it was all becoming far too concentrated. The sweet taste was initially enticing, ride any time of day, race any time you want, ride with whoever you want, as hard as you want - but like anything, too much of a good thing surely can't keep delivering the goods, right? But I was searching, still hoping to land on that magic path that would provide me with a true sense of purpose and identity.

Zwifting in the garage

I then transferred to a Bachelor of Psychology to start in July. I was searching hard for that meaning and purpose, grasping at anything that would send me forward and turn me into someone new. The online study with the Psychology degree, the online cycling platform, online coaching professional development courses, online coaching for my clients, Zoom classes, Zoom meetings all held in the virtual world. Connecting to people, whilst in our homes, in our safety bubbles, the experience was all-consuming. Glimmers of hope of lockdown ending, only to be shut down with COVID outbreaks.

Planning, looking forward to anything, was fraught with disappointment. To stay sane, I began to get outdoors daily, riding when and where I could regardless of the weather and aiming for the small things that gave me joy every day. As challenging as the situation was, this time was refreshing to magnify my focus to only a few small things that mattered.

> By late September, my state of bullshit was high. I had filled every void, striving to succeed, but why or what for? I quit my second attempt at university studies; this time, I withdrew from everything, no more deferrals.

The Victorian world of COVID had opened up slightly, and we could live again. Honestly, I was a mental mess. During this phase of the lockdowns, I had used all my resilience. Focused on being strong, I was starting to fatigue. Ambivalence and a nihilistic view on life were bubbling along nicely. I could no longer trust myself to make a good decision, flitting about from the next thing to the next, seeking peace from a feeling I would get when I found my place again.

One of my greatest strengths was about to do me in. As a coach, giving time, energy, and support to my clients aided in me carving a niche for myself. I was a friend, a mentor and became a weekly reinforcement to my client's wellbeing. It was just a natural progression for me to give. But with twenty clients to share my energy with and no one to offload to on my end, I was slowly depleting what I had left for me. I didn't realise it whilst it was happening, immersing myself in my role as coach, but slowly over time, the lines blurred - I was consumed in everyone else's life issues and ignoring my own. None of this was the fault of others; I allowed it, I didn't do anything to stop it. A week after, I decided not to make any phone calls to catch up; my energy levels perked up a notch. So I took another week of no calls for me and then another.

The hardest part of coaching during the pandemic was the various changes in lockdown, what people could and couldn't do, what events might or may not go ahead and what were we all training for anyway? The levels of purpose were all over the place, and each individual had their growing case of stress and anxieties, not just to do with their athletic goals but life in general. Coaching had just become a whole lot more complex than it ever had been. And so I persevered, but with a new strategy to stay energised and maintain self-care.

Iso haircuts - totally acceptable!

Norm and I were going a little crazy in our small two-bedroom unit, working in each others space, eating, living, and arguing a lot. The tapping of keyboards, the long meetings Norm would be in, my calls with clients, the messy kitchen only metres away, the unmade beds, the merging of life and work in our minimal space. Even with my noise-cancelling headphones, I found it challenging to concentrate with so much noise. It had become suffocating. With spare time on our hands and a strong need to change our current situation, we started to look around at what a larger house would look like for us. Where could we move, how much would it cost and did we have enough deposit? Would we have to sell our unit first? We saved up enough money to buy a new house. Yes, it was a lot of work; yes, we had to sell our unit first, but it worked, and we bought a new house with loads of room to live and work.

Toward the end of the year, I was still a mess. I had been here before, but I didn't have big race goals to work towards and give me purpose this time. Each day I would pop a new band-aid on, even though my wound was weeping.

> **My sense of self-loathing was at an all-time high, exhausted by the charades. I desperately needed time to stop and do nothing but didn't think I could do it and was too scared to try. Just like that, I fell out of love with racing my bike.**

Real-life racing was back on, no more virtual smash fests. I was looking forward to seeing how my hard work over winter would translate into reality. I showed up to my first race back. I recall feeling that male ego in our B grade bunch. The ego was intense; I could almost smell it. Had the lack of racing turned these men into hungry warriors? The vibe of the bunch was hatred and anger. Was it just me? Racing was no longer fun. My race result was ok, but more importantly, I hated the experience, but I vowed to turn up next week, improve my race tactics, and find the fun in it regardless of how others acted.

The following week came around; I was on the start line with an immense sense of regret as we pedalled off, wishing instead, to be riding around and not having to fight these warriors tonight.

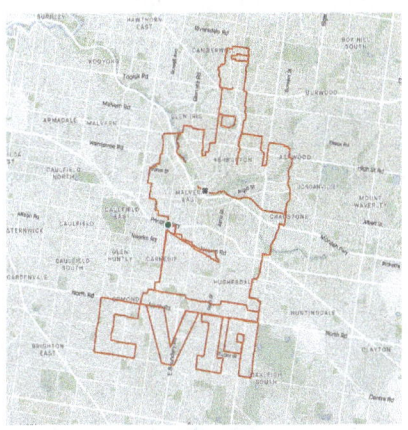

Some great Strava Art was going on at least
not mine - not sure who did it

Then it happened, the race finished, as was I. The fight, the pre-race nerves became debilitating, and I was angry at other people whilst I was racing. One minute it was all about how much power I could produce, what position I could place, how good it felt to be strong, and the very next moment, it was like I realised that none of it mattered. I was only ever doing it for me, to prove I could and get lost in the process of bettering myself.

I never showed up to another race. Though I kept pursuing indoor virtual racing as part of a women's Team Trial Team, this was fun. No more university stress; that was bliss and an increase in coaching clients.

Making time for family, Finley sleepovers, a few social engagements, do we dare dream of planning anything more? Move house, sell a home, buy a new one, finance, forms and bank approvals. But just as life was looking sweet, I did something silly. Just as I felt that being comfortable was ok, I got a job at a bike shop in Hoppers Crossing in the middle of COVID cycling retail mayhem.

> Would this change me? Would this add value to my life? Why was I so hell-bent on remaining relevant?

It was as if the only way I could prove my worth was through toil and sufferance—my signature trait, to outlast and endure. I shunned the concept of comfort and mediocracy by inviting trials of hardship, but this time I was not racing my bike or running 100 miles across the Victorian Alps. The bike shop was 70 km away, so I chose to ride each day and then catch the train home, selling this concept to myself as a way to escape and meditate before being annihilated in the trenches, otherwise known as work.

When I applied for the job online and got a phone call twenty minutes later and an interview there and then, the urgency of the situation became apparent. I got the job and started only a day or two later. The bike industry was being crushed, especially in Melbourne. People were buying into an idea, a reason to get out and exercise on local paths that gave them time to have fun and feel free, if only for an hour or two on the weekend. People were also riding to work, deciding that whilst the roads were quiet, or trains were packed, as summer was here, the commute on a bike was a great way to stay safe from the virus and enjoy life a smidge more each day. Whatever the reason people were buying bikes, it was insane. I had no idea what I had said yes to and barely had a moment to think about what had just happened. From day one, I was swimming hard, every single second of every single day I worked. With only particular stock left to sell, long, very long lead times for bikes on order and a line of people that never ended. Cranky customers, waiting too long, not enough staff, not enough stock, not enough of anything.

Lunch breaks would happen whenever they could, often much later in the day, or sometimes not at all. I had not been in the winter lockdown working at the shop. But apparently, this level of crazy had been going on all year long. I was astounded by the resilience of the long term staff. How had they found this kind of work enjoyable? How did they keep showing up each day?

In the beginning, I put it down to being a new staff member, learning the ropes. I wanted to let Norm know that I was doing well, but I would have been lying. I felt like a failure each day. I was not opposed to hard work, long hours, and the unpredictable nature of retail; in fact, I thought it was enjoyable to be under the pump. Day after day, without any sign of relief, was a whole new experience for me. There was a day, well, a few days, but one I remember well. It got busy, super busy, it was December, and it was coming up to Christmas. We were all serving customers without even drinking water before the next person locked eyes with you to help them now. It was hectic. Being bombarded in the trenches, and we couldn't get out, no matter what. They just kept coming. I remember looking at the eyes of senior staff, the ones that had trained me. They looked scared, exhausted, in shock, with genuine fear in their eyes.

> Being busy in retail is exhilarating, but this was debilitating. We were no good to anyone, yet pushed on with a sense of obligation because that's what you do; it's why you are in customer service.

Each day I worked, my godsend was the commute on bike, keeping me sane as I had my dose of meditation. Cycling 70 km, I would leave home at 5:00 am, watching the sunrise; quality time alone was perfect to set me up for my workday of war games. Only a week in, I began to wonder why I needed to work like this? I was selling bikes to people out of a sense of urgency, not because it was best for them. It was all any of us could do. I didn't even need the money; I was choosing to work here. But each day, I would show up and hope it would change, that I would get better. Maybe it would slow down a bit, and I could enjoy the customer engagement and sales process. I was still coaching as well, using the train ride home to write notes, responding to my clients, and on my days off, I would update programs to catch up. Of course, it was unsustainable, but how bad would it look, me quitting, again? I had to give it a red hot go; maybe relief was just around the corner?

For the first time in a very long time, I started to drink. Only a glass of wine at night to wind down. Living with a recovering alcoholic, I was well aware of what I was doing, promising myself to keep tabs on not letting this turn into a case of self-medication, numbing myself from my situation. Some days, as I rode to work, I wondered how I could stop this. I didn't have to show up; I could just call up and quit. But, my whole year had been a series of failures. My ego kept me going for fear of what others would think, meanwhile, the workload was crushing my spirit.

Eventually, after six weeks, I quit. It hurt me to do so, my ego bruised, but it was the right decision. What on earth had I just done for the past month and a half? It was exactly like a bike packing race or an adventure race. There was much suffering to prove I could go to new places I may never have otherwise. And just like that, I was free again. But I was also homing in closer to a sense of peace. We had moved into our new house whilst working. And with that done, I could finally enjoy my new neighbourhood, my new house. I had heard a local bike shop was under the pump, so I contacted the owner. I enjoyed this space, helping customers and learning new skills. Within a week, I was working again, only parttime and a twenty-minute bike ride from home. I had a life again. Time to ride my bike for fun. Time to do almost anything, as well as work. The balance felt manageable, and most importantly, sustainable long term and the crew and boss were all lovely people. Even though bikes were still in high demand, the flurry and hurry of most customers was a lot more low key. I honestly was feeling a sense of peace and contentment. Our new house was excellent, the balance between work and play was perfect, and I still had time to manage my coaching clients and the work I needed to do. I had loads of time to ride bikes and still had no desire to race them, so really, I could do whatever I wanted these days.

Freedom rides with Norm

It was January 2021; I had decided last year not to do the Otway Odyssey. The 100km mountain bike race had been my benchmark event for the past 14 years. I'd considered just showing up and hanging out at the back of the field, just to keep ticking over my race attendance. My instincts told me just to let it go. It was time to move on. The funny thing is when I let that be so, there was no pang of regret or what if; the feeling was one of freedom. Finally, I was making decisions not based on my past and expectations. However, I had said yes to another yearly responsibility. I said yes because previously, I had enjoyed it, not for egotistical reasons, but for the camaraderie within the volunteers, the experience away and the enjoyment of helping others.

The event was the Peaks Challenge at Falls Creek. I'd been a volunteer for a few years now with Bicycle Network and found the association and work enjoyable and rewarding. Peaks was a big ride, 245 km in the Victoria Alps and to be there to help riders reach their goals on the day had become a yearly pilgrimage.

Thankfully, the COVID-19 pandemic had slowed down enough in Australia for life to resume to a welcome sense of normality, and events were happening again. People were excited to get striving again, to get stuck into some chunky goals. On the other hand, as an athlete and coach, I was fighting off years of fatigue, convincing myself that I needed to stay relevant in the world of cycling. If I wasn't racing, I needed to keep coaching and all options open, as this was my livelihood and who I was. If I wasn't Jess, the cyclist and coach, then what?

2020 had worn me down, flip-flopping about on my trajectory and having to do so for my clients as goalposts constantly changed, events cancelled, and restrictions were forever evolving. The moral support I was giving to my clients was tremendous; I knew at the time that it would drain me of my energy, but I felt compelled to keep my clients engaged. I was afraid of losing them. My greatest fear was that I would no longer coach because I had slowly unsubscribed from caring deep down. Not because I didn't want the best for my clients, but I had given so much for so long; the pressure of the pandemic, lockdowns, cancellations and my inner struggles just brought it all ahead. I was now fatigued and had not much motivation to invest in others.

There was a change in the air. The Peaks Challenge commitment involved taking a training ride as a volunteer. A couple of years ago, I took a ride down on the Great Ocean Road, an incredible 200 km loop with loads of climbing and beautiful scenery. At this stage, early February, the actual goal event was only four weeks away. A fantastic opportunity to test the legs and gain confidence that Peaks Challenge was going to be possible.

In the lead-up, interest was high for this ride, even with cyclists from Melbourne. Perhaps a chance to visit the beach and go for a ride made for a winning weekend away for many. I had met a customer in the local bike shop I was working at. He had ridden a few of our Chase the Dog events back in the day in Forrest. He was going to come along too, as he had been training for Peaks since last March. A local Torquay outdoorsman, good at everything, was super excited to ride a local route in preparation for the big ride in March. This training ride in February and the Peaks Challenge in March were my only events planned for 2021, and I had already decided that this would be my last year of involvement.

It was Sunday, February the 7th. It was the middle of summer, but down on the Great Ocean Road, you can get any weather system, and you need to be ready for it. I had spent a reasonable amount of time putting some guidelines to with Bicycle Network and my resources on the day.

Things to consider when riding in bunches in the Otways, safety, descending, weather, eating, drinking, what to carry, cycling etiquette and more. I also needed to ensure the riders knew what to do if something happened, as it was just me leading the ride today. Thankfully I had some of my coaching clients in attendance; a few extra riders had my back and knew how things rolled in these kinds of bunch rides. We rolled off around 7:30 am, with the promise of all the weather systems, wind, rain, sun and everything else in-between—a 200 km group ride. As happens, we split into groups. The 10 km climb out of Lorne helped decide this nevertheless, and the day would move along like this, groups of the same ability riding together before regrouping at intersections or food stops. As we approached the climb out of Forrest, I suspected it would be cold and wet up on the ridge and was grateful for my jacket. Everyone was in great spirits and ready to smash down all the food at Lavers Hill. After reminding the groups to descend off Lavers with caution and to regroup at Apollo Bay, we got going again, shivering off the ridgeline until we warmed up again. Loads more climbing to make that happen. The vibe of the group was magic—what a great bunch of people. It is why I would volunteer for these things, meet and ride with them, feel energised and inspired by their stories, which I got to listen to loads of during the day.

One story stood out to me and others as well—let's call him Luke. On the Labour Day long weekend, back in March 2020, he had been up at Falls Creek riding his mountain bike and was instantly intrigued by the Peaks Challenge road event. He hung around at the finish chute until the last riders were in, and it was dark and cold. He watched them with excitement, conjuring up the dream that this would be his next year. He bought a bike, got training and signed up as soon as he could. 'Luke' had been involved in the great outdoors his whole life, so choosing a challenge like this was just part and parcel of but a small chapter of fun epic adventures. Doing this on the mountains where he loved to ski in winter and ride in summer was very fitting. Such a humble guy, so excited to be reaching his goal, full of energy and enthusiasm for life. He spoke to many people on this day, sharing his inspiring story of why he was here.

We were ¾ of the way through the ride as we arrived at Apollo Bay; time to eat, go to the toilet, refill bottles, and we would be back in Lorne in no time. Only 45km to go and a terrific WSW wind to push us back along the coastline, we would be sure to up the average speed and be back in around 1.5 hours. The promised tailwind was there, pushing us home. A wonderfully supportive group had formed, and I was in the middle of it. We were all enjoying this final bit of magic along the Great Ocean Road. No need to go too hard now. We were a troop who had worked together all day long, ridden through rain, toiled up long climbs and spent time getting to know each other.

Closing in on our halfway mark back to Lorne, our bunch settled in, but as we reached the base of a slight climb to Cape Patton, I decided to stay at the front of the group. Purely to have a clear road in front of me to descend on the other side and into Grey River. Not a long nor challenging climb, a bit of gradient change split the group up for the meantime as we settled into a tempo to suit fitness and ability. As we rolled down the other side, the lovely tailwind was now a mix of wind gusts coming off the headland, nothing unusual, but I took it easy here. I led the group to this point; there is only so much you can do to ensure each person rides to the conditions and ability. It is such a relief to regroup and find that everyone is ok and off you go again. It was always a laughing point at the start of the ride and on all rides I have ever officially led or instructed. But in all seriousness, I always warned the riders about avoiding the need to call an ambulance. Today was no different; the more you ride, the greater the chance that shit will hit the fan one day. I have said this before, many times.

I had feathered my brakes to back off my speed as I felt the wind come off the headland of Cape Patton. Nothing too alarming, but enough to make me decide on a cautious descent. I hoped that no one was sitting right on my wheel as I slowed down a bit. I was about to keep veering left and would soon be heading inland for a short bit when I heard the most gut-wrenching noise.

I knew I was about to call an ambulance. My heart sank. I wanted to pretend this was not happening and that if I had made it around the next corner, I would have never heard it. If I had been in the bunch in front, we would now be heading to Lorne. If I had pushed hard to catch up to a rider in front that broke away up Cape Patton, I would have left this for someone else to deal with today.

> The noise, the sound of crunching metal, the sound of impact and chaos and then silence.

A few of us who were in front of the incident were still descending. We cautiously came to a stop. We were a few small turns down the road, and the visual was unclear about what had just happened. Someone said to me, shall I call the ambulance? I say yes. Today is now the day I have dreaded; it's here. My brain has instantly gone into acceptance mode. Something terrible has happened, and I am going to have to deal with it. We start to ride up to the scene, and then I see it. My brain is working overtime, all the things that have to be done, but also trying to understand the situation of the body on the road. From about 100 metres away, I am still confused, and as I get closer, I can see that it is 'Luke'.

All the other riders start to come on the scene, and a few people call ambulances. It's going to be a while before we see one, though. There is so much going on, though. 'Luke' is on the road, and his body doesn't make sense. His bike is to the right of him, looking almost rideable. There are details in the scene before me, unimaginable trauma. None of it helps me better understand how and what occurred. I could only speculate. There was no redemption back to life from what took place today.

> A suffocating sense of hopelessness envelops me; this is out of my realm.

Snapping into action mode, I was now worried about the entire situation; we were on the Great Ocean Road, and cars were banking back, trying to pass the scene. We need people to manage this. I ask a few riders to help out here; we all need to get in and work it best we can. Drivers stop and help; amazingly, there are nurses and other health professionals right there with us—a couple who have been surfing offer up pillows for the crew doing CPR. Many people were helping and doing their bit.

There is a car; it is ahead of the rider on the ground. The driver is out, and he is hysterical. David, Kym, Rob and Liv are attending to 'Luke'. I went to talk to the driver. Someone else comes to take over from me. I have just seen two riders over on the other side of the road and a broken bike. It's Ren and Darren. Ren saw it all; Darren couldn't avoid 'Luke's' bike as it kept moving after the impact. Darren was ok, shaken, speechless and alive. There were other casualties now. We are all part of the most traumatic thing we will ever experience in a long time to come, and there is no getting out of it.

> **The scene is horrific, but everyone is doing their bit. 'Luke' is not going to make it today, and when the paramedics arrive, they confirm this. He has died, this information we already knew.**

The police arrive too, and I share with one of the officers who the rider is. He was known to a few of them, including the surfers. It is such a shock. The scene on the road stays there; official work is yet to happen with detectives and the coroner to come. A police officer took our names and numbers; we would need to prepare reports of what we saw and remember. I am waiting like a captain of a ship until I know that Darren is ok as he is getting taken by ambulance to get checked over. Ensuring all details are complete with the police, David and I are waiting for Norm to come and get us. We are also taking Darren's broken bike. Then the people who can, and have to, slowly and somberly ride back to their cars in Lorne. The day turned from magic to mayhem, just like that, and no one saw it coming.

I wasn't making sense to Norm as he arrived. David had been doing the breaths for CPR and was exhausted, but we were both in a hyper survival mode. Adrenaline helps us to make sense of what has just happened. We got back to Lorne, met up with a few others, went and had something to eat, and attempted to debrief before driving home. No one can prepare for this; none of us were trauma specialists, though a few had seen the aftermath from a professional view. We were a band of soldiers, the troops coming home from battle, where we all fought for each other's lives, and saw things we never want to see again. Now we had seen the unseeable; we could never unknow this.

What to do now? How do you move on from this trauma?

There was so much input from people and well-meaning support, but not all of it was helpful. Survivor guilt sets in; why him, what could have we done to prevent this? All the scenarios and what-ifs. I wasn't the only one going through this, as Darren and Ren had seen it all from behind and made it out alive, with horrific visuals to last them a lifetime, and the group looked after him; could they have done anything to bring him back to life?

I was aware that the people around me needed support, I needed help, we all just needed to know there was nothing more we could have done and that what we did was enough. My coaching clients and I caught up again in a few days at my house to purge out what we could and share our support for each other. I took the week off work and vowed to start my healing, but I had no idea what this would be. Bicycle Network CEO Craig made contact, and he and Bec came and visited me. Support coming from everywhere. Everyone had my back. All the help in the world would not assist me unless I knew what to do with it. In the first week, all I did was spend time on the phone talking to people who offered. My instinct told me to keep talking about it, don't try to solve this or see reason, just be open to what others are offering. Unsure of the outcome, I just let go and shared my pain, knowing it would somehow help me.

I was acutely aware that 'Luke' had bestowed me a gift; as he left this world, this pause I was giving myself was not to be rushed. It was his extreme loss of life; ensuring this was honoured, I listened and decided to heal, not just from what happened but from every bit of suffering I had quashed inside over the years. I never went back to work at the bike shop.

The next day I made an appointment with a new GP, as I had many things to sort out, and I crossed my fingers she would be the right one to listen. My problems were many, but I felt that my most pressing issue was sleep. If I could get this in a better place, other areas of my health would have a greater chance of improvement. So I shared with my GP what was on my mind, day and night, since the incident. I also shared with her the lifetime of depression and how I have dealt with it previously. Mostly, I was fearful of putting on my strong armour and pushing through like a bad arse in my current state. For the first time in like, forever, I knew this was a shift, a pivotal moment to make a change. The kind of transformation that I had been sensing for so long now. I had a bloody good cry, not just for my pain or the incident that occurred that fateful day, but also for the happiness I had seeping in my pores. I could sense hope, I felt the warmth of the sun on my back, and I felt worthy. But the consult didn't stop there; we had menopausal issues to sort, blood tests to organise, a full health check to book in, and my blood pressure was a bit high too.

Lucky me, I had just landed on the best GP I had ever consulted. I walked away today with a mental health plan, a psychologist booking, a script for hormone replacement therapy, a goal to reduce blood pressure, a blood test, a mammogram, a booking for a full health check and most importantly, a new sense of hope for the next phase. It had been eight days since the tragedy, and my first psychology appointment revealed many things to me. I had become so exhausted on many levels. The compassion that used to come so freely to me turned into apathy. Despite what may have appeared to the outside world, I struggled to find meaning and purpose in my life. I was not suicidal, but I wanted relief. I wanted a break from my life as I lacked energy and enthusiasm, even though I was doing my best to fake this to everyone.

Before COVID and all the many lockdowns in Victoria, my level of empathy and compassion was high. As a coach, I enjoyed this part of the job. I was helping people become their best versions of themselves. But that concentrated period where everyone was suffering to some degree, including me, slowly wore me down. I suspect I had been on the way to this for some time. But 2020, in all its glory, brought me there a smidge quicker than anticipated. Life was losing its glow. My daily grind was finding something to be grateful for and focusing on that. I started to withdraw from people and their joy, for in my mind, all I could see was the end game, that nothing mattered; we would all die anyway. It angered me to listen to petty gripes about not going on holiday or cancelling a race again, or anything trivial. I was desperate for an exit point, but in the meantime, I persevered. In this psychology appointment, so many of my hidden pains came to the surface as I babbled out everything for an entire hour. As I drove home, my mind and body felt separate, and I was numb all over like I had just taken some kind of drug. Norm wanted to know how it went; all I could do was cry; there were no words;

the pain had started to seep out through my cracks. All he could do right now was be there for me.

I tried my best to be there for my coaching clients who had been there on that day. Even if just to listen to how they were doing. But as far as my clients striving towards events and fitness goals, it was becoming a challenge to align myself with caring. I cared for them as a person. However, my apathy would seep through when events were cancelled because, after all, it was just an event. I had stopped making phone call appointments to catch up in an attempt to avoid listening to any life problems. I just couldn't take on any more. All I could do now was to look after myself, do my best for my clients as best I could with what energy I had. I hoped they could feel this, and I wished for a sense of joy again.

In the same week of my psych appointment was the yearly event of the Otway Odyssey. Norm was an MC, so he would be driving down to Apollo Bay and then back up for the finish at Forrest. I was ready to ride my bike on the Great Ocean Road and revisit the scene. As I watched the start of the mountain bike race that I would always do, I felt no pangs of missing out. Instead, it was a feeling of relief that I had moved on from this yearly commitment. I had always thought I owed others to be there because it's what I had always done, but today I released myself from that self-imposed obligation. I felt free, and a different glow of warmth appeared on my back, one of new hope and new direction; I could be whoever I wanted. My past no longer defines me, and my future is full of opportunities I have not explored yet.

Today, there were no expectations about visiting the scene where he died, but I was experiencing a hurricane of emotions. Instead of trying to control them, I let them swirl around inside, creating all sorts of physical responses. At one point, I was breathless, feeling a bit of panic, so it was time to focus on breathing, gaining back control. My legs would feel lacklustre up a climb, so I would get out of the saddle and climb, allowing the focus to be on a steady rhythm. I wondered how I would feel when I got to the spot. Would I recoil, would I cry, would I cope?

Almost deliberately, I took my time, soaking in the beauty of cycling on the Great Ocean Road and enjoying the quiet hour, where traffic was low, allowing the sites and sounds of the ocean on my right to dominate my thoughts. However, this next phase, the revisiting of 'the spot', I knew it was part of my recovery. To make sense of that day without the confusion of people, cars, and the horror of what happened.

As I descended the same part of the road, coming down off Cape Patton, my heart was in my throat; I almost couldn't breathe as I anticipated the worst. Panic had well and truly set in. There I was, not a car in sight; the sun was glistening on the horizon as I listened to the comforting sound of the waves crashing on the rocks below. The panic disappeared, and now I understood and made sense of the day only a few weeks ago. The stark realisation of how life comes and goes, how time keeps moving and how all space retains the history and will, in time, melt away. I had carried a paint texta and wrote a note on a sign nearby, for me, to never forget.

As I rode onto Lorne, I envisaged an alternate reality, where we had safely progressed past that endpoint and made it back, with happy banter of what a great day it had been. Everyone on that day, including 'Luke' and his loved ones, the driver, the emergency services people, the people who stopped on the road to help, how had this impacted them? Each crossroad we meet, each decision we make or encounter with the world and its cogs will place us in a direction. Some of our most significant angst in life comes from fighting this and wishing it was otherwise. Instead, some of our most powerful moments of peace and contentment can come from acceptance and using these moments as gifts.

I then rode back to Forrest to see the end of the Otway Odyssey, via the same way I came, stopping again at Cape Patton and making peace with this space and with me. I was glad for my own company on this day, to ride in total harmony, with my senses alert to the sounds of nature, my breathing and soaking in the beauty of being outdoors. I arrived at Forrest, said a few hellos and Norm and I went home.

The following week was 'Luke's' memorial, on a magnificent property down in the gullies of Spring Creek, at the back of Torquay. COVID restrictions for group gatherings had just been lifted, which made this possible.

The location rendered a very peaceful ambience, yet the space held a deep history of a time long ago. The welcome to country by local indigenous people exuded a sense of protection for use on the day.

Such gratitude for being here, witnessing his remarkable life, and listening to his wife, family, and friends share his adventures. Being there was a magnificent display of how one person is so intertwined with so many others. That all of our days intersect with countless people and many more experiences. Our needs, goals and aspirations are not linear, and the impact of our time on this earth is more profound than we can ever measure or imagine.

The following week I headed to Falls Creek to be a volunteer rider at Peaks Challenge, the event we were all training for on that fateful day. Darren, who had crashed on that day, would be there to ride with 'Luke's' number and other clients who had been there as well. We all had our reasons for attending. I still wasn't feeling it but hoped just by availing myself that something would click, and my enthusiasm would just click into place. It never did. So I let the people around me be excited, grateful for the opportunity to be up in the mountains on a beautiful weekend with beautiful friends.

My coaching clients and a few others went for a short easy ride the day before; the energy was supportive and friendly, we were all looking forward to the ride and enjoying each others company, no egos, no agendas. But all around us, we watched riders doing stupid things as though they owned the road, with little concern for oncoming cars or other people. The road was full of large bunches of riders doing as we were, creating a mob mentality. It annoyed me profusely, feeling anger towards these riders who seemed to not care about the consequences. The disdain for large group riding had always been there for me, especially with social groups with lots of egos and reckless behaviour. But today, I was super sensitive to it. My riding had also become very conservative, I could tell. Every noise, every potential action where things could go wrong, I was hearing it and seeing it, and I could feel every muscle fibre in my body cringing in preparation for the outcome. Yet nothing happened.

> I was here, on the mountain, but I wasn't. I was a spectator to everything, listening and making commentary in my head about how insignificant all the hustle and bustle was.

I patiently waited to get excited about the 245km bike ride tomorrow, the task I would be undertaking to support other riders out there. Instead, I wanted to disappear, perhaps use this time to go for a long bushwalk by myself instead. The next day arrived, up early, preparing everything for the ride and down to the start line. Yes, it was a beautiful morning, and it was enjoyable to watch other people being excited, but I couldn't get there myself. I wanted this to be over before it had started. This was one of those days; all I had to do was live through it, and tomorrow I could get on with life.

The time came for our group to roll off; it was a very long mountain descent to start the day. The roads are closed, and personally, it's the scariest part of the day. Everyone is passing, and some are taking questionable line choices at devastating speeds. I am not that kind of descender on the best of days, but today my reaction to everyone around me was to slow right down and get out of the way. Oh, the pain of going so slow. It wasn't just the speed hindering my progress; I had started to feel an anxiety attack, my breathing shallow, I felt hot and couldn't take on air properly. I unzipped the top of my jacket to relieve my neck and let in the fresh air, then realised what was happening.

Regaining control of the situation, I told myself, you know how to descend, take the lines you want, own your space, and breathe. And like that, I was back. I took my mind off what it was searching for, which was a hypersensitivity to danger. I had been zoning in on minute detail of peoples wheels, the fingers on their handlebars, all in super fine detail. I made it to the bottom, adrenaline pulsating through every part of me. I had a mind-body dissociation; I was numb.

Now it started to happen, other riders asking questions, wanting to talk, weaving in and out of my space, giving me the shits. One hour into the ride, I was ready to tell the entire group around me to piss off and leave me alone; in fact, I wanted to turn around, head back up the mountain and end it there. But I continued, I have suffered like this before and magically come good, you just never know, it is early days. I got slower, crankier and less engaged as we went along. When I finally saw Craig and Fiona, from the Bicycle Network team, part way up Mt Hotham, they asked if I was ok. I was not. And I just let loose and started crying, all the emotions coming out. Craig said I could get a lift, I didn't need to go on, but instead, I wanted to become invisible and took my 12-hour wave rider bib off and continued. Eventually, making it to Dinner Plain, with about 120 km down, I finally quit. I was at the halfway point, exhausted from not just the physical effort but the emotional toll. Now I could let it go as the tears flowed. My heart ached for me; why was I doing this to myself?

Why did I always feel obligated? Why did I have to be so resilient all the time? Why couldn't I accept that I was suffering and needed a freaking good hug and a hefty dose of time out from life and all my responsibilities? This moment, where I gave myself an out, was pivotal to what would come next. I was glad to be off my bike and at peace with my decision. I drove home on Monday as swiftly as possible, needing Norm and a big hug. I had to talk to him about what had happened and unpack where I was in the healing process. There was a massive shift occurring, and I wanted to honour what was happening before it got lost in the bustle of living.

The next few weeks were eventful, Norm's mum passed away, and he flew to Darwin for the funeral. I signed off on my Police statement for the accident. I also had a CPR update, which triggered a PTSD response. Then one random day, I went on a ride by myself. This ride was the next turning point, and I had no idea it would turn out this way.

There is a period when the brain buzzes, and thoughts and feedback responses churn at a constant rate. It often happens, out riding my bike, or a long run or walk through nature. This experience is far from enjoyable, similar to having the tv turned on, with music as well, the dog barking, and someone wanting to have a conversation whilst you are trying to find peace in a corner somewhere. Every speck of dust is pulsating with noise, and the only way to shut it up is to let it run out of energy. The more I fight it, the more hectic it becomes, so I let it run its course. Most times, the peace comes, but always as a surprise as my thoughts become solid yet soft and singular. One idea can sit there for a long time before I realise I am thinking it. That is what happened today.

> The words spoke to me, I ignored them, I read them to myself again, silently in my mind, and I had to repeat it, just one more time. What was I hearing, and why had this idea surfaced today?
>
> "Jess, you need to give up your coaching business, and this will give you space to heal and the opportunity to reveal new possibilities."

I meditated on this for the remainder of the ride, knowing it must have been there in my deep subconscious and interested in exploring it more. Not sharing this with anyone, it all still felt far too vulnerable. But the scary thing was, it felt right. There was no need to act upon it, only to give it some air. For the next couple of weeks, I would entertain this concept, exploring the outcomes but not becoming overly invested - just yet.

Meanwhile, I found myself content with less, leaving space in my diary for nothing. Though I still felt mildly conflicted about this, I vowed to give doing less a red hot go. Towards the end of April, I finally built up the courage to talk to Norm about my epiphany to quit coaching. I told him about the random thought that entered my mind one day and what did he think? It was instantaneous, his reaction.

"Then let it be so", he said.

"Do it. I fully support you, and we will be fine; it is the right time for you, Jess."

So that day, I entertained the best and worst-case scenarios. The only thing holding me back now was a feeling of obligation and letting down my clients. But to move forward, it was up to me to make this change, which would require some discomfort. My clients were beautiful; some saw it coming, others didn't, but they understood and took it as a time for a change in their lives as well. And just like that, life went on. I could now plan for life without coaching.

> Initially, I felt my ego get a hit and just let it be so. It was time for me to let go.

I had a clean out of gear as well. I cancelled some online training memberships, sold a few indoor trainers, sold two bikes, and felt relieved to have this clutter out of my life. My past, everything I had achieved, was there for me to cherish, but I no longer felt the need to keep proving my relevance. I was free, and the possibility of my future was endless. All the while, Norm and I had been planning a cycling holiday. We had hoped to do this in 2020, but it never happened because of bushfires and then COVID.

More adventures await

The timing was perfect. One week after announcing the news to my coaching clients, we were off on this holiday. These seven days away, riding bikes, enjoying life, immersing myself in micro-moments of time slows everything down, helping me reset and filling my days with other priorities to keep the mind busy. I couldn't recall the last time I had been able to do something like this without constant worry about business matters, so it took a few days and loads of riding chatter with Norm to accept that I was at a huge turning point. Possibly the most challenging part was to stop planning and just live right now, not to invest in tomorrow, but in today. Again, this time out was the perfect catalyst for accepting change.

Norm had been pushing me for ages to get writing my book again, to immerse myself in it. Since starting in July the year prior, I had made good progress with a first draft start of 40,000 words. And then the investment went stone-cold; I had lost momentum with university studies and work, and then that overwhelming apathy started to consume me. I just couldn't find the reason to write; my inner critic kept reminding me that no one would want to hear my story; what does it matter anyway? After returning home from the cycling holiday, I knew I had the perfect platform to get started again. My idea was to write a blog for each day on the bike, with a bit of a story behind it and when I finished day seven, get onto the book the very next day.

So I did. But as soon as I started writing again, I realised why I had stopped in the first place. To relive your life and express that time for a reader to understand requires deep introspection, and I had ceased writing at the point where life started to get a little insane. Norm and I had been under the pump and experiencing depression, even among all the fantastic things. To relive this was exhausting. But I kept true to myself.

Writing about these few years was genuinely demanding. One word at a time, just purging it out of my mind, onto my keyboard. Many times I had to walk away and rest or put my head in my hands and sob. I was crying for me; I knew that pain so intimately. I cried because I wanted to hug Jess and let her know she was worthy and what a great job she was doing in life, and how courageous she was and that I was so proud of her.

It then occurred to me that I was doing my own therapy, and it was free, and I was ultimately enjoying the process undeterred by the hard work. I cancelled my future psychologist appointments, employed myself and my methods of the 1% rule, and got on with the book. Write for one hour a day, every day. No word limits; just purge it out.

The next phase of writing another 60,000 words only took five months. It became a daily practice that I enjoyed again, waking at 4:30 am to get the best out of me. I thought less and less about escaping life and found I had replaced it with an immense sense of pride for all I have done and achieved. My inner critic quietened down, reducing my self-loathing quite a lot. I always knew they were lies, and just voices in my head, not reality, but turning down the volume was always a challenge. Now I can not only lower the noise, but I can also turn it off completely.

I am still finding it difficult to strive less and finding a purpose to combat this; I have been reminding myself to live for today; tomorrow doesn't matter yet. Instead of filling my days with ten or more things to accomplish, I have lowered my expectations to one or two solid and meaningful goals. I choose to punctuate my days with self-care and downtime, which could be a walk, a run, drawing, cooking, or nothing. During this time, my brain still buzzes with all the possibilities of life, ideas, and things I want to achieve, which is very distracting. Still, I am getting better at letting the energy dissipate on its own, like atoms buzzing around in my head, eventually running out of power.

As in a fable, I have come to realise the magnitude of all that encompassed my life. What started as a simple story about my world championship wins had become so much more. The answers had been there all along, but I needed to live it and find out on my own. That is the way most of us learn, to find out the hard way and develop wisdom retrospectively.

I am so proud of my persistence; I have chosen to grow and learn even under enormous adversity. Even when I have been in my most profound darkest depression, I have decided to seek help or find an alternative, as painful as it was. My resilience toolbox is quite extensive as a result, and I now know how to use it.

But possibly the most valuable life lesson has been to narrow my focus.

Funny that!

The whole story of learning to become a world champion started with exactly that, a simple 1% methodology. It focused on one thing at a time, with small chunks of time, over a long time, with a result compounding slowly and organically with continuous and consistent investment. It was that simple all along. It always has been.

Yes, it was a lot of hard work, but that didn't mean it wasn't fun. To achieve something spectacular, you need to put the work in and go beyond what you have ever done before. And oh, it is such a wonderful space to be in! I had gotten caught up in the success of it all.

Opportunities flooded my life, and what a blessing that was.

The dissonance was nothing more than feeling out of alignment with myself. It had pushed me well outside of my comfort zone. How bloody lucky am I?

To have been given a chance to be someone special, to do things that only others dream?

To inspire, teach, lead, and be a woman who did some marvellous things in her life!

The journey started with cracking the code, the 1% rule. But the real journey has been in persistence despite the hardships. Or perhaps because of this. LIFE is the proving ground to test out theories and to keep growing and learning. Evolving is such a beautiful gift as I keep living the rest of my wonderful life.

It seems like a bit of an anti-climax to get to the end like this.

I was never afraid or refraining from being broken; I just never realised all the gold in my life experiences was there, all along, to place the pieces back together. I was creating something even more beautiful, the cracks highlighting, not hiding, the imperfections.

I know what to do next; these last 48 years have provided me with everything I need.

I have finished my apprenticeship, and now the best is yet to come.

30th Wedding Anniversary 'business class' flight to enjoy some sunshine - Not Viotorial

Epilogue

It is December 2021. I started writing this book in the middle of 2020, thinking it would be done by the end of that year, instead, I wrote for about 3 months. Writing about yourself is hard work, and I reached a point in my recollections where it was all too much and I was exhausted.

> I told Norm, "I need a break, I will come back to it with a fresh outlook in a few weeks, I promise."

Well, it wasn't until March 2021 that I got back into it and it still wasn't any easier to get past where I left off. If you have read the contents you will know, life was full-on. At the time, it was mind-blowing, yet also suffocating, yet also beautiful. How blessed was I? I truly was living my best life. I didn't know how to say NO, but it was also conversely a positive trait, for without all the yesses where would I be today?

Starting my book again in 2021 only came about due to a life-changing experience, the road fatality I was a part of in February. As soon as it happened, I knew I needed to press PAUSE. Through this tragedy, I was allowing myself to heal, not just from what had happened on this day, but to finish this book and purge out the pain that I was holding inside. I had been strong for so long, I am still strong and resilient, but it was time, time for me to heal and give space to how awesome my life has been, exposing all the good and not so good.

The bike and I are still good friends but we go for social outings and enjoy a good coffee or cake.

> Will I race again? I have no idea.
> Maybe, maybe not, but gee I have a good story because of all that I have done.

We are now in a different chapter, and whilst I do miss being a goal-driven athlete, I am looking forward to other adventures in the outdoors, things I have not yet done. Oh and let's see if I can write another book, and improve my skills, and unleash my creative side with writing and art. I would really love to keep honing public speaking as well, which went by the wayside over Covid lockdowns.

How exciting is life? At any point, you can choose a different path. You can choose to press RESET.

I can't wait to see what the next 10 years look like!
Thanks for listening, the last 48 years has been a blast.

Who would have thought being a 'nana' would be so awesome.

Acknowledgements

Cliche yes, but where do I start? A life well-lived is not done alone. It must start with my parents, I am here! thank you. To my dad for teaching me how to ride, who would have known? To my mum, for all the people who ever said you needed to 'parent' me better, well I am grateful for your trust in me. You only gave me a few boundaries but was always there to pick me up and forgive me when I failed or made mistakes. It was hard work, you did a great job - thank you. To Tony, my stepdad, you entered our lives whilst we were giving mum a hard time, and we gave you a hard time. We all worked through it, and look at us now! Living out best lives. To all my grandparents who are no longer here, pivotal and so important to me growing up, offering me a different perspective on life and what is possible. On both sides, my Oma and Opa and then Opa Cees, later on, I loved the 'Dutchness' of this side of my upbringing, Oma's lolly drawer and Opa's never-ending paper supply. To Grandma and Pa, fishing, camping, shopping trips, teaching me how to sew and knit and just general love and support. I miss you all. My brothers Tom, Ben and sister Amber - thank you for loving me unconditionally. My wider family, Aunties & Uncles, cousins and extended family. We are all just a bunch of crazy misfits and as you well know, world championships do not change a person at all!

To the teachers who taught Bike Ed at primary school, Mr Wells and Mr Carr, you were the catalysts for a life well-lived, and ultimately my greatest success in life thus far. Amazing how teachers can plant a seed and never know about the outcome - to all the teachers in my life - thank you for your vision, passion and sacrifice. Never stop investing in future generations. Thanks to Mr Grant for saying yes to the school group and the Great Vic Bike ride.

You changed my trajectory in life. thank you to Mrs Young, my art teacher and saviour, she nurtured my artistic self for a good 2 years and we had so much fun. To Cancer, thank you for being in my life. Another Keystone that gave me the impetus to do great things.

To Pamela for being there at Saskia's birth - I may never have been able to express my gratitude, I was too young and self-involved to really offer a proper thanks. We may not be in each other lives now but to Chris and Corrine Chalmers. That time working with and for you at Physical Revolution showed me what was possible. I didn't know I had this in me. Moving forward: big thanks to people who showed me what I could do, even when I didn't know I could. On that note, Bengt Carlson - all your massages helped me too, even if I was crying on the inside. "Groomster" - thanks for your coaching and support. Mark Yeates, Janelle Crib - your energies to me through playing football propelled me to greater self-belief. To Gary Pettigrove, you too showed me how to do things I was fearful of, your calm approach was spot on. Donna Rae-Szalinski, your guidance in my journey of cycling was always a matter of fact, and I appreciated your views on how to make 'shit happen'. I never forgot anything you told me. To Canberra Off-Road Cyclists (CORC) - Sarah O'Callaghan and Russell Baker namely - but everyone involved in the sport in Canberra. I looked up to you, listened and took in what you shared with me. You all were and still are, trailblazers and movers and shakers in the sport. Actually, without all my interactions with your races, camps, people and government funding, I would not be here today with my race resume. Simple.

The photographers that shared your passion with me at races, too many to name but thank you for capturing all the joy and pain! Thank you James 'Willo' Williamson, you may no longer be on this earth, but you have inspired so many people via your actions. You were everything to me, and thanks for that pivotal intro to Giant Bikes Australia. Thank you to TCF, Lorenzo for supporting me in the early days. Then onto Jo Hall and the man himself, Darren "Ruddy" Rutherford. Time has passed and perhaps now I can truly give you the space, to truly THANK YOU! Without your belief in what Norm and I were up to, well... it's safe to say I could not have done it or at least gone so far as I did. The bikes, the relationships, the support, everything. It was huge. It really was huge. There was also a very important encounter with a person named Simon Mouatt - changing my thought patterns, the way in which I used my words and generally giving me a shakeup. THANK you! This leads me to thank Jet Black, Shimano Australia, Adidas Sunglasses, Bike Box (Schwalbe), Rapid Ascent, Iain Moore, Dave and Emma of Top Bike Tours. Stephane Vanderbruggen of GPC, coaches I have had; Brendan, Mark Fenner, Greg Meyland and David Heatley. You have all taught me little gems that are with me today, I love all your views on life and what racing means to you and your athletes.

To the village town of Forrest, that we called home for 8 years. The people and businesses in it, the support you gave our business and family. Thank you, without being able to live here and ride and enjoy the environment, the progress to World Champ status would have been that much more challenging.

To our staff at the Corner Store and MTBSkills, all our instructors and partners and staff. Wow. We had some fun times. We all worked so hard, but were so passionate and at the beginning of the ride here in Australia. You can be proud of what you have done, for us and for the people you all touched. How good was it? Thank you to Bec and Kylie for your friendships as well xx Thank you Glen Jacobs for suggesting we set up shop at Derby and at Buller. It was bloody hard work, but it was fun while it lasted. Thanks to the Dorset Council and to Mt Buller Resort Management. Especially to the crew at Buller.

There are some pretty special people that I need to thank, Haydn Tilley, who is no longer here with us, but was pivotal in the development of trails and mountain biking in Townsville. Your friendship and support helped us immensely, and the people you introduced us to, namely your bro in Brett and his family. Townsville holds so many special memories for me and it is because of you. To my friends in Alice Springs, Janine, Kathryn, Stephen, Ciara, Raby, Jess, Dave, Deb, Dorinda, Ron, Nic, Georgina, Emma, Catherine and so many more...you know who you are, I love you and love your energy and friendships. Fast forward to moving back to Geelong and building new friendships, thanks to Tina, for being in my life and all the fun times we have had, and to all those, I have formed many new friendships with since returning to my hometown. More to come.

To those who I have coached and mentored over the years, I am so proud to have helped you and been a small part of your life. To the crew who were there on that fateful day, the death of another cyclist is always hard to bear, but even harder when you are there - thank you for your support and I hope you are getting through life a bit easier each day, as am I.

It is without further ado that I thank my family. Norm and Saskia(and welcome to my son-in-law, James) You both gave up a lot for me and of course, dealt with a cranky self-centred athlete for a long time. But we all worked hard, those days in Forrest especially. Imagine the next 20 years...Finley and the new one due in Jan '22, what will they be doing? What crazy stuff will we all be up to? I am so lucky to have you in my life.

That's a wrap from me, and if I have forgotten to thank you, let me know, I can always add you in a later print run!

But honestly...I am human and certainly not perfect, so please forgive me. Over and out.

Jess xx

Wally, I promised you would get a mention in my book

My small beautiful family

Thanks to all my beautiful friends, not just J&K of course. xx

WHY NOT ME? — 319

Thank you for everything Giant Bicycles Australia x

Oh the views - Mt Buller
'selfie'

Jess Douglas describes herself as a lifelong learner.
An apprentice of life.
She met her husband, best friend and life confidant, Norm, at 17, married at 18, and a mum at 21.
Jess is an accomplished Australian cyclist, with 3 World and 3 National titles to her name. A cancer survivor, mother, wife and business owner, she learnt early on the gift of adversity, providing a platform to share what is possible. Most importantly, she loves to follow her own processes that found her success in becoming a 3 x World Champion in her sport; her 1% Rule.
Simply put, breaking big tasks into small 1% efforts, consistently over time, produce the most amazing outcomes.
And it's not just about the end result, it's what you learn along the way. Jess likes to remind you, *"That if she can do it, so can you."*

Website www.jessicadouglas.com

Instagram: www.instagram.com/jedouglas73/

Facebook: https://www.facebook.com/GtownJess/